THE
CONSTITUTION

EDITED BY

James Morton Smith

State Historical Society of Wisconsin
and
The University of Wisconsin

HARPER & ROW, PUBLISHERS

NEW YORK, EVANSTON, SAN FRANCISCO, LONDON

THE CONSTITUTION

Standard Book Number: 06-046337-6

Library of Congress Catalog Card Number: 70-168363

CONTENTS

v

The Federal Constitution

EDITORS' INTRODUCTION

This volume—and companions in the series "Interpretations of American History"—makes a special effort to cope with one of the basic dilemmas confronting every student of history. On the one hand, historical knowledge shares a characteristic common to all appraisals of human affairs. It is partial and selective. It picks out some features and facts of a situation while ignoring others that may be equally pertinent. The more selective an interpretation is, the more memorable and widely applicable it can be. On the other hand, history has to provide what nothing else does: a total estimate, a multifaceted synthesis, of man's experience in particular times and places. To study history, therefore, is to strive simultaneously for a clear, selective focus and for an integrated, overall view.

In that spirit, each book of the series aims to resolve the varied literature on a major topic or event into a meaningful whole. One interpretation, we believe does not deserve as much of a student's attention as another simply because they are in conflict. Instead of contriving a balance between opposing views, or choosing polemical material simply to create an appearance of controversy, Professor Smith has exercised his own judgment on the relative importance of different aspects or interpretations of a problem. We have asked him to select some of what he considers the best, most persuasive writings bearing on the origins of American constitutionalism, indicating in the introductory essay and headnotes his reasons for considering these accounts convincing or significant. When appropriate, he has also brought out the relation between older and more recent approaches to the subject. The editor's own competence and experience in the field enable him to provide a sense of order and to indicate the evolution and complexity of interpretations. He is, then, like other editors in this series, an informed participant rather than a mere observer, a student sharing with other students the results of his own investigations of the literature on a crucial phase of American development.

JOHN HIGHAM
BRADFORD PERKINS

THE CONSTITUTION

INTRODUCTION

Looking back at the four months of bickering and debate, the balancing of clashing views and diverse interests, at Philadelphia in 1787, James Madison assured Thomas Jefferson that the achievement of the federal Convention was nothing "less than a miracle." Clearly, the new-modeled government was something new under the sun; neither history nor political theory could furnish a model for the new federal republic. Indeed, finding the proper terminology to describe the new creation was difficult, as Madison noted in Federalist Paper No. 39:

> The proposed constitution . . . is . . . neither a national nor a federal Constitution, but a composition of both. In its foundation it is federal, not national; in the sources from which the ordinary powers of the government are drawn, it is partly federal and partly national; in the operation of these powers, it is national, not federal; in the extent of them, again, it is federal, not national; and, finally in the authoritative mode of introducing amendments, it is neither wholly federal nor wholly national.

One of the admirers of the new Constitution observed that it was "so novel, so complex, and intricate" that writing about it would never cease. It never has, of course, from that day till this, and never has it been in fuller swing than in the past two decades, though the pace is likely to quicken in the two decades ahead as we move toward a predictable flood of books in connection with the American Revolution Bicentennial celebration. Even now we are well into the midst of a quiet revolution in historical writing that has revised the revisionist views of Charles A. Beard and Vernon Louis Parrington, the chief architects of the most influential interpretations of the Constitution in the first half of the twentieth century.

Beard's book, *An Economic Interpretation of the Constitution of the United States* (1913), concluded that the Constitution "was not the product of an abstraction known as 'the whole people,' but of a group of economic interests which must have expected beneficial results from its adoption." The Constitution was essentially an economic document drafted by an unrepresentative minority of property holders by undemocratic means to secure their own personal economic interests, organizing a system whose advantages "would accrue to themselves first, from their own action." The personal property holders—especially public securities holders who "knew, not as a matter of theory, but as a practical matter of dollars and cents, the value of the new Constitution"—carried the day largely because of "the disfranchisement of the massees through property qualifications and ignorance and apathy." "A considerable proportion of the adult white male population was debarred from participating in the elections of delegates to the ratifying state conventions by the prevailing property qualifications on suffrage." An undemocratic document adopted by undemocratic means in an undemocratic society, the Constitution was presented as a counterrevolutionary instrument designed to curb the excesses of democracy unleashed by the American Revolution by instituting a complicated system of checks and balances on popular majorities. "Owners of personality" were "anxious to find a foil against the attacks of levelling democracy."

Other scholars wrote of the adoption of the Constitution as a Thermidorean reaction against the ideals of the Declaration of Independence, Parrington calling it "a carefully formulated expression of eighteenth-century property consciousness, erected as a defense against the democratic spirit that had got out of hand during the Revolution." In the only scholarly study of *The Articles of Confederation* available before World War II, Merrill Jensen identified the Articles as the constitutional embodiment "of the philosophy of the Declaration of Independence" and concluded that the Federalists who replaced the Confederation with the Constitution "engineered a conservative counter-revolution and erected a nationalistic government whose purpose in part was to thwart the will of 'the people' in whose name they acted."

In the years since World War II, Beard's "frankly fragmentary" research has been frankly fragmented, fractured by the methodological critique of

Robert E. Brown, then destroyed by the massive research of Forrest McDonald.[1] In a line-by-line analysis of Beard's historical method—his gathering of evidence from original sources, his critical evaluation of the evidence, and his presentation of conclusions with the evidence—Brown demonstrated that Beard had violated the fundamental concept of historical scholarship: his conclusions were not supported by his evidence, which was not only fragmentary but also often mishandled. McDonald's approach was different. He filled in the gaps in Beard's research pattern to see if new evidence, such as Beard had suggested would be necessary in order to verify his interpretation, would in fact buttress Beard's views. After a meticulous appraisal of the economic interest of the 55 participants in the Philadelphia Convention and the 1111 delegates in the ratification conventions in the thirteen states, McDonald concluded that Beard's "economic interpretation of the Constitution does not work." Richard Hofstadter, writing on *The Progressive Historians* in 1968, summed up the Beardian controversy in a sentence: Beard's reputation, "once the grandest house in the province, is now a ravaged survival," an "imposing ruin in the landscape of American historiography." Jackson Turner Main, a critic of both Brown and McDonald, who says that he "stands closer to Beard than to his detractors," nonetheless agrees that "Beard can no longer be accepted without serious reservations."[2] And in the most recent article on the economic interpretation of the Constitution, E. James Ferguson acknowledges that "it is impossible to sustain Charles A. Beard's distinction between realty and personalty interests" and divorces his economic emphasis from "a Beardian or anti-Beardian assessment of the role of security holders."[3]

The truth of the matter is that Beard himself abandoned the "Beard thesis" during the 1940s. In *The Republic* (1943) he reflected his concern over the spread of dictatorships by his new emphasis on the Constitution as an alternative to military dictatorship. Washington, the only Founding Father who had holdings in four of the five major economic interests listed by Beard in the *Economic Interpretation,* now attracted Beard's admiration because of his stress on civil authority over the military. In discussing the General's rejection of dictatorial powers at Newburgh, New York, in 1783, Beard concluded that "his firm resistance to

[1] Robert E. Brown, *Charles Beard and the Constitution: A Critical Analysis of "An Economic Interpretation of the Constitution of the United States"* (1956); Forrest McDonald, *We the People: The Economic Origins of the Constitution* (1958).

[2] *The Antifederalists: Critics of the Constitution, 1781–1788* (1961) 294.

[3] E. James Ferguson, "The Nationalists of 1781–1783 and the Economic Interpretation of the Constitution," *Journal of American History,* 56 (1969) 241–261.

every proposal for the seizure of power showed his unfailing devotion to constitutional methods, even in revolutionary war."[4] As for the Founding Fathers in general, they had built a Constitution in order to preserve "the sacred fire of liberty and the destiny of the republican model of government." In his popular *Basic History of the United States* (1944), Beard's interpretation of the Constitution stood in stark contrast with his earlier works. In his *Rise of American Civilization* (1927), he had entitled his chapter on the Constitution "Populism and Reaction," arguing that the system of checks and balances was a means of "dissolving the energy of the democratic majority." In 1944 that chapter became simply "Constitutional Government for the United States," and the checks and balance system was presented as an attempt to prevent the "accumulation of despotic power in any hands," even democratic majorities. In another book, *Public Policy and the General Welfare* (1941), Beard discussed the elements of the American constitutional system and stressed democracy, but he noted that "democracy is only one element in the American system and we must consider other essentials. Two of the essentials are authority and liberty—power and freedom. The Constitution of the United States provides for both; indeed, the very word 'constitution' itself implies limited government. Hence it is useful to consider the Constitution as a system of power and as a system of liberty."

Essentially that is what the recent—and not so recent—writers on the origins of American constitutionalism have done. They have been concerned with the equation between Power and Liberty, the proper political adjustment, both in theory and practice, between freedom and authority, the establishment of the right relationship of ordered liberty in a free society. The chief difficulty in the eighteenth century—and the chief analytical difficulty ever since—was to recognize the problem for what it was: an essentially federal problem of distributing governmental authority between one central and several regional units without impinging on the liberties of free Englishmen. As Benjamin Franklin remarked after the failure of imperial and colonial agents to agree on a plan of federalism at the Albany Conference in 1754, "Everybody cries, a Union is absolutely necessary, but when they come to the manner and form of the Union, their weak noddles are perfectly distracted." Both weak noddles and strong puzzled over the problem, and as the current state of the literature testifies, they still are puzzling over it.

---

[4] The most recent investigator of the Newburgh plot agrees; see Richard H. Kohn, "The Inside History of the Newburgh Conspiracy: America and the Coup d'Etat," *William and Mary Quarterly*, 3rd ser., 27 (1970) 187–220.

The current emphasis by historians on the nature of the constitutional debate in the pre-Revolutionary years owes much to the work of Edmund S. and Helen M. Morgan, *The Stamp Act Crisis: Prologue to Revolution* (1953), which focused attention on the twin problems of representation and sovereignty, and E. S. Morgan's pioneering article entitled "The American Revolution Considered as an Intellectual Movement" (1963). Indeed, most of the recent work emphasizes ideas, ideology, and the changing concepts of constitutionalism in the seventeenth and eighteenth centuries. It begins with a new look at the concept of the mixed constitution, the English Whig tradition, the idea of separation of powers, and the concept of representation.[5] Two of the most influential studies are Caroline Robbins' monumental and diffuse study with the expansive title, *The Eighteenth-Century Commonwealthman: Studies in the Transmission, Development, and Circumstances of English Liberal Thought From the Restoration of Charles II Until the War with the Thirteen Colonies* (1959), and Barnard Bailyn's careful exploration of the relationship between American constitutional thought and the libertarian tradition of English radical Whiggism, *The Ideological Origins of the American Revolution* (1967). But the most significant book on the Constitution since Beard's is the magisterial study of Gordon S. Wood, *The Creation of the American Republic, 1776–1787* (1969),[6] which starts where Bailyn leaves off and traces carefully the transformation of political and constitutional thought during the Revolutionary and Confederation eras to the crucial creation of a new and modern conception of constitutionalism.[7]

[5] See the Selective Bibliography for a discussion of these works.

[6] Other recent studies of importance include Catherine Drinker Bowen, *Miracle at Philadelphia: The Story of the Constitutional Convention, May to September 1787* (1966); Paul Eidelberg, *The Philosophy of the American Constitution: A Reinterpretation of the Intentions of the Founding Fathers* (1968); Clinton Rossiter, *1787: The Grand Convention* (1966); and Robert A. Rutland, *The Ordeal of the Constitution: The Antifederalists and the Ratification Struggle of 1787–1788* (1966). For other contributions to the study of early American constitutionalism, see the Selective Bibliography.

[7] Students who have not done much reading in political and constitutional theory may feel as "perfectly distracted" as Benjamin Franklin when they contemplate such complex concepts as sovereignty, federalism, and mixed government in the following portions of this introduction. The selections included in this anthology are designed to clarify these concepts, of course, but clarification can come only after the reader has read all of the book. It may be worthwhile, therefore, to give this introduction a preliminary reading for an overview of the dimensions of the problem which historians and political scientists have discussed and debated for so long, then come back and reread this introduction after finishing the essays in the book.

I

What are the major elements of this new view of American constitutionalism? The central issues turned on the nature of the empire or the union and the essentially federal question of the relationship between the central government and the parts, the question of how to balance Power and Liberty, and the issues of representation, sovereignty, separation of powers, and a written constitution.

Before 1763 the relationships between Great Britain and the colonies were little explored. Although theory and fact did not jibe—in theory the empire was centralized and ruled by a single, supreme, and undivided sovereign, the king-in-Parliament, but in fact it was a composite, decentralized empire with a remarkable degree of freedom, prosperity, and internal autonomy at the local level—American constitutional thought paralleled England's. Colonial Americans, like Britons at home, stressed the perfection of a government that preserved the "invaluable civil rights and privileges" of British subjects everywhere. Free English government, the security of civil liberty, the pitting of Liberty against Power, the identification of happiness with freedom—American colonists constantly reiterated these central themes, singling out freedom as the chief characteristic of the mixed constitution of Great Britain and identifying their governments with the model of the mother country.

The concept of balance was the key to the Whig theory of mixed government in England and America in the eighteenth century. The English constitution, wrote a colonist in the Boston *Independent Advertiser,* more nearly than any other form of government, properly balanced Power and Liberty: "In none that I ever met with," he observed, "is the Power of the Governors, and the Rights of the Governed, more nicely adjusted." This equilibrium was achieved by combining and blending the three classic forms of government derived from Polybius—monarchy, aristocracy, and democracy—in a mixed constitution that prevented any one order—king, lords, or commons—from exercising arbitrary authority. In the tripartite division of the supreme legislative authority, the Liberty of free Englishmen was the special interest of the House of Commons, the only elective element in the mixed constitution, but the democratic branch was checked by the other two orders. The prerogatives of Power were vested in the Crown, but the laws that the Crown executed were enacted by the balanced legislature, and their execution could be checked by courts under the control of the aristocracy and juries under the democracy. Between the monarchy and the democracy stood the aristocracy, embodied in the House of Lords, participating like the other two estates in the lawmaking process, serving as an appellate court in the interpretation of law and authority, restraining the other two elements in government and in turn being restrained by them, and standing as a buffer of Wisdom between Power and Liberty.

It was this mixed constitution of king-in-Parliament that the colonists praised as "the most compleat and regular, that has ever been contrived by the Wisdom of Man," for it preserved freedom by avoiding the triple threats of tyranny, oligarchy, and anarchy. In theory political stability in England resulted from the proper "mix" in the mixed constitution, whose parts operated independently, harmoniously, and legitimately, with self-adjusting regularity, alternating between conflict, which prevented bad legislation, and cooperation, which guaranteed good legislation.

Since neither Crown nor Commons held the upper hand in the balanced constitution, the king and his ministers solved the problem of political leadership by taking the initiative to achieve support for their program in Commons, utilizing the patronage power of the Crown, distributing favors, manipulating elections, and managing Crown placemen in the Commons to obtain a majority for ministerial measures.

Although David Hume and other orthodox commentators defended the use of Crown influence as a necessary ingredient to give cohesion and stability to mixed government, opponents of governmental policy argued that it threatened to unbalance the mixed constitution by undermining the independence of Commons, the protector of Liberty, and strengthening ministerial Power. Opposition spokesmen, like orthodox political commentators in eighteenth-century England, praised the mixed constitution as the preservative of British freedom, but they constantly emphasized the precarious nature of the balance between Liberty and Power: Power is aggressive and has a natural tendency to encroach; Liberty is fragile, submissive, "a virgin, that everyone seeks to deflower." Ministerial management of the House of Commons threatened Liberty by increasing executive Power.

The experience of the colonists, who exalted freedom, made them receptive to the theory that liberty should be protected and the use of corruption and influence to expand power opposèd, giving to American political thought in the eighteenth century an antiadministration bias. "Before the revolution," Jefferson later wrote, "we were all good whigs, cordial in their free principles, and in their jealousies of the executive magistrate." This radical Whig fear of executive Power had important consequences for the American colonies, because the administration of the colonies was performed in the name of the king, a practice established in the seventeenth century when the royal prerogative was the dominant factor in British politics. By his "royal grace and favor," the king issued royal instructions and commissions to his deputies in the provinces, the colonial governors, who not only headed the colonial administration, but also linked the colony with the king's government in England. Thus, the apex of colonial political authority was located outside colonial society. Government by "royal grace and favor," therefore, gave to the Crown a much more influential place in the colonial constitution than it had in the British constitution and magnified enormously colonial fears of executive Power.

Conflict between royal governors and colonial assemblies was perhaps inevitable under any circumstances, but the theory of "government by instruction" made the clash predictable. According to imperial theory, the king's instructions formed "the true principles of a provincial constitution." Colonial government derived from the Crown, who gave the governor authority to enforce local legislation and British statutes extending to the colonies, listed the members and duties of the Council, and authorized the establishment and outlined the privileges of the elective assembly. But the colonial legislature was strictly a subordinate governmental agency with limited lawmaking power, mere "Corporations at a distance," wrote one British official, "invested with an ability to make temporary By Laws for themselves, agreeable to their respective situations and climates."

In theory, then, the British Empire was unitary and imperial, centralized and all powerful. But in practice the political culture of the colonies had diverged radically from the British model by the middle of the eighteenth century; political authority had devolved to local governments in a decentralized system, and the colonists had achieved a remarkable degree of autonomy. Both Parliament and the local assemblies exercised the lawmaking power, but Parliament had generally confined its legislation to the regulation of imperial trade and commerce—to the external affairs of the colonies—leaving the colonial assemblies to legislate on internal affairs under the tutelage of the governors. The power to tax was exercised at the local level by town, counties, and provincial assemblies; the administration of justice was in the hands of local officials in the local courts which maintained law and order; colonial interest was identified with local government.

According to American political leaders, government came not from royal favor graciously conferred in fixed and unchanging instruction to the governor; it came instead from the consent of the governed who exercised their rights as Englishmen, inherent and unalterable rights that were the same in the colonies as in the home islands. By 1763 the colonial assemblies had successfully pitted the concept of colonial self-government against that of government-by-royal-grace-and-favor; they had acquired a new status in colonial politics. Transformed from dependent lawmaking bodies into miniature parliaments, they had won the right to initiate legislation and to assent to local laws and taxes. Spurred by the radical Whig fear of executive Power and stressing the concept of legislative supremacy in imitation of the House of Commons, the provincial assemblies had combatted the expansive prerogative of the governors; by controlling colonial finance, they had gained even more extensive authority in handling executive affairs than that of the English House of Commons. As Sir William Blackstone noted in the 1750s, the provincial assemblies were for the colonists "their houses of commons." In the colonies, as in England, the representative bodies stood for English Liberty; in both they protected freedom.

But what if the parallel lines of development between the colonial legislatures and Parliament should converge—if Parliament, which had curbed the prerogative of the ruling sovereign and now claimed complete and absolute sovereignty throughout the empire, but contained no representatives chosen by the American colonists, should levy taxes on the colonists with the consent of the Commons of Great Britain but without the consent of the colonists? Between 1763 and 1773 the British Parliament did precisely that, enacting a series of colonial taxation measures beginning with the Sugar and Stamp Acts of 1764 and 1765 and culminating with the tea tax. With each measure the colonists protested vigorously, and Parliament twice repealed revenue laws. But when Parliament pushed the enforcement of the tea tax in 1773, some Bostonians pushed the tea into the harbor, creating the supreme crisis of the pre-revolutionary years.

II

Since the question of parliamentary taxation had never really come up before and since most Americans acknowledged the theoretical sovereignty and unlimited authority of Parliament, the colonists faced an almost impossible task of formulating a logical and coherent constitutional theory which squared with the actual division of governmental authority in a system that was characterized in fact by functional decentralization. To construct arguments where none had existed before, to work out the principles of a composite federal empire when the concept of federalism had not yet been invented, to place limits on what was theoretically unlimited and illimitable became an immediate problem in politics comparable in difficulty to squaring the circle in mathematics. It was not an easy intellectual assignment, but many colonists willingly undertook it, for the passage of the Sugar Act, as James Otis observed, had "set people athinking, in six months, more than they had done in their whole lives before." In the first of the essays that follow, Andrew C. McLaughlin argues that "the discussions of the generation from the French and Indian war to the adoption of the federal Constitution, and more particularly, the discussions in the ten or twelve years before independence, were over the problem of imperial organization" and the essential qualities of what later came to be called American federalism. Indeed, he stresses the fact that the central features "of American federal organization were largely the product of the practices of the old British empire as it existed before 1764." Similarly, the essay by Corrine C. Weston sketches the origins and development of the theory of the mixed or balanced constitution, which dominated English political thought in the eighteenth century —in the colonies as well as in Great Britain—before the parliamentary taxation measures inaugurated the imperial crisis in 1764–65.

There was remarkable agreement among the colonists about the basis for their response to the parliamentary challenge. James Otis, a member of the Massachusetts Assembly and the leading spokesman in the early phase of opposition, captured the essence of the colonial defense in the title of his popular pamphlet, *The Rights of the British Colonies Asserted and Proved.* Otis agreed that Parliament was sovereign, but he also argued that the people have rights; the colonists were "by the law of God and nature, by the common law, and by act of parliament (exclusive of all charters from the crown) entitled to all the natural, essential, inherent and inseparable rights of our fellow subjects in Great Britain." Neither in Great Britain nor in the colonies could the supreme power deprive any man of any part of his property, "without his consent in person, or by representation. If he does, he deprives me of my liberty, and makes me a slave." Most colonial spokesmen agreed with George Washington, a member of the House of Burgesses, who declared that Parliament "hath no more right to put their hands into my pockets, without my consent, than I have to put my hands into yours for money." In the third essay on the colonial background of American constitutionalism, Bernard Bailyn traces the critical colonial probing of the traditional concepts of constitutions and rights between 1764 and 1776, noting the transformation of old ideas into radical concepts that "would shape the entire future development of American constitutional thought and practice."

The first critical question in that debate turned on representation and consent. Although the colonists were not actually represented in Parliament, the ministry argued that they were "virtually" represented there, as much so as were the nine-tenths of the people of Great Britain who did not possess the franchise, for the members of Parliament did not represent just the constituency that elected them but all the commons of Great

Britain—all British subjects whatever and wherever. The fact that the colonists were represented in their own assemblies did not exempt them from the authority of Parliament any more than the representation of Londoners in their Common Council was a pretence for their exclusion from the superior authority of Parliament. According to Daniel Dulany, the chief spokesman for the colonists in 1765, the essential defect of this argument was that the mutuality of interests which made the system work in England ceased to exist when the concept of virtual representation was exported to America. In England the interests of the 90 percent of Englishmen without the franchise was intimately tied to those of the 10 percent who voted for members of Parliament, as well as to those of the representatives themselves. But there was no such identity of interests, no such intimate and inseparable relation "between the electors of Great Britain and the colonists who were supposed to be virtually represented in Parliament"; on the contrary, there might be an opposition of interest. Since mutuality of interest was the basis of virtual representation and that in turn the justification of the parliamentary taxation, it followed that a total dissimilarity of situation inferred that colonial representation was different and that "the principle of the Stamp Act must be given up as indefensible on the point of representation." The second defect, Dulany contended, was that the colonial charters and constitutions of government empowered the colonies, by express compact, to levy taxes, and he argued that "by the powers vested in the inferior, is the superior limited." The power of colonial taxation, he observed, was compatible with colonial dependence and had been "expressly recognized by British Ministers and the British Parliament, upon many occasions." Indeed, it was "the fundamental and necessary principle of Constitutional Liberty."

These views were echoed by the Stamp Act Congress, the first intercolonial meeting ever held. Linking taxation to representation as "inseparably essential to the Freedom of a People, and the undoubted Right of Englishmen," the congress rejected virtual representation and parliamentary taxation, asserting "that no Taxes ever have been or can be Constitutionally imposed on them, but by their respective Legislature." Since taxes were free gifts from the people to the Crown, it was unreasonable and inconsistent with the principles of the British constitution for the representatives of the people of Great Britain to grant the property of the American colonists to the King. Like Dulany, the Stamp Act Congress resolutions distinguished between taxation and legislation; due subordination, therefore, meant to the American colonists the acceptance of parliamentary legislation—the regulation of the trade of the empire, amendments of the common law, for example—and the rejection of parliamentary taxation.

Constitutional arguments, economic pressure, and the dismissal of George Grenville, author of the Stamp Act, by George III paved the way for the repeal of the Stamp Act by the Rockingham ministry. But at the same time that it repealed the law, Parliament adopted the Declaratory Act of 1766. When he drafted that act, Rockingham used general terms, affirming Parliament's "full power and authority to make laws and statutes of sufficient force and validity to bind the colonies and people of America, subjects of the crown of Great Britain, in all cases whatsoever." Rockingham's Attorney General was critical of the ambiguous phraseology and suggested that the final clause be amended to read "as well in cases of Taxation, as in all other cases whatsoever." But Rockingham refused to insert "taxation," hopeful of carrying the majority who identified Parliament's legislative authority as encompassing the power to tax and fearful of arousing Pitt, who supported Parliament's legislative authority but denied its power to tax. Since the debates at that time were secret and unreported, however, the colonists, noting that taxation was not mentioned, could view the Declaratory Act as an endorsement of their arguments, whereas the majority of Parliament viewed it as precisely the opposite. One fact of major importance about the Declaratory Act stands out: whereas Grenville had linked taxation to representation—virtual representation but nonetheless representation—and colonial consent, the Declaratory Act omitted any reference to representation or consent; Parliament had instead based its claim to all power over the colonies in all cases whatsoever on a simple statement of its unlimited sovereignty.

In the crisis created by the Townshend taxes in 1767, the Ministry rested the right to tax on parliamentary sovereignty without reference to representation, making crystal clear the meaning of parliamentary sovereignty. But it was not until 1773 that any colonial legislature undertook a thoroughgoing discussion of the limits of parliamentary power and the nature of sovereignty. In Massachusetts the royal governor, native born Thomas Hutchinson, became alarmed because the town meetings' defense of local political control denied the unlimited extent of parliamentary authority; he therefore challenged the colonial legislature to reconsider the indivisibility of sovereignty. "I know of no line," he told the colonial legislators, "that can be drawn between the supreme authority of Parliament and the total independence of the colonies: it is impossible [that] there should be two independent legislatures in one and the same state for . . . two legislative bodies will make two governments as distinct as the kingdoms of England and Scotland before the Union."

The Massachusetts House promptly dissented. "If there be no such line," wrote John Adams in the legislature's reply, "the consequence is, either that the colonies are the vassals of the Parliament, or that they are totally independent" of Parliament. Conceding that "it is difficult to draw a line of distinction between the universal authority of Parliament over the colonies and no authority at all," the legislators made it clear that they would never agree to "be reduced to a state of vassalage," subject to an "absolute uncontrolled supreme power." By accepting the governor's terms of argument, the Massachusetts legislature articulated a new theory that Parliament, instead of having power to bind the colonies in all cases whatsoever, had no authority in the colonies whatsoever. The legislators did not argue that they were independent of Great Britain, however, for they pointed out that as long as they were "united in one head and common Sovereign [the King]" and did not interfere with each other, they could "live happily in that connection, and mutually support and protect each other."

Other colonists reached the same conclusions after Parliament passed the Coercive Acts in retaliation for the Boston Tea Party. To meet this assertion of parliamentary supremacy, the thirteen colonies met at the first Continental Congress at Philadelphia in September 1774 and adopted a resolution disavowing the authority of Parliament but claiming allegiance to the King. Ultimate authority rested not with Parliament but with the people: "The foundation of English liberty, and of all free government, is a right in the people to participate in their legislative council: and as the English colonists are not represented, and from their local and other circumstances, cannot properly be represented in the British Parliament, they are entitled to a free and exclusive power of legislation in their several provincial legislatures, where their right of representation can alone be preserved, in all cases of taxation and internal polity, subject only to the negative of their sovereign, in such manner as has been heretofore used and accustomed."

In rejecting parliamentary sovereignty, the colonists elevated their provincial assemblies to an equality with Parliament, accepting the logic of legislative supremacy in a representative government based on popular sovereignty and turning it against the British to justify the independence of colonial legislatures from parliamentary control, while protesting their loyalty to their King. After April 19, 1775, however, the Americans found themselves at war with the King's troops and condemned as rebels and seditionists in the King's proclamation in August 1775. Forced to choose between their King and their rights, most Americans chose their rights. But if the authority of King and Parliament were overthrown, in whose name would the armed men from Massachusetts to Georgia fight? If sovereignty did not rest with the king-in-Parliament, where did it lie? If the Americans had dissolved the existing bonds of government, how was government to be reconstituted? To what civilian authority was the army to be subordinated?

III

The Declaration of Independence *in theory* located sovereignty in the people, as did the state constitutions, but *in practice* that sovereignty was identified, as it had been in the pre-Revolutionary debates, with the only organ of government that spoke for the people—the legislature. The Americans became almost instant devotees of republicanism in 1776 and worked with a sense of dedication and excitement in restructuring government. "A bare conquest over our enemy is not enough," a New Hampshire writer emphasized; "Nothing short of a form of government fixed on genuine principles can preserve our liberties inviolate." That meant, as historian William Gordon noted in 1777, that the state constitutions should be shaped "so as not only to exclude kings but tyranny. . . . Now is the golden opportunity for vanquishing tyranny as well as royalty out of the American states, and sending them back to Europe from whence they are imported." And the essential focus was on the states, not the central government. After all, the revolt was against unitary, arbitrary, centralized power. No one in 1776, as John Adams recalled, thought "of consolidating this vast continent under one national Government" but only of establishing "a Confereracy of States, each of which must have a separate Government."

"To contrive some *Method* for the Colonies to glide insensibly; from under the old Government, into a peaceable and contented submission to new ones" was, according to Adams, "the most difficult and dangerous"— as well as the most important and exciting—"part of the Business Americans have to do in this mighty contest." All the colonies transformed themselves into states by adopting constitutions between 1776 and 1780, but in no state was the quest for John Adams' "method" of legitimating the people as constituent power more carefully worked out than in Massachusetts. Indeed, Andrew C. McLaughlin, in his presidential address to the American Historical Association in 1914, claimed that "if I were called upon to select a single fact or enterprise that more nearly than any other single thing embraced the significance of the American Revolution, I should select—not [the battle of] Saratoga or the French alliance, or even the Declaration of Independence—I should choose the formation of the Massachusetts Constitution of 1780." And he justified his selection by pointing out that "that constitution rested upon the fully developed [constitutional] convention, the greatest institution of government which America has produced, the institution which answered, in itself, the problem of how men could make government of their own free will."

In the fourth essay in this collection, Robert R. Palmer underscores McLaughlin's point, singling out as "the most distinctive work of the Revolution" the implementation of the idea of the people as constituent power. The Massachusetts process illustrates perfectly the way in which Americans found a method to grant *power* to government, but at the same time, by basing government on the consent of the governed, to preserve *liberty*. Starting with the fundamental proposition of *popular sovereignty*—that government rests on consent of the governed—the Americans institutionalized this revolutionary concept by perfecting the constitutional convention. By prescribing governmental *limits* with a written constitution, with built in checks and balances and with an additional bill of rights to protect liberty, they broke with the monolithic concept of governmental sovereignty—Parliament's claim to all power in all cases whatsoever—and actualized the principle of limited government.

But there were inherent tensions in the new American political system. In rejecting Parliament's sovereignty, the Americans elevated their provincial assemblies to an equality with Parliament, accepting the logic of a legislative supremacy bordering on a new legislative sovereignty and turning it against the British to justify the independence of colonial legislatures from parliamentary control. The new state constitutions were established on the sovereignty of the people, of course, but few people realized the possibility of any inconsistency—much less any clash—between the concept of legislative supremacy—or legislative sovereignty through representatives—and popular sovereignty, the people at large. And yet, during the Confederation period, the problem at the state level became in part that of securing the rights of individuals and of the minority against the majority in the legislatures—or to put it another way, of protecting individuals and assemblies of people outside the Assembly from the power of the people in the Assembly, of securing the rights of the minority from the power of temporary majorities.

Between 1776 and 1787, the American people debated constantly the meaning of republican government, just as they had debated the constitutional issues from 1760 to 1776. The implications of the underlying principles of republicanism were not grasped fully in 1776 in the Declaration of Independence, or in 1780 in the Massachusetts Constitution, or in 1781 in the Articles of Confederation. The truth of the matter is that the Americans, by transforming the rights of Englishmen into natural and universal rights, made it difficult to ever conclusively and definitively nail down the meaning of those rights in a republican form of government. As

John Adams confessed as late as 1807, he never understood what a republican government was, and he added, "I believe no other man did or ever will."

When they rejected parliamentary sovereignty, the Americans embraced the corollary idea that "it is impossible there should be two independent Legislatures in one and the same state"—that is, that sovereignty could be divided. "The same collective body," James Wilson wrote in 1776, "cannot delegate the same Powers to distinct representative bodies." It seemed "incongrous and absurd that the same Property should be liable to be taxed by two bodies independent of each other" and that "the same offense" should be "subjected to different and perhaps inconsistent Punishments."

Accordingly, the Confederation did not divide sovereignty; it placed it with the free, sovereign, and independent states. A confederation, according to Montesquieu, was the only way to obtain energy among independent states, without in any real sense contravening their sovereignty. Or as Vattel said in his *Law of Nations,* a political reference work for many Americans, "several sovereign and independent states may unite themselves together by a perpetual confederacy without each in particular ceasing to be a perfect state. . . . The deliberations in common will offer no violence to the sovereignty of each member." The Articles of Confederation, according to Ezra Stiles, the future president of Yale, was not meant to be "a body in which resides authoritative sovereignty; for there is no real cession of dominion, no surrender or transfer of sovereignty to the national council, as each state in the confederacy is an independent sovereignty."

Many histories and historians focus their attention on the attempt of a dynamic minority of nationalists to strengthen the central government by amending the Articles by adding powers to Congress, especially the taxing power and power to regulate trade. These all failed, of course, although the Confederation was strengthened by constitutional construction of the treaty power, as interpreted by John Jay, Secretary for Foreign Affairs under the Confederation, and the state courts, acting as courts of the United States. It was also strengthened by the use of implied powers when the Confederation Congress accepted cessions of western land from some of the states, then established laws pertaining to the western territories. Although there was no clause empowering Congress to abolish slavery in the territories, Congress did so in the Northwest Ordinance.

Despite these efforts to strengthen the central government by increasing its powers, it was clear by the middle of the 1780s that substantial reform of the Confederation would be impossible as long as each state was vested with freedom, sovereignty, and independence over its own affairs, and the central government had no way of enforcing sanctions upon the states or the people of the states. One of the most perceptive analyses of these problems was written by Edward S. Corwin in 1925. Instead of viewing the constitutional arrangements at the state and federal levels as being forever frozen into their only legitimate configuration in 1776, his pioneering article traced "The Progress of Constitutional Theory between the Declaration of Independence and the Meeting of the Philadelphia Convention." It is the fifth essay in this collection, and it remains, after nearly half a century, the most penetrating analysis in short form of constitutional thought during the Confederation period, discussing the changing ideas about separation of powers, the deflation of the idea of legislative sovereignty, and the evolution of the concept of judicial review in a popular government. Although he did not overlook the strengths of the Articles— "They kept alive the idea of union . . . when the feeling of national unity was at its lowest ebb; and they accorded formal recognition that the great powers of war and foreign relations were intrinsically national in character," he emphasized their shortcomings—their inadequacies for "the exigencies of the Union" and "the faulty organization of government within the states, threatening as it did, not alone the Union, but republican government itself."

To many contemporary observers it became increasingly obvious that the defects of the Confederation were organically related to the defects of state sovereignty and simple majoritarianism at the local level. One of the first critics of legislative sovereignty was Thomas Jefferson, whose term as governor of Virginia under the constitution of 1776 made him skeptical of the concentration in the legislature of "all the powers of government, legislative, executive, and judiciary." Despite a declaration about the separation of powers in the Virginia Constitution, the former governor complained, "the judiciary and executive members were left dependent on the legislature, for their subsistence in office, and some of them for their continuance in it. If therefore the legislature assumes executive and judiciary powers, no opposition is likely to be made; nor, if made, can it be effectual; because in that case they may put the proceedings into the form of an act of assembly which will render them obligatory on the other branches. They have accordingly, in many instances, decided rights which should have been left to judiciary controversy: and the direction of the executive, during the whole time of their session is becoming habitual and familiar."

Though such a possibility was unforeseen in 1776, the consolidation of governmental power in the hands of the legislature, Jefferson said, "is precisely the definition of despotic government. 173 despots would surely be as oppressive as one." And the author of the Declaration of Independence concluded, "An *elective despotism* was not the government we fought for." What kind of government did Jefferson think the Revolution was fought for? One "in which the powers of government should be so divided and balanced among several bodies of magistrates"—and Jefferson regarded the executive, judiciary, and legislative as "three branches of magistry"— "as that no one could transcend their legal limits, without being effectually checked and restrained by the others."

Writing in 1784, Madison agreed that the "union of powers" in the Virginia Constitution was, as Jefferson had complained, the very definition of "tyranny." And most of the state constitutions suffered from similar defects, according to Madison. His comprehensive critique of the politics of the Confederation period, written in 1787 on the eve of the Philadelphia Convention, was entitled "Vices of the Political System of the United States." Despite the existence of the separate state sovereignties and the Confederation government, he saw the political system as a *single* system and the problem of reform as a *single* reform.

Although the central problem of the Confederation period was the central government, the successful attempt to reform the political system of the United States came not so much from efforts at bolstering the central government from above by strengthening the Confederation Congress through the addition of new powers, as from creeping criticism of state sovereignty from below, by growing denials within the states that legislative sovereignty was the same as popular sovereignty—from denials that the representatives in the state legislatures were the sole or adequate spokesman for the represented. In short, the attack on state sovereignty was an inside job—one done inside the states. This concentration of power in the state legislature, "drawing all power into its impetuous vortex," as Madison phrased it in the *Federalist Papers,* created a legislative sovereignty dominated by a simple majoritorianism that threatened individual liberty through "unjust violations of the rights and interests of the minority, or of individuals."

As Madison wrote Jefferson, the mutability and injustice of state laws were "so frequent and so flagrant as to alarm the most stedfast friends of Republicanism" who sought constitutional means "to secure individuals against encroachments on their rights." "The evils issuing from these sources," he emphasized, "contributed more to that uneasiness which produced the Convention, and prepared the public mind for a general reform, than those which accrued to our national character and interest from the inadequacy of the Confederation to its immediate objects."

The attack on state sovereignty during the Confederation period was closely linked with the reexamination of the relationship between legislative sovereignty and popular sovereignty. In the contest between England and the colonies, the representatives in the colonial legislatures had had the support of the people, and after independence this support carried over into the contest between the state legislatures and the Confederation Congress, the ideological momentum of the Revolution favoring the states. But in the Confederation period, people began to disentangle the strands of popular sovereignty and legislative sovereignty, so easily merged during the Revolution. In this contest between the people and the state governments, the strongest argument favored the people-at-large rather than the legislature or any particular governmental group. In his analysis of the role of the public in a republic, Gordon S. Wood, like Corwin earlier, examines the creative evolution of constitutional theory during the Confederation period, a development that led to "The Transformation of Republican Thought" (essay six).

IV

By the mid-eighties the concept of popular sovereignty was emerging at the state level as a more fundamental consideration than either legislative sovereignty or state sovereignty. In the Whig theory of mixed government, the people participated as one of the social elements in the government, choosing the House of Commons, the protector of their Liberty, and pitting it against the hereditary lords, and the monarch, the weilder of executive Power. In England the government—king-in-Parliament—was sovereign; in America the source of sovereignty—the people—was located outside government. But by the exercise of the principle of representation, the people could delegate their authority to create governmental Power and to protect individual Liberty, either by establishing governments "to secure these rights," as the Declaration of Independence phased it, or by reserving these rights beyond the reach of even a legislative majority.

Thus the 1780s saw an attack on the idea of legislative sovereignty at the state level, which led to a relocation of sovereignty from the legislature to the people. That relocation made possible the extension of republicanism over a wider geographical area, if the people should decide to create a new level of representative government and delegate power to it. The Constitutional Convention did precisely that.

Seeking "a republican remedy for the diseases most incident to republican government," the Philadelphia Convention extended to the central government the representative principle which was common to all the states, overcoming Madison's criticism of the "want of ratification by the people of the Articles of Confederation" by creating a large republic based not on the states in the corporate capacity but on the people. The chief advantage of a large republic over a small one was the fact that it encompassed a greater number of interests scattered over an extensive geographical sphere of government, thus making it vastly more difficult for an unjust, dishonorable, or overbearing majority faction, bent on utilizing the forms of majority rule, to encroach on individual liberties or private rights —basic liberties which no government, regardless of form, structure, function, or source of authority, could rightfully disregard. "What remedy can be found in a republican government, where the majority must ultimately decide," Madison asked, "but that of giving such an extent to its sphere, that no one common interest or passion will be likely to unite a majority of the whole number is an unjust pursuit." In such an extensive republic, he argued, "the people are broken into so many interests and parties, that a common sentiment is less likely to be felt, and the requisite concert less likely to be formed, by a majority of the whole." According to Madison, the "great desideratum of republican wisdom" was "to secure the public good and private rights against the danger of such a faction, and at the same time preserve the spirit and form of popular government." Indeed, he concluded that it was probable that the delegates "were now digesting a plan which in its operation would decide forever the fate of republican government."

Just as representation was the key to republicanism in the states, so it was to republicanism at the federal level. "If Europe had the merit of discovering this great mechanical power [of representation] in government," Madison wrote, "by the simple agency of which, the will of the largest political body may be concentered, and its force directed to any object which the public good requires, America can claim the merit of making the discovery the basis of unmixed and extensive republics."

By unmixed Madison meant "wholly popular." Rejecting the British system of balancing three forms of government derived from different social elements—king, the monarchy; lords, the aristocracy; and commons, the democracy—Americans had discovered that it was "not necessary to intermix the different species of government," as James Wilson noted, in order "to secure the advantages of all three." The source of authority for the federal Constitution, according to Wilson, was "purely democratical," since "all authority of every kind"—legislative, executive, and judicial —"is derived by representation from the people and the democratic principle is carried into every part of the government." In the seventh essay, John P. Roche argues that the federal Convention is "a case study in democratic politics." After noting the agreement among the framers on political and constitutional fundamentals, he quietly abandons ideology to concentrate on the Convention as "a nationalist reform caucus which . . . [sought] to achieve the one definitive goal—popular approbation." The establishment of popular government is also the central theme of Martin Diamond's discussion of "Republicanism and Democratic Thought in

The Federalist," which is the eighth essay in this collection. What distinguished popular government from other types of government, Diamond declares, "was that in it, political authority is 'derived from the great body of society, not from . . . [any] favoured class of it.' " The novelty of this experiment in representative government, he concludes, "consisted in solving the problems of popular government by means which yet maintain the government 'wholly popular.' "

While the delegates to the Constitutional Convention were meeting in 1787, the Confederation Congress was working out the machinery for statemaking, breaking with the colonial concept of subordinating new territories to older areas. Reconciling through equality and popular sovereignty the ancient conflict between liberty and empire, the Northwest Ordinance established an "Empire for Liberty," as Jefferson phrased it, and the new Constitution authorized the admission of new states on the basis of equality with the older ones. In the concluding essay, Daniel J. Boorstin traces the "stages through which a Territory would pass on its way from complete control by Congress to equality as a new State within the Union," a process which created "A Spacious Republic" based on federalism.

The solutions worked out in theory and practice between 1763 and 1789—popular sovereignty and republicanism, a new concept of equality, a new constitutionalism of limited government that established a stable political order while protecting liberty, a new form of functional federalism, an anticolonial "colonial system" that established an expansive system of republicanism by accepting new states on the basis of equality with the old—these were the supreme achievements of the Revolutionary era, creative contributions which institutionalized American ideas of liberty, sovereignty, and equality. The federal republic was a very complicated political machine, depending, as Jefferson observed, on a "proper complication of principles." It was divided, separated, limited, unmixed or popular government; it was federalistic, pluralistic, constitutionally restrained republicanism. By 1789 the pre-Revolutionary theory of mixed government—of monarchy, aristocracy, and democracy—had been replaced by what Madison called an "unmixed" government, a democratic form of republican rule which placed limitations on simple majoritarianism to preserve individual liberty while creating a more powerful general government and a more perfect Union.

That more perfect Union, like all human creations, was not perfect; there were then, and ever would be, tensions between ideals and realities, aspirations and achievements. But Thomas Jefferson, who had formalized the American theory of self government in the Declaration of Independence, seemed to summarize, in his inaugural address of 1801, a quarter of a century of experience under the American experiment in republicanism, that paradoxical system of self-imposed limitations on self government. He stressed the fact that both Power and Liberty flowed from the people. As for Power, he said that "I believe this . . . the strongest government on earth," a "successful experiment . . . which has so far kept us free and firm"—indeed, "the world's best hope." On Liberty—on reconciling majority rule and individual rights—he observed that absolute acquiescence in the decisions of the majority was "the vital principle of republics, from which there is no appeal but to force." But he also stressed the "sacred principle" that "though the will of the majority is in all cases to prevail, that will to be rightful must be reasonable," for "the minority possess their equal rights which equal laws must protect and to violate would be oppression."

In the essays reprinted in this collection, footnotes have been omitted except where they clarify the text or contribute to the author's line of argument. Each essay is reprinted by permission of the publisher listed in the credit line at the beginning of the selection.

THE
COLONIAL
BACKGROUND

The Background
of American Federalism

ANDREW C. McLAUGHLIN

William Gladstone, British Prime Minister in the nineteenth century, once praised the federal Constitution as "the most wonderful work ever struck off at a given time by the brain and purpose of man." The creative work of the Constitutional Convention of 1787 has long been recognized, but, as Professor McLaughlin points out in the following essay, there was also continuity between the colonial period of constitutional growth and the creation of the American republic. Writing only five years after Charles A. Beard had published his *Economic Interpretation of the Constitution,* McLaughlin concentrated his attention not on the economic influences that affected the immediate origins of the Constitution, but instead explored the historical background of colonial development for an explanation of the central principle of American federalism, "that system of political order in which powers of government are separated and distinguished and in which these powers are distributed among governments, each government having its quota of authority and each its distinct sphere of activity." He found that the essential qualities of American federal organization were largely the product of the *practices* —not the *theory*—"of the old British empire as it existed before 1764," and he noted especially that "the discussions of the generation from the French and Indian war to the federal Constitution, and, more particularly, the discussions in the ten or twelve years before independence, were over the problem of imperial organization."

McLaughlin later incorporated this essay on federalism in his Phelps Lectures at New York University in 1932—published as *The Foundation of American Constitutionalism*—where he stressed the necessity for studying the legislative debates and the political thought of the Revolutionary era. "To teach . . . that the heroes of the Revolutionary controversy were only those taking part in tea parties and various acts of violence is to inculcate the belief that liberty and justice rest in the main

Andrew C. McLaughlin, "The Background of American Federalism," *American Political Science Review,* 12 (1918), 215–240. Reprinted by permission.

on lawless force." The establishment of a system of ordered liberty, he wrote, "can scarcely be understood without some appreciation of the old philosophy which assumed the existence of men before government, of personal rights which are not supposed to be granted by government, of the right and the power of men to organize a political system and establish government . . . that only a government constitutionally limited can be the government of a free people."

THE PURPOSE OF THIS PAPER IS TO MAKE PLAIN TWO FACTS: FIRST that the essential qualities of American federal organization were largely the product of the practices of the old British empire as it existed before 1764; second, that the discussions of the generation from the French and Indian war to the adoption of the federal Constitution, and, more particularly, the discussions in the ten or twelve years before independence, were over the problem of imperial organization. The center of this problem was the difficulty of recognizing federalism; and, though there was great difficulty in grasping the principle, the idea of federalism went over from the old empire, through discussion into the Constitution of the United States. By federalism is meant, of course, that system of political order in which powers of government are separated and distinguished and in which these powers are distributed among governments, each government having its quota of authority and each its distinct sphere of activity.[1]

We all remember very well that, until about thirty years ago, it was common to think of the United States Constitution as if it were "stricken off in a given time by the brain and purpose of man." About that time there began a careful study of the background of constitutional provisions and especially of the specific make-up of the institutions provided for by the instrument. It is probably fair to say that the net result of this investigation was the discovery that the Constitution was in marked degree founded on the state constitutions, and that they in turn were largely a formulation of colonial institutions and practices; the strong influence of English political principles and procedure was apparent, though commonly that influence had percolated through colonial governments and experiences.

In such studies as these just mentioned, we do not find, nor have recent

[1] This paper is limited to the subject stated above. It does not pretend to assert or deny economic influences. It confines itself to the intellectual problem of imperial order. Only one other subject vies with this in importance—the problem of making real the rights of the individual under government.

works furnished us, any historical explanation of the central principle of American federalism. And still, one may well hesitate to give the historical explanation, because, when stated, it appears as obvious as it is significant. No better occasion than this, however, is likely to arise for acknowledging the fact that out of the practices of the old empire, an empirical empire, an opportunistic empire, an empire which today is seeking formulation in law or in public acknowledgment of institutional coördination, an empire which the Englishmen even of a century and a half ago did not understand—no better time than now to acknowledge that to the practices of English imperialism we owe the very essence of American federalism. It is a striking fact that there are two great empires in the world: one the British empire based on opportunism and on the principles of Edmund Burke; the other the American empire based on law, the law of imperial organization. The first of these, an empire without imperial law, was profoundly influenced by the experience of the American Revolution and by slowly developing liberalism; the other—an empire with a fundamental law of coördination, also influenced by its experiences and by Revolutionary discussion—institutionalized and legalized, with some modifications and additions, the practices of the prerevolutionary imperial system of Britain.

If we go back to the old empire as it was, let us say in 1760, we find that it was a composite empire, not simple and centralized. We are not speaking of any theory of the law of the empire but of its actual institutions and their practical operation.

First: The active instrument or authority of imperial government was the crown. It operated of course most immediately and effectively in the royal colonies. It operated by the appointment of some officials, by instructions, and by disallowance of colonial acts. The generalization is probably just, that instruction and disallowance were exercised chiefly for essentially nonlocal, imperial purposes, the maintenance of the character and aim of the empire. The process of review of cases appealed from the colonies can probably be similarly classified—its operation was for homogeneity in part but substantially for imperial purposes. This central authority of the empire had charge of foreign affairs, navy and army, war and peace, subordinate military authority being left to the individual colonies.[2] It managed the post office; it was beginning to take charge of Indian affairs and trade with the Indian tribes; it had charge of the back lands and of crown lands within the limit of the colonies; it was preparing

---

[2] Working out the principle of federalism in military affairs was a big problem in the French and Indian war, in the decade before independence, in the Revolution, in the Federal Convention, in the War of 1812, in the Civil War, in the Congress of 1916, in the War of 1917.

to take in hand the building up of new colonies (our territorial system); it exercised executive power in carrying out the legislation of Parliament which was chiefly concerned with trade and navigation.

Second: Parliament had legislated little if at all for strictly local internal affairs of the colonies. If we omit for the moment acts of trade and navigation, we should find the act making colonial real estate chargeable with debts, the post office, the Naturalization Act of 1740, the Bubble Act, the act against the land bank, the act against paper money. Each one of these acts was of imperial scope or nature, because it was directed against an evil of more than local extent, or because, as in the case of the post office, it was of more than local interest. The acts of trade and navigation were in some instances, for example the act against the smelting of iron, a somewhat rude intrusion upon the sphere of local action; but to see these things properly, we must associate them together with the general policy of mercantilism, and see them as a part of a system, not always wisely developed, of making a self-sustaining empire. On the whole, Parliament, as was perfectly natural, had to a very marked extent interested itself in regulation of trade; it was perfectly natural that the empire as far as Parliament was concerned should have been largely a commercial empire; the part played by mercantilistic doctrine in the seventeenth and eighteenth centuries made such parliamentary interests and activities inevitable.[3]

Third: The colonies managed their own "internal police," some of them under charters, all by governments in which there were representative assemblies. They levied taxes for local purposes, and voluntarily contributed, after a wholesome or a ramshackle manner, to the defense of the empire. They managed local trade, and in short did the thousand and one things—sometimes under pressure from the representatives of the royal prerogative—that concerned the daily life of the colonist.

Any one even slightly familiar with American constitutional system will see at once that to a very marked degree we have here the distribution of powers characteristic of American federalism. In fact if we add to the powers of the central authority in the old empire the single power to obtain money by direct or indirect taxation immediately from the colonists for imperial purposes, we have almost exactly the scheme of distribution

---

[3] I have left out of consideration the question of the absorption by the colonies of common law and the acceptance of legislation modifying common law, especially criminal law. It is a big and complicated question. Limited space does not permit the treatment. I content myself with a general picture of the make-up of the empire, which I believe is substantially correct. It is also noteworthy that there was in the empire national or imperial and local citizenship, and that naturalization by colonial authorities was after 1740 under imperial law.

of our own constitutional system.[4] Of course there had to be found a thorough working legal basis and a legal method of operation. The legal basis was found when the constitutional convention of 1787 declared that the Constitution should be law. The operation of the central government directly upon its own citizens, a most important quality of our own federalism, probably came in part from the old empire, but was distinctly worked out in the debates of the convention.

If any one wishes to criticize unfavorably some detail of the scheme of empire which has just been sketched, he will still scarcely deny that Britain had a working federal empire by the middle of the eighteenth century. If Great Britain, in 1760, had reached out and said, "this is the law of the empire; thus the system is formed," she would have seen herself as the most considerable member of a federal state based distinctly on law and not on practice alone. If Britain by a formal constitution could have formulated the empire she had, if the imperial order could have been frozen, petrified, in the form that time had made for it, the British empire would have been legally a federal empire. But though she did not, she made her contribution; her imperial history had selected and set apart the particular and the general, according to a scheme which was of lasting significance in the development of American imperial order. On that general scheme of distribution the Constitution of the United States was founded.

Let us now discuss this subject more in detail and with some consideration for chronological sequence, with some deference, that is to say, to the order and time in which events occurred and arguments were put forth. The scheme of imperial order presented by the Albany congress is so well-known, that it does not need extended comment; it is of interest as a plan for redistribution of powers in certain essential particulars and it is of lasting significance as an effort to select certain things of extra-colony rather than intra-colony importance, those things which needed general control by a colonial representative body. It tried chiefly to solve the problem of imperial order as far as that centered in the need of securing men and money for imperial security; and for the time the plan failed.

[4] The reader may object that Congress can now provide for standards of weights and measures, patents, and copyrights. He might point out, possibly with justice, that coining money and regulating the value thereof did not belong in the old empire to the central authority; but I leave the old practice to justify my assertion and refer again in passing to the act against paper money. The bankruptcy power, as a part of the general power of our central government, probably can be traced back with certainty at least to colonial conditions, and the Bubble Act and its extension to the colonies must not be forgotten.

This matter of imperial security, augmented in weight by the experiences of the war, became the center of dispute in the decade or so after the peace of 1763. Could England by parliamentary enactment secure money for imperial defense? While this question was the center of dispute, the discussion was soon narrowed, or, if you like, broadened, to this: Did the colonies, as constituent parts of the whole, possess certain indefeasible legal rights and especially the right to hold on to their own purse strings? The dispute was narrowed because it came to be confined to the field of theory; it was not a question as to whether Parliament could get money from the colonies but whether they would acknowledge the abstract legal right to get it. The dispute was broadened, because it involved the whole question of interdependence and relationship.

Any amount of argument over the theoretical legal right to exercise sovereignty in the empire does not get one very far. There is no great practical value in trying to determine whether the colonies by the principles of English law were subject to taxation by Parliament. It may not be amiss, however, to point out that most of this argument, as far as it seeks to make out that Parliament did have the taxing power, whether that argument was made in 1765 or in 1917, has for its basis the constitution of the island and not that of the empire. It is largely insular argument, based on insular experience and founded on insular history. The unwritten constitution of the empire is the other way, and that is just what the men, especially the Englishmen, of a hundred and fifty years ago could not see. They could not think and talk imperially, when it came to a matter of constitutional law. If the practical working empire of 1760 had been frozen into recognizable legal shape, the right to tax the colonies would not have been within the legal competence of Parliament, even as an imperial legislature. And because the Englishmen did not think imperially, because they did not realize that time had wrought out for them a composite federal empire, because they insisted on the principle of centralization in theory, they failed patiently to set about the task of determining some way by which, while recognizing federalism and colonial integrity, they could on a basis of justice and consent obtain authoritatively an acknowledged legal right to tax for strictly imperial purposes. Men that could not comprehend federalism, who denied the possibility of its existence, were incapable of dealing with a crisis of an imperial system in which federalism already existed.

Some one may say, and with considerable justice, that the colonists were also incapable, quite as incapable as the parliamentarian and the British pamphleteer, of understanding the nature of a composite empire. It long remained true as Franklin said in disgust after the failure of the Albany plan: "Everybody cries, a Union is absolutely necessary, but when they come to the Manner and Form of the Union, their weak noddles are perfectly distracted."[5] That was the trouble—weak noddles. But, withal, the idea was hard to grasp, simple as it may appear to us; and it took the discussions and experience of a generation to find the manner and form of imperial order, though, when they did find it, it was the old scheme only in part modified, representing in its method of distributing powers the familiar practices of the empire.

And yet it is not quite correct to say that colonial noddles utterly failed. It is true that the colonists often spoke as Englishmen, they claimed rights as Englishmen, they, too, argued on the basis of insular law; and indeed the principles of insular law were not at variance with the rights which they set up as citizens in the empire. But some of them went further, and defended the rights of the colonies, as distinguished from the rights of Englishmen; they defended, to use later phraseology, states rights as distinguished from individual rights; they argued from the structure of the empire rather than from the principles which aim to protect the individual from governmental wrong. As far as they did this, they grasped the nature of an imperial system in which the outlying portions had their own indefeasible share, legal share, of political authority.

If there were space to examine critically the whole mass of constitutional arguments, we should see a groping after the idea of classification of powers, and on the other hand the emphatic declaration that to deny to a government the right to make any particular law or any special kind of laws is to deny all power and authority—government must have full sovereign power or none. In examining some of the materials throwing light on the nature of the arguments, it will be well on the whole to exclude those assertions from which we can gather only inferentially that the writer or speaker grasped the principle of differentiation. As we have already seen, the Albany plan was distinctly based on the idea of classification and distribution. The controversy of 1764 regarding the revenue act brought out occasional indications that certain distinctions were close at hand, if not as yet fully comprehended; at least there was a recognition of the old exercise of power over trade and an objection to the newly

[5] This statement needs modification; for Burke, rejecting legalism, still displayed statesmanship of the highest order. He resented any attempt to fossilize or ossify the empire and sought to hold out the idea of parliamentary duty rather than legal power. In these latter days it would be stupid to declare that one must grasp and apply legal federalism if he is to deal with the elements of a composite empire; Burke's principles of duty and of freedom have been proved to be the cement of the British Empire. But, withal, it is quite plain that the statesmen of the Revolution on both sides thought there was need of fixing legal authority; and those incapable of seeing the principle of distributed authority—federalism—were in a bad way.

proposed schemes of revenue. In the main, however, the American opposition at that time was not clearly and precisely directed against taxation because it violated a principle of imperial structure, but rather because it violated a principle of English personal liberty. Otis, in his *Rights of the Colonies Asserted,* denies the authority of Parliament to tax, and admits their right to regulate trade; but his argument against taxation is English not imperial argument, on the whole. It is probably safe to say he relied on personal right rather than on the principles of empire.

Still in these early days of 1764 and '65 certain fundamentals did appear, even when lines were not drawn with the precision of later days. Dulaney recognized a supreme authority in Parliament to preserve the dependence of the colonies; he spoke of the subordination of the colonies, which still however retained rights despite their inferiority; for "in what the Superior may rightly controul, or compel, and in what the Superior ought to be at Liberty to act without Controul or Compulsion, depends upon the nature of the dependence, and the Degree of the Subordination." He suggests that a line may be drawn "between such Acts as are necessary, or proper, for preserving or securing the Dependence of the Colonies, and such as are not necessary or proper for that very important Purpose." He thus clearly points to the possibility of an empire managed in the large by a central authority but in which the outlying parts are possessed of indefeasible authority on subjects belonging of right to them, subjects which do not contravene the general superintending power lodged in the central authority. He naturally dwells on those particular exercises of authority then under dispute, and declares that there is "a clear and necessary Distinction between an Act imposing a Tax for the single Purpose of Revenue, and those Acts which have been made for the Regulation of Trade, and have produced some Revenue in Consequence of their Effect and Operation as regulations of Trade." This pamphlet of Dulaney's was a statesmanlike production, and contained at least the foundations for the conception of federalism.

Unhappily in 1766, Franklin in his examination before the committee of commons does not indulge in clear and precise thinking. Had he then enlarged on the character of the imperial structure, and had he sharply drawn the lines of demarcation between imperial superintendence and colonial legal right, possibly the listening commons might have understood the vital distinctions. Franklin's examination admirably discloses the opportunistic and nonlegalistic nature of his statesmanship. In this examination he does, of course, emphasize the colonial objection to revenue acts; but he became hopelessly confused in discussing the basis for trade regulation, and impressed on his listeners that what was objectionable was internal taxation as distinguished from external; he appears to have impressed this distinction so firmly, that the Englishmen never lost the notion that it was peculiarly dear to the American heart; and, when within a year or two external taxes were levied, the English administrators were hurt in their minds by the prompt rejection of their schemes. It is true that Lyttleton (1766) called the attention of the lords to the fact that the Americans made no such distinction and that it could not be found in Otis's pamphlet; but the idea seems to have persisted, aided probably by the loose use of terms by occasional American writers.

It was partly to clear up such confusion as this and to draw the line properly, that John Dickinson penned his *Farmer's Letters*. The thinking of Dickinson was plain, straightforward and able. Possibly in his first letter he enters upon indefensible ground; for, having in mind the effort to compel the New York legislature to furnish quarters for troops and thereby to incur certain expense, he insists that an order to do a thing is the imposition of a tax. But in no other place does he become entangled in dubious assertions. Dickinson spoke as an imperialist, as one who saw and felt the empire; he is hardly less emphatic in his declarations concerning the imperial power of Parliament and the existence of a real whole of which the colonies are parts, than in defending the indefeasible share of empire which the colonies possessed. Hitherto the colonies, save as they had been restrained in trade and manufacture by parliamentary legislation under the general principles of mercantilism, had been regulated even for purposes of empire largely by the exercise of the royal prerogative. Dickinson realized the necessity of parliamentary control and guidance; he saw as did Dulaney the need of a superintending authority, and he openly acknowledged that it lay with Parliament. It was perfectly inevitable that a statesman—colonial or English—should think of the control of trade as the big duty, and thus Dickinson emphasized that duty and the right of Parliament to direct the trade of the whole system. He saw an empire, composite and not simple or centralized, with a Parliament possessed of indubitable power to maintain the whole and chiefly to look after the interests of the whole by the regulation of trade.

It was just because Dickinson was thinking imperially and was doing more than to acknowledge that Parliament might regulate trade, that his words deserve especial weight. He was not speaking as a disgruntled colonist merely finding fault; he was not setting up purely insular constitutional principles; he was not talking as a frontier individualist; he saw the existence of an imperial reality and he presented strongly certain principles of imperial structure. He denied that Parliament had the right to tax; scouting the supposed distinction between internal and external taxation, he openly admitted the authority of Parliament to regulate trade.

Taxation is an imposition for the raising of revenue; it at times seems strange, not that Dickinson should have made the distinction between taxation and regulation, but that men at all experienced with actual practices of the empire and familiar with mercantilistic doctrine should not have readily accepted it. That distinction had been touched on before Dickinson wrote; but he made the thing so evident that men ought to have been able to see it. Still it is not plain that men did see it. At least they were not quite able to see that he was proposing not only a perfectly valid distinction between powers, but a real theory of imperial structure. Consequently Dickinson's words did not have the weight they deserved in pointing the way to composite empire, an empire in which there was an indefeasible participation of the parts under a government charged with the maintenance of the whole. Federalism, we must remember, necessitates singling out of specific branches of authority, which we commonly call "powers." Nothing is simpler in the primer of our constitutional law than the distinction between the taxing power and the power to regulate interstate and foreign commerce. Any person, though he be unlearned in jurisprudence, will talk glibly of the commerce power, the treaty making power, the taxing power and many other powers, fully realizing that we take certain authorities of government and label them, put them in certain receptacles, and leave to our astute courts the duty of deciding whether a legislative act is to be classified thus or so and whether it is a due exercise of "powers" that have been authoritatively granted. And so it is amazing to us, this difficulty in seeing the validity of this most commonplace distinction, and that writers should still think Dickinson was speaking in confusion instead, as was the fact, talking the A, B, C of American constitutional law.

Dickinson's position distinguished the power to regulate trade from the power to tax. The distinction deserves to be called proper, because we have had it in active operation under our Constitution for a century and over. But it was proper also, because it carried on the practices of the old empire. Parliament had regulated trade; it had not taxed. For a century or more the empire had acknowledged in practice, not to speak of in charters and commissions and instructions, the existence of colonies with the authority to tax for local concerns, and had refrained from taxation for imperial purposes. To a marked degree we may say again the empire was a commercial empire. Its commercial purposes were expressed in navigation acts, and a large portion even of the administrative control by the Royal council had been directed to the support of those enactments and that commercial policy.

Before passing on to other and particularly later appreciations of federalism, let us turn to the other side of the matter. Englishmen, whether they defended the colonists or opposed them, were likely to take refuge in insular (i.e., English) law, not discussing the question openly as to whether Parliament had become imperial, or whether, if it had, its power was unlimited; blank assertion took the place of argument.[6] They occasionally spoke learnedly or superficially of whether places without the realm could be taxed, or whether such places must be brought within the realm and given representation before they could be taxed; and thus, in referring to past conditions in the history of Britain, they really recognized the fact that even Britain herself had been a growth and had been compounded, but curiously enough they were blind to the composite empire already in existence and to the practices of a century. The freedom from taxation they discussed from the viewpoint of insular institutions, and, as the world knows, made the ludicrous blunder of attempting to impute the insular system of representation to the whole empire. They fumbled with the whole principle of representation; but their chief error was the insistence on applying to the whole empire certain rigid principles which they believed were logically irrefutable. Scarcely any one of them saw that, in the development of empire, had arisen new principles of law and organization. Of course they rejected the distinction between internal taxation and external taxation, as there may have been reason for doing on practical as well as theoretical grounds; from the beginning they denied the possibility of classification of powers; they asserted the indivisible character of legislative power, and almost at once took a position which, if insisted on in practice, left nothing to the colonists but a choice between acceptance of an absolute government at the head of a centralized empire on the one hand, and the total denial of all parliamentary authority on the other.[7]

The pamphlet entitled *The Controversy Between Great Britain and her colonies,* commonly attributed to the pen of William Knox, probably deserves the praise bestowed upon it as being the best presentation of Britain's case.[8] It is true that in one flagrant instance it falsely juggles with Locke's second essay, and it shows more than usual cunning in making Locke's theories support governmental authority; but the argument from the history of Parliament and the empire to support the claim for imperial authority is able and has the strength of historical statement as contradistinguished from bald assertion and adroit legalism. Knox, however, has a merry time with Dickinson, proving to his own satisfaction the

[6] Special exceptions should of course be made. Thomas Pownall, in his *Administration of the Colonies* (London 1764 and later amplified editions), struggles to find expression. Of course there were others.

[7] Pitt's statement distinguishing taxation from legislation is omitted from this discussion in the text. See for partial support of position above Grenville, Speech of January 14, 1766. *Parl Hist.,* XVI, 101. See also *Ibid.,* 167.

[8] Except Hutchinson's speeches of 1773.

folly of distinguishing between taxation and regulation of commerce; and he thus fails utterly to see anything but a centralized empire with all authority in Parliament. "There is no alternative: either the colonies are a part of the community of Great Britain, or they are in a state of nature with respect to her, and in no case can be subject to the jurisdiction of that legislative power which represents her community, which is the British Parliament." Nothing could more fully discredit legalism when dealing with a practical problem of statesmanship; this was denying that Parliament could not recognize the illegality of doing what in practice it actually had not done and what the passing years were proving it could in reality not do.

Even before 1770, many American opponents of parliamentary taxation had been hurried along to the position in which they denied that Parliament possessed any power over them. It would appear, however, that the more sober-minded did not as yet openly go so far; it was easy for the thoughtless to resent British assertion of authority by the simple denial of all authority. There is no such declaration, however, in the American state papers. There was still readiness, as there continued to be after 1770, to acquiesce in British regulation of the trade of the empire, and in such royal control as was consistent with practice and the charters.

In 1770 when the long controversy arose between Hutchinson and the Massachusetts legislature over the right to remove the legislature to Cambridge, Hutchinson declared that the Boston men, having denied the power of Parliament over them, were now prepared to deny the power of the crown. It is perfectly true that that controversy concerned the power of the crown; it involved the question whether the prerogative could be used freely and arbitrarily and in disregard of established laws and the charter; but certainly till that time the colonists had not committed themselves to the doctrine that Parliament was totally powerless, nor did they deny *in toto* the authority of the crown. As before 1770 they had asserted that there were bounds to the authority of Parliament, so now they rejected the notion that sufficient excuse for a governor's acts was his simple declaration that he had received orders from Westminster. Even in the exercise of the prerogative, there must be recognition of the legal entity and the legal competence of the colony as an integral portion of an integral empire; that was the position of the Massachusetts legislature translated into modern terms.

Students of the Revolution that believe the movement was economic in origin, character and purpose, may not deny that, after 1768, Parliament had no express hope or intention of obtaining revenue from America. From that time on, British interest was largely, if not wholly, confined to asserting parliamentary omnipotence, or, if this seems too strong, confined to an insistence upon the supreme power of Parliament and to resisting what they believed, under the tutelage of American governors, was a conscious tendency toward independence. Indeed, especially after 1768, but to a considerable extent from 1766, the question was not so much whether the colonies would pay taxes as whether they would acknowledge the legal obligation; and to an amazing extent the conflict was over the existence or nonexistence of an abstract right. As we have already seen, much of the colonial argument was in defense of individual liberty, not of states rights; but the center of the controversy was whether or not Parliament was possessed of limitless authority.

The colonists at least claimed to be satisfied with the old régime, in which power had been divided, and in which Parliament had chiefly shown its power by the regulation of trade. The parliamentarians insisted that in the law of the empire the will of Parliament was nothing more or less than supreme and all-inclusive. The colonists insisted, though they did not use this phraseology, that old practices of the empire were the law of the empire and thus, in modern phraseology, they demanded the recognition of a composite empire based on law. Even if we admit the presence of many economic and social forces, we find in actual conflict two theories of imperial order; and in this discussion after 1768, if not before, the English parliamentarians and pamphleteers were victims of certain dogmas of political science, curiously similar to the doctrine of indivisible sovereignty. How often did Burke deprecate the continual harping on Parliament's authority, on the necessity of acknowledging the theoretical supremacy of Parliament! He deplored the common talk about the legal rights. Beyond Burke's speeches little needs be cited to show the essentially legalistic character of the whole discussion.

It may be rash to assert that the colonists were less insistent upon knowing what the constitution of the empire was than were the Englishmen, though there seems no reason to doubt that the colonists would have willingly accepted the old practice as sufficient, if it were not threatened. Still, the colonists desired to know precisely what were American rights; and in this respect possibly America was more legalistic than Britain, because Parliament insisted on the existence of unlimited power—asserted, one might not unjustly say, that Parliament was above the law—while the colonists asserted that Parliament was bound by rigid law. "The patchwork government of AMERICA," wrote Bernard in 1765, "will last no longer; the necessity of a parliamentary establishment of the governments of AMERICA upon fixed constitutional principles, is brought out with a precipitation which could not have been foreseen but a year ago; and is become more urgent, by the very incidents which make it more difficult." At this time, it will be remembered, he proposed an extraordinary Parliament, in which there were to be American representatives, which should form and establish "a general and uniform system of American government;" "and let the relation of America be determined and ascertained by a solemn Recognition; so that the rights of the American governments, and their subordination to that of Great Britain, may no longer be a subject of doubt and disputation." In 1766 he declares that "the Stamp Act is become in itself a matter of indifference; it is swallowed up in the importance of the effects of which it has been the cause. . . . And as the relation between Great Britain and the colonies has not only been never settled, but scarce even formally canvassed, it is the less surprising, that the ideas of it on one side of the water and on the other are so widely different, to reconcile these, and to ascertain the nature of the subjection of the colonies to the crown of Great Britain, will be a work of time and difficulty."

There can be little doubt that Bernard was right; the problem of the day was the problem of imperial organization: were Englishmen or Americans capable of finding a law of the empire?[9] If so, that law must be consonant with practical realities; it must be a formulation of the principles of relationship which recognized not centralization but distribution.[10] As an indication of the fact that men were discussing legal rights, and losing sight of financial returns, it may be sufficient for the earlier days to refer to the comments in the *Parliamentary History* on the debate about the Circular Letter. It was insisted by opponents of the ministry in debate on the Massachusetts Circular Letter and in respect to the revenue laws "that the inutility of these laws was so evident, that the ministers did not even pretend to support them upon that ground, but rested their defense upon the expediency of establishing the right of taxation." And if we turn again to Dickinson, we find the same thing in a different guise—the necessity of law in the empire—not a law securing centralized authority but freedom. There could be no freedom without legal restriction: "For who are a free people? Not those, over whom government is reasonably and equitably exercised, but those, who live under a government so constitutionally checked and controlled that proper provision is made against its being otherwise exercised."

[9] By "law" I do not mean that there was a demand for a parliamentary act; I mean at the least an evident understanding, at the most a formal acknowledgment of power and the extent of it, a formal recognition of the complete authority of Parliament or, on the other hand, of the width and depth of the actual colonial legal competence.

[10] Only one other question—and that intimately associated with the first—vied with it in importance: Were there or were there not rooted in the British constitution fundamental principles of individual liberty superior to legislative authority and must they be recognized in the British legislation for colonial affairs?

We might wisely spend much time in considering the dispute in 1770 already referred to—the dispute as to whether instructions could *ipso facto* dispose of all matters of constitutional right of the colonies, or whether even the crown was limited in imperial authority by the fact of the existence of competent and legally recognized colonial legislatures. But passing over those three years or so of legalistic dispute, let us come to "the great controversy" of 1773. In considering this we can echo John Adam's expression of amazement at Hutchinson's audacity in throwing down the gauntlet. The truth probably is that Hutchinson had been grievously tried for years, not alone by what he considered the unmannerly conduct of the rabble, but by the doctrines which he heard in the market place and perhaps in legislative halls. He believed that the theories of the malcontents were unsound and that he in the plenitude of his wisdom could establish their invalidity; and he prepared therefore to bring his heaviest artillery to bear upon the unreasoning followers of Samuel Adams and against the arch agitator himself. What he wished to do, be it noticed, was to demolish a false theory of the empire and bring every one to ac-knowledge, not the wisdom of obnoxious legislation, but the legal au-thority of Parliament. By this time doubtless there was much talk about complete freedom from parliamentary control, but there had been little if any formal public announcement by the radicals of anything more than a freedom from taxation.

Hutchinson, it must be said, had considerable reason for having con-fidence in his massed attack; for his argument was able and compelling, serving by its weight to bring into play all the open and masked batteries of the opposition. He finally reached in his first paper a position from which he believed he could discharge one final and conclusive volley; he was prepared to use an undeniable principle of political science; he be-lieved he could silence his enemies with its mere pronouncement: "It is impossible there should be two independent Legislatures in the one and the same state." Despite all the discussion that had gone on, despite the fact that Britain had been practicing federalism, Hutchinson could see nothing but the theory of centralized legislative omnipotence and could not conceive of distribution of power between mutually independent legislative bodies. And yet this undeniable axiom of political science was to be proved untrue in the course of fifteen years by the establishment of fourteen independent legislatures in the single federal state, the United States of America.

The two branches of the legislature met Hutchinson's general arguments somewhat differently. The house argued valiantly for complete freedom from parliamentary control; in facing the alternative of complete freedom from Parliament and complete subservience, they unhesitatingly chose the former, though they did seem to recognize the possibility of drawing a line between the supreme authority of Parliament and total independence. The council, wiser and more conservative than the house, announced federalism; they contended that the colony had "property in the privileges granted to it," i.e., an indefeasible legal title: "But, as in fact, the two powers are not incompatible, and do subsist together, each restraining its acts to their constitutional objects, can we not from hence, see how the supreme power may supervise, regulate, and make general laws for the kingdom, without interfering with the privileges of the subordinate powers within it?"[11] This is a clear, precise and thorough description of federalism. It is plain enough, then, that there were some clearheaded men, who, in the years just before the final break with England, were not silenced by the fulminations of British pamphleteers or the dogmatic assertions of Hutchinson into a belief that the empire was simple and unitary; nor were they as yet ready to accept the learned and technical argument of John Adams, though buttressed by pedantic reference to Calvin's case, that the empire was held together by the king, a personal union only.

The American theory of federalism is stated with such amazing accuracy in an answer to Doctor Johnson's *Taxation No Tyranny,* that it deserves quotation at considerable length:

"Now this, in abstract, sounds well. When we speak of the Legislature of a community, we suppose only one Legislature; and where there is but one, it must of necessity have the right you speak of; otherwise, no taxes at all could be raised in that community. . . . Now the present dispute is not with respect to this Island alone, which certainly has but one Legislature, but with respect to the *British* Empire at large, in which there are many Legislatures; or many Assemblies claiming to be so. . . . From the state of the *British* Empire, composed of extensive and dispersed Dominions, and from the nature of its Government, a multiplicity of Legislatures, or of Assemblies claiming to be so, have arisen in one Empire. It is in some degree a new case in legislation, and must be governed therefore more by its own circumstances, and by the genius of our peculiar Constitution, than by abstract notions of Government at large. Every Colony,

---

[11] I omit, to save space, the extended argument, but I must call attention to their assertion of legal possession of constitutional right by the colonies as integral portions of the empire, and also to their declaration, in a delicate manner, that Hutchinson was dealing with theories and disregarding the fact, and that fact was the distribution of powers not centralization: "What has been here said [i.e. by Hutchinson], concerning supreme authority, has no reference to the manner in which it has been, in fact, exercised; but is wholly confined to its general nature." *Ibid.,* p. 413. These arguments are also to be found in *Mass. State Papers,* as well as in the appendix to Hosmer's *Hutchinson.*

in fact, has two Legislatures, one interiour and Provincial, viz: the Colony Assembly; the other exteriour and imperial, viz: the *British* Parliament. . . . Neither will the unity of the Empire be in danger from the Provincial Legislature being thus exclusive as to points. It is perfectly sufficient, if the *British* Legislature be supreme as to all those things which are essential to *Great Britain's* being substantially the head of the Empire; a line not very difficult to be drawn, if it were the present subject. Neither is there any absurdity in there being two Assemblies, each of them sufficient, or, if you will, supreme, as to objects perfectly distinct; for this plain reason, that the objects being perfectly distinct, they cannot clash. The Colonist, therefore, allowing that the supreme power or Legislature, where there is but one, must have the right you speak of, will say that with respect to him, there are two, and that the Provincial Legislature is the supreme power as to taxation for his Colony. And so the controversy, notwithstanding your position, will remain just where it began."[12]

The discussions in the Continental Congress of 1774 show us the trouble that the colonists had in reaching a satisfactory theory. By that time, many had come to the conclusion that Parliament possessed no power to pass laws governing the colonies. But the situation and the experience were too plain, and Congress "from the necessities of the case" announced that parliamentary regulation of trade would be accepted, but not taxation external or internal. They proposed as a working basis for the whole system—perhaps no longer to be termed an empire if there was no legislature with any imperial power legally speaking—the distinction between taxation and regulation of commerce, and they really put themselves back, as far as practice was concerned, nearly if not quite in the position of eleven years before. It cannot be supposed, as they accepted the king as their king, that the Congress of 1774 would deny the general right of the mother country, through the executive head, to make war and peace, manage diplomacy, hold the back lands, control Indian affairs and probably the post office—in other words, to exercise the significant powers bestowed on the central government of the United States under our Constitution. They were prepared to acknowledge a political order, in which all the great powers bestowed on our central government under the Constitution with the exception of the power to tax should be in the hands of the central authorities at Westminster; and they evidently accepted and promulgated the possibility of distribution of power.[13]

In drawing up the Declaration of Independence the Continental Con-

---

[12] *An Answer to a Pamphlet entitled "Taxation No Tyranny,"* found in Force's *American Archives,* Fourth Series, I, 1450, latter part of paragraph on p. 1451.

[13] I omit in this paper mention of various plans of imperial order. They are important as disclosures of effort to distribute powers on a legal basis.

gress accepted the theory that Parliament had had no legal authority over them; but the Articles of Confederation were drawn on the principle of distribution of powers. Of course it may properly be said that the Articles did not provide for the creation of an imperial state. If, however, we look to see how far they carried on the actual distribution which had existed in practice in the old empire, we see much in common between the empire and the Confederation. We do not find in the new system, of course, any right in the Congress—the new central authority—to exercise some of the functions formerly exercised by the crown in council; there was no right to appoint governors, or to instruct them, or to disapprove of the state laws. But the great powers of war and peace, foreign affairs, the post office and Indian affairs belonged to Congress; and it was understood before adoption that the tremendously important matter of the ownership of the back lands, and the administration of the back settlements—in other words the extension of the empire—was to be in the hands of Congress. Only a detailed examination would show how much of the old practical system of the empire was formulated in the Articles. It is sufficient now to say, and it is quite unnecessary to say it, that very much of the old system was there formulated, and the Articles carried on very distinctly the principle of distribution of powers and on the whole provided for governments with distinct spheres of action.[14] A student of the Articles will of course be carried back to the Albany plan and even to the New England Confederacy of 1643; but he will be hopelessly at sea unless he grasps the fact that the contents of the documents are distinctly the products of imperial history, and they constitute, (1) the first quasi-legal formulation of imperial existence, (2) the immediate preparation for ultimate real and full formulation in the Constitution.

The two powers of which there had been much discussion in the ten years before independence were not adequately provided for in the Confederation. Congress, the new general government, was not given the right to raise money by taxation, the Articles accepting the principle of requisitions which the colonists as part of the British empire had insisted on. Everybody knows that requisitions proved a failure in the new system, and this fact in a way gave a tardy justice to the arguments of the parliamentarians in the days before the Revolution. It is more surprising, however, that Congress was not given the right to regulate trade, inasmuch as, almost to the last, the colonies had either openly acknowledged parliamentary authority in the matter or openly professed a willingness to acquiesce in the practical exercise of such authority. The failure to grant

---

[14] Even the system of admiralty jurisdiction was carried forward through the Articles into the Constitution of the United States.

the authority to Congress shows how particularism had grown, or it discloses an inability to see that the need of imperial regulation of trade was just as vital in the new system as in the old. Because Congress did not possess these two powers, taxation and regulation of commerce, the Confederation proved a failure.

The Confederation might very well, we may suppose, have proved a failure even if Congress had been given these two essential powers. As to that little or nothing need be said; it is a very old story; the states suffered from the natural effects of a Revolution, and, had Congress had authority on paper, license and particularistic folly might have made it impossible to go on, until the natural reaction in favor of nationalism and order set in. However that may be, these two powers had to be bestowed, conditions proved it; and in the new Constitution Congress was given power to tax for national purposes and to regulate commerce. The principle of federalism was recognized, formulated and legalized in the Constitution; the new government was given its distinct sphere of action and was made the recipient of a body of powers, carefully named and carefully deposited in their proper places; but in the selection and deposition little needed to be done but to follow the practices of the old British colonial system.

The Convention of 1787 had difficulty in seeing the whole complicated scheme as a working mechanism; but how could the members possibly have imagined it at all, or provided for the scheme which in its essentials was the basis of federalism the world over, without the aid of the historical forces and the old practices? Save perhaps with the old troublesome problem of the militia, the military question in the federal state, they had little trouble in determining what should be the distribution and classification of powers. Their chief difficulty was again the old one—colonial disobedience, which was now state willfulness; and this difficulty was surmounted, as we know, by firm adherence to the principle of distinction between local and general authority, and by recognizing that each governmental authority was competent and supreme within its own sphere and had the legal power to enforce its lawful acts on its own citizens. Perhaps both parts of this principle of cohesion and of authority—of cohesion because of division, and of authority because of immediate operation— were inherited from the old empire; certainly the former one was.

The Theory of the Mixed
or Balanced Constitution

CORRINE COMSTOCK WESTON

The American colonists praised the excellence of the English constitution in the pre-Revolutionary years because it carefully balanced the
rights and interests of the three social orders so that none could over-
power the others and threaten their rights. "See here the grandeur of the
British government!" wrote James Otis in 1764. "This is government!
This is a constitution!"

The theory of the mixed or balanced government originated with
Aristotle and Polybius, who discussed the classical forms of government
—monarchy, aristocracy, and democracy. Polybius especially analyzed
the mixture of the simple forms of government in the Roman constitution, based upon a system of checks and balances. Corrine C. Weston
traces the evolution of the theory of mixed government in English
political thought from its classical beginnings to the critically important
acceptance by Charles I in his answers to Parliament's Nineteen Propositions on the eve of the English Civil War in 1642. That marked the end
of the theory of divine right kingship; by the second half of the eighteenth
century, the theory of mixed or balanced government was universally
praised as the protector of English political liberty, both in the realm
and in the dominions.

AS EARLY AS THERE WAS THEORIZING ABOUT THE NATURE OF THE
English government, it was suggested that it was a mixed government. The most notable early expression of this view appeared in
the writings of Sir John Fortescue, Chief Justice of the Court of King's
Bench in the reign of Henry VI and one of the first legal writers in England to deal systematically with the nature of the English constitution.

Corrine Comstock Weston, *English Constitutional Thought and The House of
Lords, 1556–1832* (New York, Columbia University Press, 1965), 9–12, 23–26,
31, 87–88, 123–132, 142. Reprinted by permission.

Standing as it were on the thin line separating medieval from modern times, Fortescue may perhaps be taken as representative of constitutional thought in fifteenth-century England. As is well-known, he distinguished sharply between what he called *dominium regale,* the type of government found in France, and *dominium politicum et regale,* a form of mixed government existing in England. *Dominium regale* has been translated as absolute monarchy, and *dominium politicum et regale* as limited monarchy. . . . He saw the English king as a limited monarch who could neither make laws nor levy taxes without the assent of his subjects. The constitutional treatises in which he distinguished between the two types of government, though they exerted little influence in his day, shaped Tudor political thought and made him in the seventeenth century a recognized authority on constitutional law.

Fortescue has a place in the evolution of the theory of mixed government because he made Englishmen familiar with the concept of mixture in their government. Since, however, the form in which the theory flourished in England owed less to him than to the writings of Aristotle and Polybius, the theory may appropriately be called the classical theory of the English constitution. According to its tenets government by king, lords, and commons represented a combination and blending of the simple forms of government—monarchy, aristocracy, and democracy; and to this *triple* mixture political thinkers attributed what they regarded as the peculiar virtues of the English system.

Writing under the influence of the Renaissance, Tudor publicists may have borrowed from Aristotle's *Politics* a system of classifying governments and from the *Histories* of Polybius the general form that the theory of mixed government took in modern England. Aristotle classified governments according to the numbers of those in whom the ruling power was placed and in terms of whether the ruler or rulers acted for their own or the public interest. In a pure state the ruler or rulers acted for the public benefit; in a corrupt state for his or their own. The three pure forms of government were monarchy (the rule of one), aristocracy (the rule of a few), and polity (the rule of the many). Their corresponding corrupt forms were tyranny, oligarchy, and democracy. A similar classification appeared in the *Histories* although democracy was used to denominate the rule of the many in the public interest while the name ochlocracy or mob-rule was used for its impure form.

The theory of mixed government expressed in the *Histories* strikingly resembled the classical theory that became current in modern England. In his famous sixth book Polybius discoursed on the workings of the Roman constitution, to which he attributed the unparalleled triumph of Rome over the Mediterranean world. Convinced that the most permanent of practical constitutions combined a mixture of monarchy, aristocracy, and democracy with a check and balance system, he found his most important examples in the constitutions of Sparta and Rome, particularly the latter. Unhappily monarchy if left unchecked degenerated into tyranny; aristocracy, into oligarchy; democracy, into mob-rule. To avert their tendencies towards instability the simple forms of government, Polybius pointed out, should be combined as in the Roman republic of consuls, senate, and assemblies, where the principles of the simple forms were so expertly blended that even those living under this constitution scarcely knew what to call the whole. This Roman constitution, based upon a system of checks and balances, had inherent strength for correcting all abuses. If one part attempted to encroach upon another, their mutual interdependence was such that 'the possibility of the pretensions of any one being checked and thwarted by the others, must plainly check this tendency; and so the proper equilibrium is maintained by the impulsiveness of the one part being checked by its fear of the other'.

There was no need for sixteenth-century Englishmen to turn to the writings of antiquity to become familiar with the theory of mixed government. Expressions of admiration for the theory appeared in the Middle Ages and permeated the literature of the Renaissance and Reformation. . . . It is not surprising, then, to find in late sixteenth-century England a growing tradition that the English *dominium politicum et regale* was a mixture of monarchy, aristocracy, and democracy. . . . On June 21st, 1642, almost exactly two months before [the English Civil] war began, Charles I publicly associated the theory of mixed government with the English constitution and thus gave the classical theory a vogue that it could have acquired so rapidly in no other way.

The remarks of Charles I on the mixed nature of the English government were contained in his Answer to the Nineteen Propositions, the cardinal document in the history of the classical theory of the English constitution and a pronouncement that proved to be one of the most influential ever made on the nature of the English government. The Nineteen Propositions to which the King addressed himself had been sent to him early in June by the Long Parliament, and their acceptance would have made the two Houses masters of the state. Briefly stated, they included parliamentary demands for naming the King's councillors, ministers, and judges, for controlling the militia, and for reforming the church with parliamentary participation. In his Answer Charles I offered an elaborate series of counter proposals as a basis for continued negotiation, which he seems to have expected. But he characterized the tone of the Nineteen Propositions as emanating from conquerors as he stated his firm resolution not to abandon his royal rights, nor, as he said, 'to subvert (though in a Parliamentary way) the ancient, equall, happy, well-poised, and never-enough commended Constitution of the Government of this Kingdom'.

The King based his rejection of the Nineteen Propositions on the ground that the two Houses, because of the constitutional reforms that had been completed by August 1641, possessed sufficient power to prevent the growth of royal tyranny and that further concessions would upset the balance among king, lords, and commons and eventually encompass the destruction of the mixed and balanced government that he was describing. In words that had an almost magical effect upon contemporaries he praised the existing government as a salutary mixture of the simple forms of government as these had been classified by Aristotle and later political philosophers. There were, he noted, three main forms of government— monarchy, aristocracy, and democracy—representing respectively the rule of the one, the few, and the many. Each had its own virtues and vices or, as he said, conveniences and inconveniences. The virtue of monarchy was in its uniting a nation under one head to resist invasion from abroad and insurrection at home; of aristocracy, in the conjunction of council in the ablest persons of a state for the public benefit; and of democracy, in the courage and industry which liberty begets. On the other hand, the vice endemic to monarchy was tyranny; to aristocracy, faction and division; and to democracy, tumults, violence, and licentiousness. Fortunately, for England, Charles I informed his subjects in a memorable statement: 'The experience and wisdom of your Ancestors hath so moulded this [government] out of a mixture of these [monarchy, aristocracy, and democracy], as to give to this Kingdom . . . the conveniences of all three, without the inconveniences of any one as long as the Balance hangs even between the three Estates [the King, the House of Lords, and the House of Commons], and they run joyntly on in their proper Chanell. . . .'

Delineating what came to be called the King's Constitution, Charles I implied that the mixture could be seen in the joint participation in law-making of the King, the House of Lords, and the House of Commons. Furthermore, each of these 'three Estates', as he termed them, had independent powers with which to check the others. The King was charged with the government: he made treaties of war and peace, chose councillors of state, judges, and others, raised armies, created peers, gave pardons, etc. Armed with these powers, he could command the respect of the nobility and the reverence of the people. In order that the King might not make use of his powers to the detriment of his subjects or make use of the name of public necessity for the gain of his favorites and followers, the House of Commons, an excellent conserver of liberty, was intrusted with raising money and the power of impeachment. Charles I denied that the House of Commons was ever intended to share in the government, presumably the administration, or to choose those who governed. The equipoise in the balanced constitution was maintained by the House of Lords, 'an excellent Screen and Bank between the Prince and People', assisting each against the encroachments of the others and by means of its judicial power preserving the law, which ought to be the rule of all three. 'Since therefore the Power Legally placed in both Houses' was 'more than sufficient to prevent and restrain the power of Tyranny' and since the adoption of the Nineteen Propositions would mean the total subversion of 'that excellent Constitution of this Kingdom', Charles I refused the demands of the two Houses, repeating the dictum ascribed to the barons at Merton in 1236, *Nolumus Leges Angliae mutari.*

The adoption of this interpretation of the English constitution meant that Charles had abandoned the theory of the divine right of kings which his father James I had preached and he himself had practiced. He probably acted from motives of expediency. Whatever his private thoughts and reservations may have been, the King by publicly enunciating the classical theory of the constitution had cloaked it with a sanctity which the circumstances of his death must have heightened. Since he used the classical theory, he stamped it with royal approval; and this was a fact of fundamental importance. . . .

The widespread use of the royal definition of the three estates after the appearance of the Answer to the Nineteen Propositions is a hallmark of its influence. Before its appearance the term three estates had been used officially and popularly to designate the lords spiritual, the lords temporal, and the commons. . . . The royal definition of the three estates spread rapidly during the period of the Civil Wars and Interregnum and was a subject of controversy in the reign of Charles II. Publicists after 1660 recognized that the royal definition of the three estates and the theory of mixed monarchy went hand in hand, and they traced both ideas squarely to the civil-war period though not necessarily to the statements of Charles I. . . . In the eighteenth century the royal definition of the three estates was a commonplace in parliamentary oratory, and it was driven from the schoolbooks only by the scorn of nineteenth-century historians....

> The full, the perfect plan
> Of Britain's matchless Constitution, mixt
> Of mutual checking and supporting powers,
> King, Lords, and Commons.
> JAMES THOMPSON, 'Liberty' (1736)

The theory of mixed government spread steadily in the reign of Charles II and after, and in the second half of the eighteenth century received its perfected form in the writings of Montesquieu, Sir William Blackstone, John Louis De Lolme, William Paley, and Edmund Burke. Two corollaries were of increasing importance as the theory developed. The first was the belief that the secret of the constitution lay in the maintenance of a balance among three independent, powerful branches of government, that is, among the three estates. . . . The second corollary was that the House of Lords, the second estate, provided the equipoise of the mixed and balanced government. . . . The theory of mixed government expressed in the Answer to the Nineteen Propositions was elaborated and systematized in the eighteenth century in the writings of publicists such as Montesquieu, Sir William Blackstone, John Louis De Lolme, William Paley, and Edmund Burke. In their several ways each contributed to the supremacy of the classical theory and to the popular assumption that the House of Lords, representative as it was of landed property, maintained, or ought to, the equipoise of the constitution, its membership constituting in Burke's neat phrase, 'the ballast in the vessel of the commonwealth'. Each publicized England's matchless constitution. Montesquieu brought it an international reputation. More than the others, Blackstone and De Lolme formulated the classical expression of its theory. . . . Paley rationalized the operation of influence as an integral part of mixed government. And Burke rallied his countrymen with the cry of the constitution in danger. . . .

In his *Spirit of the Laws,* published in French in 1748, Montesquieu by stating that the direct end of the English constitution was political liberty brought that constitution an international prestige on a scale hitherto unknown. He had admired the English constitution, as Burke said later, and held it out to the admiration of mankind. It becomes, then, of particular interest to note the terms he used. On first sight Montesquieu appears to have broken with the tradition of mixed government. He was interested primarily in establishing that English political liberty was due to what he believed to be the sharp separation of powers among the executive, legislative, and judicial branches of the government; that is, among king, parliament, and bench. He thus applied to the English government what has since become a commonplace classification of the powers of government and professed to find the secret of the English government in the equilibrium among three divided and mutually antagonistic branches. Political liberty, he asserted, was attainable only if there were no abuse of power by government; and the mechanism to secure this was the separation of powers. Of the European kingdoms, England alone had been able to separate the executive and legislative powers; others had achieved only the separation of the judicial power from the other two.

Montesquieu seemed to be attributing political liberty in England to the balance maintained among king, parliament, and bench, whereas believers in mixed government claimed that the desideratum was a balance among king, lords, and commons. Until he modified this major thesis, he was saying that political liberty in England was due to the separation of powers in the government and not to the combination and balance of the three simple forms of government in such a way that their virtues were retained while their vices were eliminated. The distinction is fundamental. But it was [as] though Montesquieu hesitated and then decided to throw in his lot with English publicists. He shifted his emphasis from a balance among king, parliament, and bench to a balance among king, lords, and commons; he encouraged the already prominent tendency among Englishmen to attribute the stability of their complex government to the moderating influence of the House of Lords; and he noticed, by indirection, the monarchic, aristocratic, and democratic elements in the English constitution.

His first step was to dismiss from consideration the judicial branch. It was 'in some measure next to nothing'. There remained to be considered only the executive and legislative branches of government, and these required a regulating power to moderate them that could properly be supplied by the nobility as part of the legislature. Thus Montesquieu's newly minted separation of powers, as applied to the English government, had melted into the tradition of mixed government as he described what he called the fundamental English constitution in these words: 'The legislative body being composed of two parts, they check one another by the mutual privilege of rejecting. They are both restrained by the executive power, as the executive is by the legislative.' Like Harrington earlier, Montesquieu was convinced that a nobility was essential to a limited monarchy. Neither could survive without the other. Abolish the nobility, he warned; and either a despotism or a popular state would result.

In a much-quoted phrase Montesquieu added that 'this beautiful system was invented first in the woods'. This 'Gothic' construction had originated among the Germans who conquered the Roman Empire. By reading Tacitus one could see how these people, while in Germany, had assembled for public business; but after the conquest they had adopted the use of representatives with a resulting government of monarchy mixed with aristocracy. At that time the people were bondsmen; but, once they were enfranchised, there followed a perfect harmony among the civil liberty of the people, the privileges of the nobility and clergy, and the prerogative of the prince. Thus Montesquieu had fused two separate ideas: the separation of powers (executive, legislative, and judicial) and mixed government (monarchy, aristocracy, and democracy).

But he was interested primarily in the provision for political liberty made by the separation of the legislative and executive branches of government, and to him the doctrine of mixed government was secondary. Englishmen, imbued with the maxims of the classical theory, probably found confirmation of their preconceived ideas in the *Spirit of the Laws*; but the uninitiated were more likely to carry away a realization of the importance of the separation of powers to political liberty rather than an awareness of the adaptation of that doctrine to the classical theory. Montesquieu's contribution to the supremacy of the theory of mixed government was in bringing world-wide attention to the English system and in his emphasizing the moderating role of the nobility in the English government. In brief, he made but an indirect contribution to the classical theory, of which others wrote more fully and more specifically.

It was Sir William Blackstone, sometimes called the high priest of the cult of constitutionalism, who gave Montesquieu's separation of powers its classical English form. The announcement of a course of lectures at Oxford from which stemmed the *Commentaries on the Laws of England* (1765-9) was posted on June 23rd, 1753; but the first volume of the *Commentaries,* in which he included his well-known description of the English constitution, did not appear until 1765. Few books have been so successful. It went through eight editions in Blackstone's lifetime and made him a comfortable fortune. Burke thought as many volumes had been sold in the English colonies in America as in England.

Blackstone's exposition of the English constitution was, if stereotyped, at least complete. He drew together what his predecessors in the field had said earlier. In his long introduction to Book I he pointed out that the writers of antiquity would admit no more than three regular forms of government—monarchy, aristocracy, and democracy—for others were either corruptions or reducible to the simple forms. Each had its respective virtues and vices: in a democracy public virtue or goodness of intention was more likely to exist than in other forms of government; in an aristocracy, less honesty than in a democracy but more wisdom; and in a monarchy, more power than in the others but more likelihood of tyranny. In general, according to the Commentator, the ancients had no idea of any other permanent form although Cicero thought that the best-constituted republic would combine monarchy, aristocracy, and democracy. Tacitus, on the other hand, had thought such a combination visionary, which, if it could be effected, could not last.

A standing exception to the validity of Tacitus' argument was the English constitution, in which the executive power was lodged in a single person so that the advantages of absolute monarchy were secured, while the legislative power was lodged in three distinct powers entirely independent of one another. They were the king, the lords spiritual and temporal ('an aristocratical assembly of persons selected for their piety, their birth, their wisdom, their valor, or their property'); and the House of Commons, freely chosen from the people and thus a kind of democracy. Among these powerful branches of government, Blackstone discerned a perfect equilibrium; for in this aggregate body, actuated by different motives and interests, there could be no 'inconvenience' attempted by one of the three branches which could not be withstood by one of the others, armed with a negative power adequate to repel any inexpedient or dangerous innovation.

He enlarged upon the merits of the English constitution. In the legislature was lodged the sovereignty of the English people as beneficially as possible for any society. There could be found the three great qualities of government. If the supreme power were lodged in only one branch, the English must be exposed to the inconveniences of absolute monarchy, aristocracy, or democracy and so lack two of the three principal ingredients of good polity, either power, wisdom, or virtue. If power were lodged in two branches such as the king and the House of Lords, laws might be well made and executed but the good of the people might well be neglected. On the other hand, if power were lodged in the king and the House of Commons, then the 'circumspection and mediatory caution, which the wisdom of the peers' afforded, would be lacking. Finally, if the king had no veto on the proceedings of the two houses, they might abolish the office and destroy the executive power. Fortunately for Englishmen, concluded Blackstone, 'the constitutional government of this island is so admirably tempered and compounded, that nothing can endanger or hurt it, but destroying the equilibrium of power between one branch of the legislature and the rest'. Like Montesquieu, whose terminology of the separation of powers he had adopted, the Commentator forecast the end of the constitution if the independence of one branch should be lost.

This description of the English government dominated for almost 100 years the thinking of the great majority of Englishmen who gave any thought at all to their government. Blackstone and the constitution were practically synonymous in the pamphlet literature of the time, and after 1832 the Radicals who attacked the constitution aimed their diatribes at Blackstone. Not untypical was a tract entitled the *Matchless Constitution* (1835), in which an obscure follower of Jeremy Bentham was critical of the Commentator for having taught the Tories that the constitution contained within itself all the necessary checks on all abuses of power.

The relationship between Blackstone's *Commentaries* and John Louis De Lolme's *Constitution of England* (1770) was succinctly, if ironically, expressed in the epigrammatic comment of the dissenter David Williams, who was one of the first Englishmen in the eighteenth century to reject the theory of mixed government. Williams thus summed up the connection: 'Englishmen learnt their political creeds from these romances copied into political breviaries. . . . See Blackstone's Introduction copied from Montesquieu; and De Lolme's Constitution of England copied from Blackstone.' In 1770 De Lolme published in Holland his *Constitution of England,* written in French; and five years later an English translation was in print. The times were auspicious for its success. English national pride was troubled by the Wilkes affair and the *Letters of Junius,* both revealing defects in the much vaunted constitution. While De Lolme's thesis that the mechanism of the English constitution insured English liberty was soothing, it was also flattering that a foreigner should have devoted a full-length treatise to the history of the development of the English constitution, followed by a discussion of its principles. By 1784 the *Constitution of England* had passed through four editions, and it continued to enjoy high repute until superseded in the second half of the nineteenth century by Walter Bagehot's *English Constitution,* first published in 1867. It was perhaps inevitable that De Lolme should have been compared with his illustrious predecessor who had given the English constitution its international reputation. He has been called the English Montesquieu, and it has been suggested that his *Constitution of England* was but an elaboration of Book eleven, chapter six of the *Spirit of the Laws.*

De Lolme treated the English constitution as a piece of machinery in which king, lords, and commons, each armed with an independent veto, served as balancing weights. The desideratum of this mechanism was not progress but stability. This stability had come into being because the early strong power of the crown had created a popular force as a counterweight. In the Conquest William I had so centralized his government, De Lolme explained, that he had aligned against himself and succeeding kings the combined force of the nobles and the people. The main problem of government was the equalization of the two forces. Since the king could not originate laws, he had been unable to invade successfully the popular power. And the royal power had remained intact because of the division of the legislature into two bodies, each jealous of the other and zealous to prevent the other from engrossing the power of the crown. In this way the views of the House of Commons and the House of Lords cancelled each other like equal quantities on opposite sides of an equation. Thus De Lolme had postulated a double balance in the English constitution; first, a balance between the king and the popular power (nobles and people) and secondly, a subsidiary balance between the lords and commons, the net result of which was constant protection of the royal power.

Not only did the English constitution possess a double balance; it also had the unique advantage of combining monarchic, aristocratic, and democratic elements. Had this constitution been planned, this was the reasoning its planner probably followed. Recognizing that nothing was more chimerical than a state of perfect liberty or equality, he would have anticipated the rise of a despot by establishing a sovereign whose powers could be bound and rendered innocuous. Around such a person in every state there usually grew up a privileged class, whose potentialities could be turned to the use of the state by the granting of titles and by the formation of a House of Lords. Since the House of Commons, the true representative of the people, was by this circumstance the more powerful house, what the House of Lords lacked in real strength it had to receive in outward splendor and greatness. When De Lolme ended with a warning to those who would tamper with this delicate mechanism without understanding its principles, he placed himself squarely against the rising demand for a reform in the House of Commons, even as did Paley and Burke.

Another important contributor to the spread of the classical theory was William Paley, Archdeacon of Carlisle, whose *Principles of Moral and Political Philosophy* (1785) went through fifteen editions during his lifetime, was adopted as a textbook at Cambridge, and was widely read, studied, and criticized. In 1792 the chapter on the English constitution was reprinted separately. His most original contribution to the classical theory was in his justification of influence as an integral part of mixed government. By influence he meant the control exercised by the king and peers over the membership of the House of Commons, a control exercised through patronage and the manipulation of small electorates in some of the boroughs.

Paley's exposition of the principles of the English constitution was memorable for the attention that he gave to the operation of influence, the equilibrium of the constitution, and the role of the House of Lords. Like Blackstone, the theologian traced distinction among governments to the location of the legislative power. A mixed government existed when the legislature combined two or more simple forms of government. In whatever proportion a simple form entered the constitution, its advantages and disadvantages were reproduced. This observation afforded a rule for directing the construction and improvement of mixed government. For example, a monarchy was usually considered to have great energy and also a propensity towards tyranny. It became the duty of the other estates to refrain from officious interference with the executive functions, which should be reserved for the administration of the prince, but to be on their guard against military domination and needless wars.

A foreign element sometimes appeared in the combination of simple forms without its being indigenous to any of them separately. This quality Paley called corruption, by which he seems to have meant influence. Whereas influence would not exist in a pure monarchy or pure democracy, it would be present in a government combining them. A considerable portion of influence, he pointed out, was viewed by many wise and virtuous politicians as necessary to give cohesion and stability to a mixed government. Paley's account of how royal influence had arisen showed perspicacity. It had developed as a result of a shift in the power of the king, which he dated from the accession of James I. Earlier kings had carried their measures in parliament through the use of force, but after 1660 they had adopted new methods. The result was the growth of influence, which was needed to check the pretensions of a popular assembly. Accordingly, the theologian viewed the aim of reformers to limit the patronage at the disposal of the crown as a threat to the constitution and even to the state.

Like De Lolme, Paley was particularly interested in the balance of the constitution, which he saw as two-fold: a balance of power and a balance of interest. By the balance of power, he explained, no branch of the government possessed a power, the abuse or excess of which was not checked by an antagonistic power elsewhere in the constitution. For example, the power of the two houses to legislate was checked by the king's veto, while an attempted arbitrary administration could be frustrated by the two houses' refusal to grant supplies. The accompanying balance of interest which gave efficiency to the balance of power meant that whenever there was an attempted encroachment by one estate, the other two would unite in resistance. It was to the interest of the House of Lords, for example, to prevent the king from expanding his power at the expense of the House of Commons. If the king became arbitrary, the nobility would lose the 'hereditary share they possess in the national counsels' and would become but part of the 'empty pageantry of a despotic court.' On the other hand, if the House of Commons should attempt to encroach upon the royal prerogative, the House of Lords would take instant alarm and side with the crown. Every principle that actuated human conduct would draw the peers to the side of the king. Finally, if the peers sought to regain their feudal privileges, king and people would unite against them.

Paley dwelt at length upon the usefulness of a House of Lords. It added stability to the monarchy, it provided a means by which the king could reward his servants, and, most important, it stemmed the popular fury. If one man in a hundred could think for himself and not allow himself to be swayed by demagogues, he continued, an hereditary nobility would not be necessary to check the people. For when allowance was made for the difference in rank and education, the decision of a nation was usually right for its interests. Unfortunately, large bodies of men were subject to certain frenzies and the only way to stop the 'fermentation' was 'to divide the mass' by erecting different orders in the community with different prejudices and interests. It was not that the nobility was free of prejudice, he emphasized. It was that their prejudices being different, they might counteract those of others. Certainly, Paley's justification of the House of Lords differed from the usual, although he too gave great weight to its moderating influence. He justified the control exercised by individual peers over the membership of the House of Commons on the grounds that in this way an alliance was formed between the two Houses and that the government of the country could thus be kept in the Commons, where it would not stay if 'so powerful and wealthy a part of the nation as the peerage compose, were excluded from all share and interest in its constitution'. . . .

The mixed character of the English constitution was [then] a fundamental assumption of eighteenth-century England. Although the theory of mixed government received its classical form in the writings of Blackstone and De Lolme, perhaps the keynote of the eighteenth century was equally well expressed in a sermon preached before the House of Commons in 1701 by Francis Atterbury, later Bishop of Rochester and leader of the English Jacobites. ' 'Tis natural for Men to think that Government the Best, under which they drew their first breath,' he explained, 'and to propose it as a Model and Standard for all Others. But if any People upon Earth have a just Title thus to boast, 'tis We of this Island; who enjoy a Constitution, wisely moulded, out of all the different Forms and Kinds of Civil Government.' It was a 'Constitution, nicely poiz'd between the Extremes of too much Liberty, and too much Power; the several Parts of it having a Proper Check upon each other. . . .'

Constitutions and Rights

BERNARD BAILYN

Starting where Professor Weston leaves off, Bernard Bailyn traces the transformation of the colonists' view of the English constitution from its traditional definition in 1760, through the critical probing of constitutional concepts which began in 1764, to the radically altered emphasis that ultimately reshaped American thought about politics and government. Like Professor McLaughlin, Bailyn concentrates on the decade of debate before independence and the shifts in American thinking that led to a redefinition of representation and consent, constitutions and rights, and sovereignty. Wrestling with problems that had puzzled political philosophers for centuries, the American colonists, according to Professor Bailyn, "struggled to work out the implications of their beliefs in the years before Independence" in an "effort to express reality as they knew it and to shape it to ideal ends." Trying to square the theory of the English constitution with the practice of colonial self-government, they ended by rejecting English political institutions and establishing American ones, replacing the unwritten English constitution with written constitutions designed to guarantee the basic rights and liberties of the people.

T HE WORD "CONSTITUTION" AND THE CONCEPT BEHIND IT WAS OF central importance to the colonists' political thought; their entire understanding of the crisis in Anglo-American relations rested upon it. So strategically located was this idea in the minds of both English and Americans, and so great was the pressure placed upon it in the course of a decade of pounding debate that in the end it was forced apart, along the seam of a basic ambiguity, to form the two contrasting concepts of

Reprinted by permission of the publishers from pp. 67–69, 161 and 176–198 of Bernard Bailyn, *The Ideological Origins of the American Revolution*. Cambridge, Mass., The Belknap Press of Harvard University Press, Copyright, 1967, by the President and Fellows of Harvard College.

constitutionalism that have remained characteristic of England and America ever since.

At the start of the controversy, however, the most distinguishing feature of the colonists' view of the constitution was its apparent traditionalism. Like their contemporaries in England and like their predecessors for centuries before, the colonists at the beginning of the Revolutionary controversy understood by the word "constitution" not, as we would have it, a written document or even an unwritten but deliberately contrived design of government and a specification of rights beyond the power of ordinary legislation to alter; they thought of it, rather, as the constituted —that is, existing—arrangement of governmental institutions, laws, and customs together with the principles and goals that animated them. So John Adams wrote that a political constitution is like "the constitution of the human body"; "certain contextures of the nerves, fibres, and muscles, or certain qualities of the blood and juices" some of which "may properly be called *stamina vitae,* or essentials and fundamentals of the constitution; parts without which life itself cannot be preserved a moment." A constitution of government, analogously, Adams wrote, is "a frame, a scheme, a combination of powers for a certain end, namely,—the good of the whole community."

The elements of this definition were traditional, but it was nevertheless distinctive in its emphasis on the animating principles, the *stamina vitae,* those "fundamental laws and rules of the constitution, which ought never to be infringed." Belief that a proper system of laws and institutions should be suffused with, should express, essences and fundamentals— moral rights, reason, justice—had never been absent from English notions of the constitution. But not since the Levellers had protested against Parliament's supremacy in the mid-seventeenth century had these considerations seemed so important as they did to the Americans of the mid-eighteenth century. Nor could they ever have appeared more distinct in their content. For if the ostensible purpose of all government was the good of the people, the particular goal of the English constitution—"its end, its use, its designation, drift, and scope"—was known to all, and declared by all, to be the attainment of liberty. This was its peculiar "grandeur" and excellence; it was for this that it should be prized "next to our Bibles, above the privileges of this world." It was for this that it should be blessed, supported and maintained, and transmitted "in full, to posterity.". . .

This critical probing of traditional concepts—part of the colonists' effort to express reality as they knew it and to shape it to ideal ends— became the basis for all further discussions of enlightened reform, in Europe as well as in America. The radicalism the Americans conveyed to the world in 1776 was a transformed as well as a transforming force. . . .

The first suggestions of change came early in the period, the full conclusions only at the very end. At the start [1764] what would emerge as the central feature of American constitutionalism was only an emphasis and a peculiarity of tone within an otherwise familiar discourse. While some writers, like Richard Bland, continued to refer to "a legal constitution, that is, a legislature," and others spoke of "the English constitution . . . a nice piece of machinery which has undergone many changes and alterations," most of the writers saw the necessity of emphasizing principles above institutions, and began to grasp the consequences of doing so. The confusions and difficulties inherent in this process are dramatically illustrated in the troubled career of James Otis.

The heart of the problem Otis faced in the early 1760's was the extent to which, indeed the sense in which, the "constitution" could be conceived of as a limitation on the power of lawmaking bodies. In the writs of assistance case in 1761 he had struck a bold and confident note—so bold, indeed, that John Adams later wrote, rather romantically, that "then and there the child Independence was born." On that famous occasion Otis had said not only that an act of Parliament "against the constitution is void" but that it was the duty of the courts to "pass such acts into disuse," for the "reason of the common law [could] control an act of Parliament." But what was the "constitution" which an act of Parliament could not infringe? Was it a set of fixed principles and rules distinguishable from, antecedent to, more fundamental than, and controlling the operating institutions of government? And was there consequently a "constitutional" limitation on Parliament's actions? Otis' answers were ambiguous, and proved to be politically disastrous. . . .

Otis, drawing the language of seventeenth-century law into the constitutional struggle of the eighteenth century, found himself veering toward positions he was neither intellectually nor politically prepared to accept. "If the reasons that can be given against an act are such," he wrote in his *Rights of the British Colonies* in 1764, "as plainly demonstrate that it is against *natural* equity, the executive courts will adjudge such act void.". . . Was this not to limit the power of Parliament by the provisions of a fixed constitution distinct from and superior to the legislature, a constitution interpreted and applied by the courts? Others, in time, would say it was. . . .

But . . . Otis . . . did not draw its implications. He ignored them, in fact, in working out his own view of the constitution and of the limits of Parliament's powers. If an act of Parliament violated natural laws, "which are *immutably* true," he wrote, it would thereby violate "eternal truth, equity, and justice," and would be "consequently void."

. . . and so it would be adjudged by the Parliament itself when convinced of their mistake. Upon this great principle Parliaments repeal such acts as soon as they find they have been mistaken . . . When such mistake is evident and palpable . . . the judges of the executive courts have declared the act "of a whole Parliament void." See here the grandeur of the British constitution! See the wisdom of our ancestors! . . . If the supreme legislative errs, it is informed by the supreme executive in the King's court of law . . . This is government! This is a constitution! to preserve which . . . has cost oceans of blood and treasure in every age; and the blood and the treasure have upon the whole been well spent.

Parliament was thus itself part of the constitution, not a creature of it, and its power was "uncontrollable but by themselves, and we must obey. They only can repeal their own acts . . . let the Parliament lay what burdens they please on us, we must, it is our duty to submit and patiently bear them, till they will be pleased to relieve us." Yet Parliament's enactments against the constitution—against, that is, the whole system of laws, principles, and institutions based on reason and justice of which it was a part—were void, Otis argued; the courts will adjudge them so, and Parliament itself, by the necessity of the system, will repeal them.

It was a strange argument, comprehensible only as an effort to apply seventeenth-century assumptions to eighteenth-century problems. For Otis continued to assume, with Coke, that Parliament was effectively a supreme judicial as well as a supreme legislative body and hence by definition involved in judicial processes. He continued to believe, too, that moral rights and obligations were not "differentiated as they would be today from legal rights and obligations," and that they naturally radiated from, rather than restricted, enacted law. And he expected fundamental, or higher, law to "control" positive acts of government not in the sense of furnishing judges with grounds for declaring them nonexistent because they conflicted with the "constitution" but only in the sense of providing judges with principles of interpretation by which to modify gross inequities and to interpret "unreasonableness" and self-contradiction in ways that would allow traditional qualities of justice to prevail.

But these assumptions were no longer applicable, in the same way, in the eighteenth century. Parliament was in reality no longer a court but an all powerful sovereign body, and the problem at hand concerned the structure and authority of government, not private law. Otis' theory of the constitution that included a self-correcting Parliament sensitive to the principles of justice and responsive to the admonitions of the courts was, insofar as it was realistic at all, an anachronism, and it came under attack by both the administration, which charged him with attempting to restrict the power of Parliament, and by the colonial radicals, who accused him of preaching passive obedience and nonresistance.

Otis had been faithful, in this way, to the seventeenth-century sources of constitutional thought which he, like so many Americans, revered. Others—poorer scholars, perhaps, but better judges of the circumstances that surrounded them—were less faithful, and in the end more creative. The dominant view of the constitution in 1764 was still the traditional one, unencumbered by Otis' complexities. While Otis was quoting Coke together with Vattel without grasping the implications of their conjunction, others were referring to constitutions as "a sort of fundamental laws"; as the common law; as Parliament; and as the whole complex of existing laws and public institutions. The transition to more advanced ground was forced forward by the continuing need, after 1764, to distinguish fundamentals from institutions and from the actions of government so that they might serve as limits and controls. Once its utility was perceived and demonstrated, this process of disengaging principles from institutions and from the positive actions of government and then of conceiving of them as fixed sets of rules and boundaries, went on swiftly.

In 1768 Samuel Adams, accustomed to drawing more extreme conclusions than most of his contemporaries, wrote in a series of letters in behalf of the Massachusetts House of Representatives that "the constitution is fixed; it is from thence that the supreme legislative as well as the supreme executive derives its authority," and he incorporated the same language into the famous Massachusetts Circular Letter of that year. At the same time a Philadelphian, William Hicks, wrote that if one were to concede that statutes were "a part of [the] constitution" simply because they were once promulgated by government, one would have no basis for restraining the actions of any government. There is nothing sacrosanct, he wrote, in the "variant, inconsistent form of government which we have received at different periods of time"; they were accidental in origins, and their defects should be corrected by comparison with ideal models. In 1769 the emerging logic was carried further by Zubly, who flatly distinguished legislatures from the constitution, and declared that the existing Parliament "derives its authority and power from the constitution, and not the constitution from Parliament." The constitution, he wrote, "is permanent and ever the same," and Parliament "can no more make laws which are against the constitution or the unalterable privileges of British subjects than it can alter the constitution itself . . . The power of Parliament, and of every branch of it, has it bounds assigned by the constitution."

In 1770 the constitution was said to be "a line which marks out the enclosure"; in 1773 it was "the standing measure of the proceedings of

government" of which rulers are "by no means to attempt an alteration
. . . without public consent"; in 1774 it was a "model of government";
in 1775 it was "certain great first principles" on whose "certainty and
permanency . . . the rights of both the ruler and.the subjects depend;
nor may they be altered or changed by ruler or people, but [only] by the
whole collective body . . . nor may they be touched by the legislator."
Finally, in 1776 there came conclusive pronouncements. Two pamphlets
of that year, brilliant sparks thrown off by the clash of Revolutionary
politics in Pennsylvania, lit up the final steps of the path that led directly
to the first constitutions of the American states. "A constitution and a
form of government," the author of *Four Letters on Important Subjects*
wrote, "are frequently confounded together and spoken of as synonymous
things, whereas they are not only different but are established for different
purposes." All nations have governments, "but few, or perhaps none,
have truly a constitution." The primary function of a constitution was to
mark out the boundaries of governmental powers—hence in England,
where there was no constitution, there were no limits (save for the effect
of trial by jury) to what the legislature might do. In order to confine the
ordinary actions of government, the constitution must be grounded in
some fundamental source of authority, some "higher authority than the
giving out temporary laws." This special authority could be gained if the
constitution were created by "an act of *all,*" and it would acquire permanence if it were embodied "in some written charter." Defects, of course,
might be discovered and would have to be repaired: there would have to
be some procedure by which to alter the constitution without disturbing
its controlling power as fundamental law. For this, the means "are easy":

> some article in the constitution may provide that at the expiration of
> every seven or any other number of years a *provincial jury* shall be
> elected to inquire if any inroads have been made in the constitution,
> and to have power to remove them; but not to make alterations, unless
> a clear majority of all the inhabitants shall so direct.

Thus created and thus secured, the constitution could effectively designate
what "part of their liberty" the people are to sacrifice to the necessity of
having government, by furnishing answers to "the two following questions: first, what shall the form of government be? And secondly, what
shall be its power?" In addition, "it is the part of a constitution to fix the
manner in which the officers of government shall be chosen, and determine
the principal outlines of their power, their time of duration, manner of
commissioning them, etc." Finally, "all the great rights which man never
mean, nor ever ought, to lose should be *guaranteed,* not *granted,* by the
constitution, for at the forming a constitution, we ought to have in mind

that whatever is left to be secured by law only may be altered by another law."

The same ideas, in some ways even more clearly worked out, appear in the second Pennsylvania pamphlet of 1776, *The Genuine Principles of the Ancient Saxon or English Constitution,* which was largely composed of excerpts from Obadiah Hulme's *An Historical Essay on the English Constitution,* published in London in 1771, a book both determinative and representative of the historical understanding that lay behind the emerging American constitutionalism. Here too was stated the idea of a constitution as a *"set of fundamental rules* by which even the supreme power of the state shall be governed" and which the legislature is absolutely forbidden to alter. But in this pamphlet there are more explicit explanations of how such documents come into being and of their permanence and importance. They are to be formed "by a convention of the delegates of the people appointed for that express purpose," the pamphlet states, and they are never to be "added to, diminished from, nor altered in any respect by any power besides the power which first framed [them]." They are to remain permanent, and so to have the most profound effect on the lives of people. "Men entrusted with the formation of civil constitutions should remember they are *painting for eternity:* that the smallest defect or redundancy in the system they frame may prove the destruction of millions."

Accompanying this shift in the understanding of constitutionalism, and part of it, was another change, which also began as a relocation of emphasis and ended as a contribution to the transforming radicalism of the Revolution. The *rights* that constitutions existed to protect were understood in the early years of the period, as we have seen, to be at once the inalienable, indefeasible rights inherent in all people by virtue of their humanity, and the concrete provisions of English law as expressed in statutes, charters, and court decisions; it was assumed that the "constitution" in its normal workings would specify and protect the inalienable rights of man. But what if it did not? What if this sense proved false, and it came to be believed that the force of government threatened rather than protected these rights? And what if, in addition, the protective machinery of rights—the constitution—came to be abstracted from the organs of government and to be seen not as an arrangement of institutions and enactments but as a blueprint for institutions, the ideal against which the actual was to be measured?

These questions were first posed early in the controversy, in the course of one of the most vituperative exchanges of constitutional views of the entire period. It is true, Judge Martin Howard, Jr., of Rhode Island wrote in response to Stephen Hopkins' *Rights of Colonies Examined* (1765), that the common law carries within it and guarantees with special force the "indefeasible" personal rights of men; for Britons it is the common law that makes these natural rights operative. But Parliament's power is no less a part of that same common law. "Can we claim the common law as an inheritance, and at the same time be at liberty to adopt one part of it and reject the other?" If Parliament is rejected, so too must political and even personal rights. If rights are accepted as inextricable parts of laws and institutions, the laws and institutions must be accepted in all their normal workings.

James Otis accepted the challenge. But in his stinging reply—a bitter, sarcastic, half-wild polemic—he again displayed a commitment to tradition that kept him from following through the logic of his own argument; again, he succeeded in dramatizing but not in resolving the issue. The judge's "truly *Filmerian*" performance, he wrote, has "inaccuracies in abundance, declamation and false logic without end . . . and the most indelicate fustian." His central error is that he "everywhere confounds the terms rights, liberties, and privileges, which, in legal as well as vulgar acceptation, denote very different ideas." The source of this confusion, Otis said, was a misreading of Blackstone; from his *Commentaries,* Howard had mistakenly derived the idea that the rights of natural persons are the same as those of artificial persons: that is, "bodies politic and corporate." Corporate rights are indeed "matters of the mere favor and grace of the donor or founder"; but that is not to say that the rights of natural people are too. Britons are entitled to their "natural absolute personal rights" by virtue of "the laws of God and nature, as well as by the common law and the constitution of their country so admirably built on the principles of the former." Only such a one as Judge Howard, with his "Filmerian sneer," who "cannot see any difference between power and right, between a blind, slavish submission and a loyal, generous, and rational obedience"—only such a person could fail to understand that the origin of "the inherent, indefeasible rights of the subject" lay in "the law of nature and its author. This law is the grand basis of the common law and of all other municipal laws that are worth a rush. True it is that every act of Parliament which names the colonies . . . binds them. But this is not so, strictly and properly speaking, by the common law as by the law of nature and by the constitution of a parliament or sovereign and supreme legislative in a state."

Otis had shifted the emphasis of discussion to the priority of abstract rights, but he had not attempted to follow through the implications of his own thought: he continued to assume that the actual law would express, and naturally protect, the universal rights of man. But if he did not draw the conclusions implicit in his own logic, others did: there is in the proliferating discussion of constitutionalism a steadily increasing emphasis on the universal, inherent, indefeasible qualities of rights. John Dickinson, also a lawyer—indeed, a more professionally trained lawyer than Otis—attacked in a more knowing and thorough way the idea that rights are matters of "favor and grace." True, in 1764 he had vehemently defended the charter of Pennsylvania against the attacks of Joseph Galloway and others, but not because he believed that "the liberties of the subject were mere favors granted by charters from the crown." The liberties of Pennsylvanians, he had proclaimed in a ringing oration in the Pennsylvania Assembly, are "founded on the acknowledged rights of human nature." The value of a charter like that of Pennsylvania was that it stated the true character of such liberties beyond any misunderstanding, and freed them from the entanglements of those ancient, archaic customs "that our ancestors either had not moderation or leisure enough to untwist." Two years later (1766) he elaborated the point significantly. Charters, he wrote in his *Address to the Committee of Correspondence in Barbados,* like all aspects of the law, are *"declarations* but not *gifts* of liberties." Kings and Parliaments cannot give "the *rights essential to happiness."*

> We claim them from a higher source—from the King of kings, and Lord of all the earth. They are not annexed to us by parchments and seals. They are created in us by the decrees of Providence, which establish the laws of our nature. They are born with us; exist with us; and cannot be taken from us by any human power without taking our lives. In short, they are founded on the immutable maxims of reason and justice.

Written laws—even the great declarations like Magna Carta—do not create liberties; they "must be considered as only declaratory of our rights, and in affirmance of them."

Ultimately, the conclusion to be drawn became obvious: the entire legitimacy of positive law and legal rights must be understood to rest on the degree to which they conformed to the abstract universals of natural rights. Not all were willing, even in 1775, to go as far as Alexander Hamilton, who wrote in bold, arresting words that "the sacred rights of mankind are not to be rummaged for among old parchments of musty records. They are written, as with a sunbeam, in the whole *volume* of human nature, by the hand of divinity itself, and can never be erased or obscured by mortal power." But if some found this statement too enthusiastic, few by 1774—few even of the Tories—disagreed with the calmer formulation of the same idea, by Philip Livingston. Had he understood his antagonist, the Rev. Thomas Bradbury Chandler, correctly? Had Chandler really meant to say "that any right . . . if it be not confirmed by some statute law is not a legal right"? If so, Livingston declared, "in the name of America, I deny it." Legal rights are "those rights which we are entitled to by the eternal laws of right reason"; they exist independent of positive law, and stand as the measure of its legitimacy.

Neither Hamilton nor Livingston, nor any of the other writers who touched on the subject, meant to repudiate the heritage of English common and statutory law. Their claim was only that the source of rights be recognized, in Jefferson's words, as "the laws of nature, and not as the gift of their chief magistrate," and that as a conseqence the ideal must be understood to exist before the real and to remain superior to it, controlling it and limiting it. But what was the ideal? What precisely were the ideal rights of man? They were, everyone knew, in some sense Life, Liberty, and Property. But in what sense? Must they not be specified? Must not the ideal now be reduced from a radiant presence and a conglomerate legal tradition to specific enumerated provisions? Must not the essential rights of man be specified and codified if they were to serve effectively as limits on the actions of courts and legislatures? In 1765 James Otis had fulminated at the mere suggestion that a document might profitably be drawn up stating the "rights of the colonies with precision and certainty." Insolence, he had called it, pedantry and nonsense; Britons had no need for "codes, pandects, novels, decretals of popes." "The common law is our birthright, and the rights and privileges confirmed and secured to us by the British constitution and by act of Parliament are our best inheritance." But thought had shifted rapidly in the decade that followed, Arthur Lee exhorting his countrymen in 1768 to draw up a petition of rights *"and never desist from the solicitation till it be confirmed into a bill of rights,"* and Andrew Eliot a year later despairing of all solutions save that of "an American bill of rights." No voice was raised in objection when in 1776 the idea was proclaimed, and acted upon, that "all the great rights . . . should be *guaranteed"* by the terms of a written constitution.

These closely related changes—in the view of what a constitution was and of the proper emphasis in the understanding of rights—were momentous; they would shape the entire future development of American constitutional thought and practice. Yet they did not seem to be momentous at the time. They were not generally experienced as intrusive or threatening alterations. They were hardly seen as changes at all: they drifted into consciousness so gradually and easily and were accepted with so little controversy that writers would soon feel called upon to remind Americans that the fundamental principles of their political and constitutional thought were "of recent date, and for [them] the world is indebted to America; for if [the distinction between constitutional law and that of the ordinary legislature] did not originate in this country, it was here that it was first reduced to practice, exemplified, and its utility and practicability first established." For in this area too, as in so many other developments in political and social thought, the way had been paved by the peculiar circumstances of colonial life. Whatever Otis may have thought of the issue when he came to consider it in theoretical terms, the fact was that written constitutions—documents not different essentially from the "codes, pandects, novels" he denounced—had existed, had been acted upon, had been assumed to be proper and necessary, for a century or more. Some, like the charter of the Massachusetts Bay Colony, had originated as commercial charters, concessions of powers by the crown to enterprisers willing to undertake the risks of exploration and settlement. These, in the colonial setting, had quickly changed in character, and "by some metamorphosis or feat of legerdemain had . . . become the frame of government for a state." The Massachusetts Bay charter in particular "approximated a popular constitution," Professor McIlwain has written, "more closely than any other instrument of government in actual use up to that time in America or elsewhere in modern times." It is hardly surprising, he concludes, that the Fundamental Orders of Connecticut of 1639, "'the first American constitution accepted by the people,'" should have been written by men who emigrated from Massachusetts.

Later crown charters, like those of Connecticut and Rhode Island, were designed in the first place to be basic instruments of government; and if the seventeenth-century proprietary grants—those of New York, Maryland, and the Carolinas—were anachronistic in their feudal terminology, they too created "governing powers" and provided for public institutions that were expected to be "incapable of alteration or amendment except by concession from the grantor." Most important of all, because most deliberately "constitutional" in character, were the foundations laid down by William Penn for the establishment of government in New Jersey and Pennsylvania. This remarkable man—courtier and sectarian; saint, schemer, and scholar—whose imaginative grasp of the possibilities of constitution-making led him eventually to propose not only a "Plan of Union for the Colonies" but also a scheme for "The Establishment of a European Diet, Parliament, or Estates," devoted himself enthusiastically to constructing a proper framework of government for the Quaker colonies. In consultation with the leading political theorists of his time, he drew up and published a series of concessions, frames of government, and charters, which were, in effect, blueprints for "civil administration, elections, court procedure, the exercise of justice, fines, penalties, and . . . the duties and obligations of officeholders." These schemes, again and again revised in an effort to adjust soaring idealism to the demands of ordinary human realities, could hardly have been more clearly fundamental, more manifestly constituent, in nature.

By the Revolutionary period, the surviving charters, which in origins had been the instruments of the aggressive creation, or legitimation, of power, had become defensive bulwarks against the misuse of power. In Connecticut, Rhode Island, and Massachusetts they were cherished still, as they had been for a century and more, as special confirmations of "the ancient common law of England, and of the common rights of Englishmen." In Pennsylvania, in the years immediately preceding the Stamp Act, the attack launched against the Penn family's tax privileges, which had been written into the original charter, was fended off by impassioned pleas, like that of John Dickinson, to preserve intact, Proprietary tax privileges and all, the "laws and liberties framed and delivered down to us by our careful ancestors . . . Any body of men acting under a charter must surely tread on slippery ground when they take a step that may be deemed a surrender of that charter." Nor were the benefits of these famous compacts "between the sovereign and the first patentees" valued only in the particular provinces in which they had survived. Everywhere in the colonies the existing charters were prized as "evidential of the rights and immunities belonging to all the King's subjects in America."

For some people, in fact, the charters had acquired, in the course of the years, an additional, transcendent sanction. Those who viewed the world in the light of covenant theology could see the colonial charters as valid not merely in the eyes of the law but in the eyes of God as well: "our charter . . . was a solemn *covenant* between [the King] and our *fathers*"—a "sacred" covenant by which the crown had contracted with a morally regenerate people to maintain their "rights, liberties, and privileges . . . inviolably firm and free from the least innovations, in the same manner that King David stood engaged by the covenant of the people." For "the covenant people of God" in particular, these charters, on the eve of the Revolution, were known to contain "the first great principles, or stamina, of their governments . . . prescribing the forms of their several governments, determining and bounding the power of the crown over them within proper limits, and ascertaining and securing their rights, jurisdictions, and liberties."

It took no wrench of mind, no daring leap, to accept, by then, the concept of a fixed, written constitution limiting the ordinary actions of government. Famous examples of the fact had long been present: the explicit idea, following, brought this experience into consciousness, gave it new meaning and propulsive power.

The same, though perhaps less obviously so, was true of the change in emphasis in the meaning of rights. The abstraction of rights from their embodiments in ancient, customary law, and their purposeful compilation and publication were not entirely new things for the colonists. Experience in such matters was buried deep in the colonial past; the process, and its results, had been familiar a century before it became systematically important in constitutional theory.

Denied the guidance of experts in the law, lacking sure ideas of what precisely the law provided and what rights were theirs, yet passionately devoted to the belief that English laws and English rights *were* theirs if they would but claim them, the first settlers in British America had found it necessary to compile the law they knew, enumerate its provisions, and specify some, at least, of the rights it guaranteed. The process could hardly have begun earlier than in fact it did. The Pilgrims, responding not to theory but to the practical needs of everyday life, drew up a code of law as early as 1636: "it contains," a leading authority on the early history of American law has written, "a rudimentary bill of rights," which, when elaborated and enlarged in the later years of the seventeenth century, became "a recognizably modern bill of rights." The Puritans did the same, also within two decades of settlement. Their *Laws and Liberties* of 1648 was in design an abridgement of the laws they had themselves enacted; but, "the culmination of an extraordinarily creative period" of legal and constitutional thought, it went beyond restating and digesting the laws in force, to define "the just rights and privileges of every freeman." It quickly became famous, and influential, in all the colonies. It proved to be

the fountainhead of Massachusetts law during most of the seventeenth century, and even thereafter, and its provisions were widely copied by other colonies, or used by them as models in framing their own laws. Through such intercolonial borrowing, its influence spread into other parts of New England, beyond to New York and even to Delaware and Pennsylvania.

But the other colonies were not entirely dependent on New England models. Acting independently, in response to needs similar to those that had motivated the Massachusetts codifiers, they too drew up, on various occasions, their own formulations of rights. The ill-fated "Charter of Liberties and Privileges" passed by the first General Assembly of New York in 1683, contained not only "the outlines of a constitution for the province" but a "bill of rights" as well. Even more elaborate, and explicit, were the provisions of the "Rights and Privileges of the Majesty's Subjects" enacted eight years later, in 1691, by the same body. This remarkable statute, objected to in England because of its "large and doubtful expressions" and disallowed there, listed the rights of the individuals in the form of a series of categorical prohibitions on government: the individual was to be free from unlawful arrest and imprisonment, arbitrary taxation, martial law and the support of standing armies in time of peace, feudal dues, and restrictions on freehold tenure; in addition, he was guaranteed due process of law, especially trial by jury, and, if Protestant, full liberty to "enjoy his or their opinion, persuasions, [and] judgments in matters of conscience and religion throughout all this province."

But, again, it was William Penn who saw farthest and accomplished the most. His "Laws, Concessions, and Agreements" for the province of West New Jersey, which he drafted probably in collaboration with Edward Byllynge and published in 1677, provided not only for the distribution of land and the organization of government but also, and in great detail, for "the common laws or fundamental rights and privileges" of the inhabitants. The central purpose of this remarkably enlightened document was, in fact, to state, so that they might be known and be preserved intact in the New World, "such liberties as were guaranteed by law for the good government of a people, in accord with, as near as conveniently might be, 'the primitive, ancient, and fundamental laws of the people of England.'" Most explicit of all were Penn's statements of rights and privileges in the provisions he made for his own province of Pennsylvania. In his original Concessions and in his Frames of Government, but even more in the so-called "Laws Agreed upon in England" and in the Charter of Liberties and the Charter of Privileges, he laid out, point by point, the rights, duties, and proper regulations of "every phase of human life, civil and social."

By no means all of these documents were bills of rights as we know them. Most of them were not thought of as defining rights antecedent to government and law, rights to which government and law must accommodate themselves. The most common assumption behind them was, rather, that these were rights that the law—English law if not colonial—already provided for and that were now being compiled simply to make them better known and more readily available for reference in a wilderness environment. Presumed to be neither "basic" in some special way nor logically comprehensive, they were mainly devoted to eliminating arbitrary procedures in the enactment and execution of laws. But some of them are nevertheless astonishingly modern, containing some of the precise prohibitions on governmental powers and some of the exact guarantees of individual action that would later come to be thought of as necessary parts of fully evolved bills of rights. The eighteenth century would add nothing to the declaration, in the "Concessions . . . or Fundamental Rights" of West New Jersey, that "no men nor number of men upon earth hath power or authority to rule over men's conscience in religious matters";

nor would much improvement be made in the clause providing that no one "shall be deprived or condemned of life, limb, liberty, estate, [or] property . . . without a due trial and judgment passed by twelve good and lawful men of his neighborhood." And it is doubtful if James Madison, writing a full century later, would better the statements in New York's *Act Declaring What Are the Rights and Privileges* guaranteeing "due course of law," trial by jury, and freedom from the obligation to quarter troops in peacetime.

All of these codes and declarations—whatever the deliberate assumptions of their authors, and however archaic or modern-sounding their provisions—were, at the very least, efforts to abstract from the deep entanglements of English law and custom certain essentials—obligations, rights, and prohibitions—by which liberty, as it was understood, might be preserved. As English law in America became better known in the eighteenth century through the work of an increasingly professional bar, and as governmental and judicial processes became stabilized in the colonies, the original need that had given rise to these documents faded. Except where they were embedded in, or protected by, crown charters, they tended to drop from prominence—but not from awareness. In some places surviving intact from the settlement period to the Revolution, well remembered in others where they had been eliminated from the statutes, and everywhere understood to be reasonable and beneficent, these documents formed a continuous tradition in colonial American life, and drifted naturally into the thought of the Revolutionary generation. So in 1774 Alexander Hamilton asserted, as a conclusive argument, that New York's "very remarkable" Act of 1691 "confutes all that has been said concerning the novelty of our present claims, and proves that the injurious reflections on the [Continental] Congress for having risen in their demands are malicious and repugnant to truth."

CONSTITUTIONAL DEVELOPMENTS DURING THE REVOLUTION AND CONFEDERATION

The People
as Constituent Power

ROBERT R. PALMER

In his book on *The Ideological Origins of the American Revolution*, Bernard Bailyn singles out the "pivotal question of sovereignty" as the absolutely crucial issue over which the Revolution was fought. That issue involved two questions, one the nature and the other the location of the ultimate power in the state. At the beginning of the controversy between Great Britain and the American colonies, Sir William Blackstone outlined the orthodox answer to both questions in his classic *Commentaries on the English Law*. First, in all forms of government "there is and must be . . . a supreme, irresistible, absolute, uncontrolled authority, in which the . . . rights of sovereignty, reside." Second, the sovereignty of the British constitution was lodged in king-in-Parliament, the trinity of king, lords, and commons, whose actions, as Blackstone pointed out, "no power on earth can undo."

The Declaration of Independence replaced parliamentary sovereignty with the sovereignty of the people, but the institutionalization of that concept, as Robert R. Palmer suggests, "developed unclearly, gradually, and sporadically during the American Revolution." As he clearly demonstrates, however, the implementation of the idea of the people as constituent power was "the most distinctive work of the Revolution."

I F IT BE ASKED WHAT THE AMERICAN REVOLUTION DISTINCTIVELY contributed to the world's stock of ideas, the answer might go somewhat along these lines. It did not contribute primarily a social doctrine—for although a certain skepticism toward social rank was an old

From R. R. Palmer, *The Age of Democratic Revolution: A Political History of Europe and America, 1760–1800*, Vol. I, *The Challenge* (copyright © 1959 by Princeton University Press; Princeton Paperback, 1969), pp. 213–232. Reprinted by permission of Princeton University Press.

American attitude, and possibly even a gift to mankind, it long antedated the Revolution, which did not so much cut down, as prevent the growth of, an aristocracy of European type. It did not especially contribute economic ideas—for the Revolution had nothing to teach on the production or distribution of goods, and the most advanced parties objected to private wealth only when it became too closely associated with government. They aimed at a separation of economic and political spheres, by which men of wealth, while free to get rich, should not have a disproportionate influence on government, and, on the other hand, government and public emoluments should not be used as a means of livelihood for an otherwise impecunious and unproductive upper class.

The American Revolution was a political movement, concerned with liberty, and with power. Most of the ideas involved were by no means distinctively American. There was nothing peculiarly American in the concepts, purely as concepts, of natural liberty and equality. They were admitted by conservatives, and were taught in the theological faculty at the Sorbonne. Nor could Americans claim any exclusive understanding of the ideas of government by contract or consent, or the sovereignty of the people, or political representation, or the desirability of independence from foreign rule, or natural rights, or the difference between natural law and positive law, or between certain fundamental laws and ordinary legislation, or the separation of powers, or the federal union of separate states. All these ideas were perfectly familiar in Europe, and that is why the American Revolution was of such interest to Europeans.

THE DISTINCTIVENESS OF AMERICAN POLITICAL IDEAS

The most distinctive work of the Revolution was in finding a method, and furnishing a model, for putting these ideas into practical effect. It was in the implementation of similar ideas that Americans were more successful than Europeans. "In the last fifty years," wrote General Bonaparte to Citizen Talleyrand in 1797, "there is only one thing that I can see that we have really defined, and that is the sovereignty of the people. But we have had no more success in determining what is constitutional, than in allocating the different powers of government." And he said more peremptorily, on becoming Emperor in 1804, that the time had come "to constitute the Nation." He added: "I am the constituent power."

The problem throughout much of America and Europe, for half a century, was to "constitute" new government, and in a measure new societies. The problem was to find a constituent power. Napoleon offered himself to Europe in this guise. The Americans solved the problem by the device of the constitutional convention, which, revolutionary in origin, soon became institutionalized in the public law of the United States.

The constitutional convention in theory embodied the sovereignty of the people. The people chose it for a specific purpose, not to govern, but to set up institutions of government. The convention, acting as the sovereign people, proceeded to draft a constitution and declaration of rights. Certain "natural" or "inalienable" rights of the citizen were thus laid down at the same time as the powers of government. It was the constitution that created the powers of government, defined their scope, gave them legality, and balanced them one against another. The constitution was written and comprised in a single document. The constitution and accompanying declaration, drafted by the convention, must, in the developed theory, be ratified by the people. The convention thereupon disbanded and disappeared, lest its members have a vested interest in the offices they created. The constituent power went into abeyance, leaving the work of government to the authorities now constituted. The people, having exercised sovereignty, now came under government. Having made law, they came under law. They put themselves voluntarily under restraint. At the same time, they put restraint upon government. All government was limited government; all public authority must keep within the bounds of the constitution and of the declared rights. There were two levels of law, a higher law or constitution that only the people could make or amend, through constitutional conventions or bodies similarly empowered; and a statutory law, to be made and unmade, within the assigned limits, by legislators to whom the constitution gave this function.

Such was the theory, and it was a distinctively American one. European thinkers, in all their discussion of a political or social contract, of government by consent and of sovereignty of the people, had not clearly imagined the people as actually contriving a constitution and creating the organs of government. They lacked the idea of the people as a constituent power. Even in the French Revolution the idea developed slowly; members of the French National Assembly, long after the Tennis Court oath, continued to feel that the constitution which they were writing, to be valid, had to be accepted by the King as a kind of equal with whom the nation had to negotiate. Nor, indeed, would the King tolerate any other view. On the other hand, we have seen how at Geneva in 1767 the democrats advanced an extreme version of citizen sovereignty, holding that the people created the constitution and the public offices by an act of will; but they failed to get beyond a simple direct democracy; they had no idea of two levels of law, or of limited government, or of a delegated and representative legislative authority, or of a sovereign people which, after acting as a god from the machine in a constituent convention, retired to the more modest status of an electorate, and let its theoretical sovereignty become inactive.

The difficulty with the theory was that the conditions under which it could work were seldom present. No people really starts *de novo;* some political institutions always already exist; there is never a *tabula rasa,* or state of nature, or Chart Blanche as Galloway posited for conservative purposes. Also, it is difficult for a convention engaged in writing a constitution not to be embroiled in daily politics and problems of government. And it is hard to live voluntarily under restraint. In complex societies, or in times of crisis, either government or people or some part of the people may feel obliged to go beyond the limits that a constitution has laid down.

In reality, the idea of the people as a constituent power, with its corollaries, developed unclearly, gradually, and sporadically during the American Revolution. It was adumbrated in the Declaration of Independence: the people may "institute new government." Jefferson, among the leaders, perhaps conceived the idea most clearly. It is of especial interest, however, to see how the "people" themselves, that is, certain lesser and unknown or poorer or unsatisfied persons, contributed to these distinctive American ideas by their opposition to the Revolutionary elite.

There were naturally many Americans who felt that no change was needed except expulsion of the British. With the disappearance of the British governors, and collapse of the old governors' councils, the kind of men who had been active in the colonial assemblies, and who now sat as provincial congresses or other *de facto* revolutionary bodies, were easily inclined to think that they should keep the management of affairs in their own hands. Some parallel can be seen with what happened in Europe. There was a revolution, or protest, of constituted bodies against authorities set above them, and a more popular form of revolution, or protest, which aimed at changing the character or membership of these constituted bodies themselves. As at Geneva the General Council rebelled against the patriciate, without wishing to admit new citizens to the General Council; as in Britain the Whigs asserted the powers of Parliament against the King, without wishing to change the composition of Parliament; as in Belgium, in 1789, the Estates party declared independence from the Emperor, while maintaining the preexisting estates; as in France, also in 1789, the nobility insisted that the King govern through the Estates-General, but objected to the transformation of the three estates into a new kind of national body; as in the Dutch provinces in 1795 the Estates-General, after expelling the Prince of Orange, tried to remain itself unchanged, and resisted the election of a "convention"; so, in America in 1776, the assemblies that drove out the officers of the King, and governed their respective states under revolutionary conditions, sought to keep control of affairs in their own hands, and to avoid reconstitution at the hands of the "people."

Ten states gave themselves new constitutions in 1776 and 1777. In nine of these states, however, it was the ordinary assembly, that is, the revolutionary government of the day, that drafted and proclaimed the constitution. In the tenth, Pennsylvania, a constituent convention met, but it soon had to take on the burden of daily government in addition. In Connecticut and Rhode Island the colonial charters remained in force, and the authorities constituted in colonial times (when governors and councils had already been elected) remained unchanged in principle for half a century. In Massachusetts the colonial charter remained in effect until 1780.

Thus in no state, when independence was declared, did a true constituent convention meet, and, as it were, calmly and rationally devise government out of a state of nature. There was already, however, some recognition of the principle that constitutions cannot be made merely by governments, that a more fundamental power is needed to produce a constitution than to pass ordinary laws or carry on ordinary executive duties. Thus, in New Hampshire, New York, Delaware, Maryland, North Carolina, and Georgia, the assemblies drew up constitutions only after soliciting authority for that purpose from the voters. In Maryland and North Carolina there was a measure of popular ratification.

CONSTITUTION-MAKING IN NORTH CAROLINA, PENNSYLVANIA, AND MASSACHUSETTS

The popular pressures that helped to form American political doctrine are best illustrated from North Carolina, Pennsylvania, and Massachusetts.[1]

In North Carolina class lines had been sharply drawn by the Regulator movement and its suppression. The people of the back-country even inclined to be loyalist, not eager for an independence that might only throw them into the hands of the county gentry. In the turbulent election of October 1776 the voters knew that the assembly which they elected would draft a state constitution. There was no demand for a convention to act exclusively and temporarily as a constituent power. But several counties drew up instructions for the deputies, in which the emerging doctrine was set forth clearly.

Orange and Mecklenburg counties used identical language. This is a

[1] Here I am indebted, without sharing all his conclusions, to E. P. Douglass, *Rebels and Democrats: the Struggle for Equal Political Rights and Majority Rule during the American Revolution* (Chapel Hill, 1955).

sign, as in the case of identical phrasing in the French *cahiers* of 1789, where the matter has been carefully studied, that some person of influence and education, and not some poor farmer ruminating in his cabin, had probably written out a draft. Still, the public meetings of both counties found it to their taste. "Political power," they said, "is of two kinds, one principal and superior, the other derived and inferior. . . . The principal supreme power is possessed only by the people at large. . . . The derived and inferior power by the servants which they employ. . . . The rules by which the inferior power is exercised are to be constituted by the principal supreme power. . . ." In other words, government was not a form of guardianship. Office was to be no longer a perquisite of the gentry, or "an aristocracy of power in the hands of the rich," to use their own language, but a form of employment by the people, whom they did not hesitate to call "the poor." Mecklenburg favored a unicameral legislature, Orange a bicameral one, but both called for a separation of powers. It was not that any organ of government should enjoy independence from the electorate (the essence of balance-of-power theory in the European, British, and loyalist view), but rather that the various functions of government should be defined and distributed among different men, to prevent what had happened in colonial times. The fact that before 1776 the council had possessed executive, legislative, and judicial functions, and that members of the assembly had served as justices of the peace, or had their relatives appointed judges and sheriffs, was the basis on which North Carolina had been dominated by small groups of gentry. It was popular objection to this situation, probably more than a reading of European books, that made the separation of powers a principal American doctrine.

The North Carolina constitution, as written and adopted, enlarged the electorate by granting all taxpayers the right to vote for members of the lower house. It equalized the representation by giving more deputies to the western counties. It required a freehold of 100 acres for members of the lower house, and of 300 acres for those of the upper house, who were to be elected only by voters possessing 50 acres. The governor, elected by the two houses, had to have a freehold worth £1,000. The constitution was a compromise between populace and landed gentry. It lasted until the Civil War.

The situation in Pennsylvania was complex. The Quaker colony, idealized by European intellectuals as the haven of innocent equality and idyllic peace, had long been plagued by some of the most acrimonious politics in America. Quaker bigwigs had long clashed with the non-Quaker lesser orders of Philadelphia and the West. In the spring of 1776 Pennsylvania was the only colony in which the assembly was still legal under the old law. It still showed a desire for reconciliation with England, and, with it, maintenance of the old social and political system. This persistence of conservatism in high places made a great many people all the more radical. A year of open war with Britain had aroused the determination for independence, and in May 1776 a mass meeting of 4,000 people in Philadelphia demanded the calling of a constitutional convention. Various local committees got to work, and a convention was elected by irregular methods. Where the three eastern counties had formerly been heavily overrepresented, the situation was now not equalized, but reversed. The West, with the same population as the three eastern counties, had 64 delegates in the convention to only 24 for the East. "The Convention in Pennsylvania was a political expedient, and not, as in Massachusetts, the cornerstone of constitutional government." Its real function was to promote the Revolution, and assure independence from England, by circumventing the assembly and all other opposition. Like the more famous French Convention elected in 1792, it rested on a kind of popular mandate which did not reflect an actual majority of the population; like it, it became the government of the country during war and revolution; like it, it behaved dictatorially. The constitutions drafted in Pennsylvania in 1776, and in France in 1793, were, in their formal provisions, by far the most democratic of any produced in the eighteenth century. The Pennsylvania constitution of 1776, unlike the French constitution of the Year I, was never submitted even to the formalities of popular ratification. But the two constitutions became a symbol of what democrats meant by democracy.

The Pennsylvania constitution vested legislative power in a single house. For the executive it avoided the name and office of governor, entrusting executive power to a council and "president," a word which then meant no more than chairman. All male taxpayers twenty-one years of age had the vote, and were eligible for any office. To sit in the assembly, however, it was necessary publicly to acknowledge the divine inspiration of the Old and New Testaments. Voters elected the legislators, the executive councillors, sheriffs, coroners, tax-assessors, and justices of the peace. Voting was by ballot. The president was chosen by the legislature and the executive council; he had no veto or appointive powers, and what powers he did have he could exercise only in agreement with his council. All officers were elected for one year, except that councillors served for three. Rotation of office was provided for; legislators, councillors, president, and sheriffs could be reelected only a certain number of times. Doors of the legislative assembly must always be open to the public. There was a kind of referendum, in that no bill passed by the assembly, short of emergency, became law until submitted for public consideration and enacted in the assembly of the following year, if there was no public objection. Officeholders received pay, but if revenues of any office became too large the assembly could reduce them. All officers and judges could be impeached by the assembly. Judges of the Supreme Court could be removed by the assembly for "misbehavior." There was an elected council of censors, or board of review, which every seven years ascertained whether the constitution had been preserved inviolate, and called a convention if amendment seemed necessary.

The Pennsylvania constitution represented the doctrine of a single party, namely the democrats, people of the kind who had formerly had little to do with government, and whose main principle was that government should never become a separate or vested interest within the state. This was indeed an understandable principle, at a time when government, in all countries in varying degree, had in fact become the entrenched interest of a largely hereditary governing class. The Pennsylvania constitution substituted almost a direct democracy, in which no one in government could carry any responsibility or pursue any sustained program of his own. Many people in Pennsylvania objected to it from the beginning. It must be remembered that the democratic constitution did not signify that Pennsylvania was really more democratic than some of the other states; it signified, rather, that Pennsylvania was more divided, and that conservatism was stronger, certain upper-class and politically experienced elements, which elsewhere took a leading part in the Revolution, being in Pennsylvania tainted with Anglophilism. Whether the constitution of 1776 was workable or not, these people soon put an end to it. It lasted only until 1790.

The most interesting case is that of Massachusetts. Here the great political thinker was John Adams, who became the main author of the Massachusetts constitution of 1780, which in turn had an influence on the Constitution of the United States. In his own time Adams was denounced as an Anglomaniac and a Monocrat. In our own time some sympathizers with the eighteenth-century democrats have considered him very conservative, while on the other hand theorists of the "new conservatism" would persuade us that John Adams was in truth the American Edmund Burke. I confess that I see very little in any of these allegations.

Adams in January 1776 published some *Thoughts on Government,* for the guidance of those in the various colonies who were soon to declare independence and begin to govern themselves. This was in some ways a conservative tract. Adams thought it best, during the war, for the new states simply to keep the forms of government that they had. He obviously approved the arrangement under the Massachusetts charter of 1691, by which the popular assembly elected an upper house or council. In other ways he was not very conservative. He declared, like Jefferson, that the aim of government is welfare or happiness, that republican institutions must rest on "virtue," and that the people should support a universal system of public schools. He wanted one-year terms for governors and officials (the alternative would be "slavery"), and he favored rotation of office. He quite agreed that someday the state governors and councillors might be popularly elected, as they were in Connecticut already. He gave six reasons for having a bicameral legislature, but in none of these six reasons did he show any fear of the people, or belief that, with a uni-cameral legislature, the people would plunder property or degenerate into anarchy. He was afraid of the one-house legislature itself. He never committed the folly of identifying the deputies with the deputizers. He was afraid that a single house would be arbitrary or capricious, or make itself perpetual, or "make laws for their own interest, and adjudge all controversies in their own favor." He himself cited the cases of Holland and the Long Parliament. The fear of a self-perpetuating political body, gathering privileges to itself, was certainly better grounded in common observation than vague alarms about anarchy or pillage.

The *Thoughts* of 1776 were conservative in another way, if conservatism be the word. Adams had not yet conceived the idea of a constitutional convention. He lacked the notion of the people as constituent power. He had in mind that existing assemblies would draft the new constitutions, when and if any were drafted. Adams was familiar with all the high-level political theory of England and Europe. But the idea of the people as the constituent power arose locally, from the grass roots.

The revolutionary leadership in Massachusetts, including both Adamses, was quite satisfied to be rid of the British, and otherwise to keep the Bay State as it had always been. They therefore "resumed" the charter of 1691. They simply undid the Massachusetts Government Act of 1774. Some of the commonalty of Boston, and farmers of Concord and the western towns, envisaged further changes. It is hard to say what they wanted, except that they wanted a new constitution. Experts in Massachusetts history contradict each other flatly; some say that debtors, poor men, and Baptists were dissatisfied; others that all kinds of diverse people naturally owed money anyway, that practically no one was too poor to vote, and that Baptists were an infinitesimal splinter group in a solidly Congregationalist population. It may be that the trouble was basically psychological; that many people of fairly low station, even though they had long had the right to vote, had never until the Revolution participated in politics, were aroused by the Revolution, the war, and excitement of soldiering, and, feeling that affairs had always been managed by people socially above them, wanted now to act politically on their own.

Demands were heard for a new constitution. It was said that the charter of 1691 was of no force, since the royal power that had issued it was no longer valid. It was said that no one could be governed without his consent, and that no living person had really consented to this charter. Some Berkshire towns even hinted that they did not belong to Massachusetts at all until they shared in constituting the new commonwealth. They talked of "setting themselves apart," or being welcomed by a neighboring state. Echoes of the social contract floated through the western air. "The law to bind all must be assented to by all," declared the farmers of Sutton. "The Great Secret of Government is governing all by all," said those of Spencer. It began to seem that a constitution was necessary not only to secure liberty but to establish authority, not only to protect the individual but to found the state.

The house of representatives proposed that it and the council, that is, the two houses of legislation sitting together, should be authorized by the people to draw up a constitution. All adult males were to vote on the granting of this authorization, not merely those possessing the customary property qualification. In a sense, this was to recognize Rousseau's principle that there must be "unanimity at least once": that everyone must consent to the law under which he was to live, even if later, when constitutional arrangements were made, a qualification was required for ordinary voting. The council objected to a plan whereby it would lose its identity by merging with the house. A little dispute occurred, not unlike that in France in 1789 between "vote by head" and "vote by order." The plan nevertheless went through. The two houses, sitting as one, authorized by the people, produced a constitution in 1778. It was submitted for popular ratification. The voters repudiated it. Apparently both democrats and conservatives were dissatisfied. This is precisely what happened in Holland in 1797, when the first constitution of the Dutch revolution was rejected by a coalition of opposite-minded voters.

A special election was therefore held, in which all towns chose delegates to a state convention, "for the sole purpose of forming a new Constitution." John Adams, delegate from Braintree, was put on the drafting committee. He wrote a draft, which the convention modified only in detail. The resulting document reflected many influences. It is worth while to suggest a few.

There is a modern fashion for believing that Rousseau had little influence in America, particularly on such sensible characters as John Adams. I do not think that he had very much. Adams, however, had read the *Social Contract* as early as 1765, and ultimately had four copies of it in his library. I suspect that, like others, he found much of it unintelligible or fantastic, and some of it a brilliant expression of his own beliefs. He himself said of the Massachusetts constitution: "It is Locke, Sidney, Rousseau, and de Mably reduced to practice."

Adams wrote in the preamble: "The body politic is formed by a voluntary association of individuals. It is a social compact, by which the whole people convenants with each citizen, and each citizen with the whole people, that all shall be governed by certain laws for the common good." The thought here, and the use of the word "covenant," go back to the Mayflower compact. But whence comes the "social" in *social* compact? And whence comes the word "citizen"? There were no "citizens" under the British constitution, except in the sense of freemen of the few towns known as cities. In the English language the word "citizen" in its modern sense is an Americanism, dating from the American Revolution.[2] It is entirely possible that Jean-Jacques Rousseau had deposited these terms in Adams' mind. The whole passage suggests Chapter vi, Book 1, of the *Social Contract.* The convention adopted this part of Adams' preamble without change.

In the enacting clause of the preamble Adams wrote: "We, therefore, the delegates of the people of Massachusetts . . . agree upon the following . . . Constitution of the Commonwealth of Massachusetts." The convention made a significant emendation: "We, therefore, the people of Massachusetts . . . agree upon, ordain and establish. . . ." The formula, *We the people ordain and establish,* expressing the developed theory of the people as constituent power, was used for the first time in the Massachusetts constitution of 1780, whence it passed into the preamble of the United States constitution of 1787 and the new Pennsylvania constitution of 1790, after which it became common in the constitutions of the new states, and in new constitutions of the old states. Adams did not invent the formula. He was content with the matter-of-fact or purely empirical statement that the "delegates" had "agreed." It was the popularly elected convention that rose to more abstract heights. Providing in advance for popular ratification, it imputed the creation of government to the people.

Adams wrote, as the first article of the Declaration of Rights: "All men are born equally free and independent, and have certain natural, essential and unalienable rights," which included defense of their lives, liberties, and property, and the seeking of "safety and happiness." The Virginia Declaration of Rights, drafted by George Mason in June 1776, was almost identical, and Adams certainly had it in mind. The Massachusetts convention made only one change in this sentence. It declared: "All men are born free and equal." The convention, obviously, was thinking of the

[2] This may be readily confirmed from the Oxford Dictionary, or by comparison of definitions of "citizen" in British and American dictionaries, or by tracing the article "citizen" through successive editions of the Encyclopaedia Britannica, where the modern meaning does not appear until the eleventh edition in 1910.

Declaration of Independence, that is, Jefferson's more incisive rewording of Mason's Virginia declaration.

The convention had been elected by a true universal male suffrage, but it adopted, following Adams' draft, a restriction on the franchise. To vote, under the constitution, it was necessary to own real estate worth £3 a year, or real and personal property of a value of £60. The charter of 1691 had specified only £2 and £40 respectively. The state constitution was thus in this respect more conservative than the charter. How much more conservative? Here we run into the difference between experts already mentioned.[3] A whole school of thought, pointing to a 50 per cent increase in the voting qualification, has seen a reaction of property-owners against dangers from below. Closer examination of the values of money reveals that the £3 and £60 of 1780 represent an increase of only one-eighth over the figures of 1691. Even if half the people of Boston were unfranchised, all Boston then had only a twentieth of the population of the state. In the rural areas, where farm ownership was usual, it was mainly grown sons living for a few years with their parents who lacked the vote. There seems to have been only sporadic objection to the suffrage provision.

Adams put into the constitution, and the convention retained it, that ghost of King, Lords, and Commons that now assumed the form of governor, senate, and house of representatives. Partisans of the British system, in England or America, would surely find this ghost highly attenuated. The point about King and Lords, in the British system, was precisely that they were not elected by anyone, that they were immune to popular pressure, or any pressure, through their enjoyment of life tenure and hereditary personal rights to political position. Governor and senators in Massachusetts, like representatives, both in Adams' draft and in the final document, were all elected, by the same electorate, and all for one-year terms. To Adams (as, for example, to Delolme), it was of the utmost importance to prevent the executive from becoming the mere creature of the legislature. He even wished the governor to have an absolute veto, which the convention changed to a veto that could be overridden by a two-thirds majority of both houses. Adams continued to prefer a final veto. Jeffersonians and their numerous progeny found this highly undemocratic. In all states south of New York, at the end of the Revolution, governors were elected by the legislative houses, and none had any veto. Adams justified the veto as a means "to preserve the independence of the execu-

[3] For emphasis on the conservative or reactionary character of the Massachusetts constitution, see Douglass, *op. cit.*, 189–213, and more specialized writers cited there; for the opposite view, which I follow in part, see R. E. Brown, *Middle-Class Democracy and the Revolution in Massachusetts, 1691–1780* (Ithaca, 1955), 384–400.

tive and judicial departments." And since governors could no longer be appointed by the crown, an obvious way to prevent their dependence on legislatures was to have them issue, like legislators, from the new sovereign, the people. It was legislative oligarchy that Adams thought the most imminent danger. As he wrote to Jefferson in 1787: "You are afraid of the one—I, of the few."

As for the phantom "lords," or senators, though they were directly elected by the ordinary voters for one-year terms, they were in a way supposed to represent property rather than numbers. They were apportioned among the counties of Massachusetts not according to population but according to taxes paid, that is, according to assessed value of taxable wealth. Suffolk County, which included Boston, thus received 6 senators out of 40, where on a purely numerical basis it would have received only four. The Maine districts, Cape Cod, and the western counties were numerically somewhat underrepresented. The three central and western counties received 11 senators, where a representation in proportion to numbers would have given them 12 or 13. Inequalities in wealth in Massachusetts, as between individuals or as between city and country, were not yet great enough to make a senate apportioned according to "property" (which included the small man's property as well as the rich man's) very different from a senate apportioned according to numbers.[4]

The Massachusetts constitution prescribed certain qualifications for eligibility. The governor was required to have a freehold worth at least £1,000, senators a freehold of £300 or £600 total estate, representatives a freehold of £100 or £200 total estate. (British law at this time required £300 or £600 *annual income* from land to qualify for the House of Commons.) These Massachusetts requirements resembled those in North Carolina, where the governor had to have a £1,000 freehold, and members of the upper and lower houses freeholds of 300 or 100 acres respectively. In the absence of comparative statistics on land values and distribution of land ownership in the two states, it is impossible to compare the real impact of these legal qualifications for office. In Massachusetts, however, whatever may have been true in North Carolina, the average 100-acre one-family farm was worth well over £300, and there were a great many such farms, so that the ordinary successful farmer could qualify for either house of the legislature, and a few well-to-do ones in almost every village might

[4] Compare the apportionment of senators in the Massachusetts constitution with the population of counties in the census of 1790. The fact that the senate represented property rather than numbers is stressed by those who see the Massachusetts constitution of 1780 as a very conservative or reactionary document. I confess to sharing the impatience of Professor Brown at academic theories which dissolve under a little grade-school computation.

if they chose have aspired to the office of governor. The requirements in Massachusetts, as set forth by John Adams, were, if anything, Jeffersonian or agrarian in their tendency, since they favored the farm population, and made it even harder for middle-class townspeople, who might own no land, to occupy public office. The aim was clearly to limit office to the substantial segment of the population, but the substantial segment was broadly defined. Still, there were people who by this definition were not "substantial," and some of them objected to these provisions, though not many would in any case have ventured to run for office or been elected if they did, in the Massachusetts of 1780.

It was Article III of the Declaration of Rights, both in Adams' draft and in the finished constitution, that caused most debate in the convention and most disagreement among the voters during ratification. This article, declaring religion to be the foundation of morality and of the state, authorized the legislature to "enjoin" people to go to church, and required the use of public funds to maintain the churches, while allowing any "subject" to have his own contribution paid to the denomination of his choice. While it received a large majority of the popular vote, 8,885 to 6,225, it was the one article which most clearly failed to obtain a two-thirds majority, and the one which may have never been legally ratified, though declared so by the convention. Those voting against it expressed a desire to separate church and state. These, in turn, included perhaps a few Baptists who favored such separation on religious principle, a great many Protestants who feared that the article might legalize Roman Catholicism, and an unknown number of people, one suspects, who were no longer very regular in attending any church at all.

The Massachusetts constitution of 1780 was adopted by a two-thirds majority in a popular referendum from which no free adult was excluded. The vote was light, for opinion on the matter seems not to have been excited.[5] It was six years since the rebellion against King George, and four

---

[5] About 23 per cent of adult males voted on ratification of the constitution of 1780, a figure which may be compared with 30 per cent of adult males voting on ratification of the French constitution of 1793, with the difference that in the France of 1793 only those voting "yes" took the trouble to vote at all (1,801,918 "ayes" to 11,610 "no's" with some 4,300,000 abstentions). It is a question whether a vote by 23 per cent of the population should be considered "light." This percentage may have been a good measure of the politically interested population; in the annual elections of the governor the ratio of persons actually casting a vote to the total of adult white males ranged between 9 per cent and 28 per cent until it began to rise with the election of 1800. See J. R. Pole, "Suffrage and Representation in Massachusetts: A Statistical Note," in *William and Mary Quarterly,* xiv (October 1957), 590–92, and J. Godechot, *Les institutions de la France sous la Révolution et l'Empire* (Paris, 1951), 252.

years since the British army had left Massachusetts; doubtless many people wished to be bothered no longer. The action of the people as constituent power is, after all, a legal concept, or even a necessary legal fiction where the sovereignty of any concrete person or government is denied. It does not signify that everyone is actually engrossed in the fabrication of constitutions. On the other hand, it does not seem necessary to believe that the convention, when it declared the constitution ratified, put something over on an innocent or apathetic or reluctant people. The people of Massachusetts had rejected the constitution proposed in 1778. They could have rejected the one proposed in 1780. It was adopted, not because it was thought perfect or final by everyone, but because it offered a frame of government, or basis of agreement, within which people could still lawfully disagree. It has lasted, with many amendments, until the present day.

A WORD ON THE CONSTITUTION OF THE UNITED STATES

The idea that sovereignty lay with the people, and not with states or their governments, made possible in America a new kind of federal structure unknown in Europe. The Dutch and Swiss federations were unions of component parts, close permanent alliances between disparate corporate members. For them no other structure was possible, because there was as yet no Dutch or Swiss people except in a cultural sense. It was in the Dutch revolution of 1795 and the Swiss revolution of 1798 that these two bundles of provinces or cantons were first proclaimed as political nations. In America it was easier to make the transition from a league of states, set up during the Revolution, to a more integral union set up in the United States constitution of 1787. The new idea was that, instead of the central government drawing its powers from the states, both central and state governments should draw their powers from the same source; the question was the limit between these two sets of derived powers. The citizen, contrariwise, was simultaneously a citizen both of the United States and of his own state. He was the sovereign, not they. He chose to live under two constitutions, two sets of laws, two sets of courts and officials; theoretically, he had created them all, reserving to himself, under each set, certain liberties specified in declarations of rights.

It has been widely believed, since the publication in 1913 of Charles A. Beard's *Economic Interpretation of the Constitution,* that the federal constitution of 1787 marked a reaction against democratic impulses of the Revolution, and was a device by which men of property, particularly those holding securities of the state or continental governments, sought to protect themselves and their financial holdings against the dangers of popular rule. The Philadelphia convention has been represented as an almost clandestine body, which exceeded its powers, and which managed (as has also been said of the Massachusetts convention of 1780) to impose a conservative constitution on a confused or apathetic people. Recently the flimsiness of the evidence for this famous thesis has been shown by Professor Robert Brown. The thesis takes its place in the history of historical writing, as a product of that Progressive and post-Progressive era in which the common man could be viewed as the dupe or plaything of private interests.

It seems likely enough that there was a conservative reaction after the American Revolution, and even a movement among the upper class (minus the old loyalists) not wholly unlike the "aristocratic resurgence" which I shall soon describe in the Europe of the 1780's. The difference is that these neo-aristocrats of America were less obstinate and less caste-conscious than in Europe. They did not agree with each other, and they knew they could not rule alone. The men at Philadelphia in 1787 were too accomplished as politicians to be motivated by anything so impractical as ideology or mere self-interest. They hoped, while solving concrete problems, to arouse as little opposition as possible. They lacked also the European sense of the permanency of class status. Thinking of an upper class as something that individuals might move into or out of, they allowed for social mobility both upward and downward. The wealthy Virginian, George Mason, at the Philadelphia convention, on urging that the upper class should take care to give adequate representation to the lower, offered it as one of his reasons that, however affluent they might be now, "the course of a few years not only might, but certainly would, distribute their posterity through the lowest classes of society." No one seems to have disputed this prognostication. Such acceptance of future downward mobility for one's own grandchildren, if by no means universal in America, was far more common than in Europe. Without such downward mobility there could not long remain much room for newcomers at the top, or much assurance of a fluid society. With it, there could not be a permanent aristocracy in the European sense.

It was the state legislatures that chose the delegates to the Philadelphia convention, in answer to a widely expressed demand for strengthening the federal government under the Articles of Confederation. The Philadelphia convention proceeded, not to amend the Articles, but to ignore and discard them. It repudiated the union which the thirteen states had made. Beard in 1913 found it satisfying to call this operation a revolution, a revolution from above to be sure, which he compared to a *coup d'état* of Napoleon. His critic, Professor Brown, in 1956, found it satisfying and important to deny any revolutionary action in what happened.

What did really happen? The men at Philadelphia did circumvent the state governments, and in a sense they betrayed those who sent them. They did so by adopting the revolutionary principle of the American Revolution, which had already become less purely revolutionary and more institutionalized as an accepted routine, as shown in the Massachusetts convention of 1780, which had been followed by a New Hampshire convention, and new constitution for New Hampshire in 1784. The Philadelphia convention went beyond the existing constituted bodies, that is, the state governments and the Congress under the Articles, by appealing for support directly to the people, who in each state elected, for this purpose only, conventions to discuss, ratify, or refuse to ratify the document proposed by the convention at Philadelphia. The authors of the proposed federal constitution needed a principle of authority; they conceived that "the people were the fountain of all power," and that if popularly chosen conventions ratified their work "all disputes and doubts concerning [its] legitimacy" would be removed. In each state, in voting for ratifying conventions, the voters voted according to the franchise as given by their state constitutions. No use was made of the more truly revolutionary idea, still alive in Massachusetts in 1780, that on the acceptance of a government *every* man should have a vote. In some states the authorized voters were a great majority; in none were they a small minority. The actual vote for the ratifying conventions was light, despite protracted public discussion, because most people lost interest, or never had any, in abstract debates concerning governmental structure at the distant federal level. Eleven states ratified within a few months, and the constitution went into effect for the people of those eleven states. The remaining two states came in within three years. The whole procedure was revolutionary in a sense, but revolution had already become domesticated in America. The idea of the people as the constituent power, acting through special conventions, was so generally accepted and understood that a mere mention of the word "convention," in the final article of the proposed constitution, was thought sufficient explanation of the process of popular endorsement.

Nevertheless, men of popular principles, those who would soon be called democrats, and who preferred the arrangements of the Pennsylvania constitution, with its single-house legislature to which the executive was subordinated, found much in the new federal constitution not to their liking, at least at first sight. The new instrument reproduced the main features of the Massachusetts constitution of 1780: the strong president, the senate, the house of representatives, the partial executive veto, the independent judiciary, the separation and balance of powers. In fact, the longer tenure of offices—four years for the president, six for senators, two for representatives, in place of the annual terms for corresponding functionaries in Massachusetts—shows a reaction away from revolutionary democracy and toward the giving of more adequate authority to those entrusted with public power. The president was not popularly elected, like the governor in Massachusetts; but neither was he designated by the legislative assembly, like the president in Pennsylvania and governors in the Southern States. He was elected by an electoral college, with each state free to determine how its own share of these electors should be chosen. Although as early as 1788 almost half the states provided for popular election of presidential electors, it was not until 1828 that this became the general and permanent rule. In the federal constitution the unique feature, and key to the main compromise, was the senate. Not only did large and small states have the same number of senators, but it was the state legislatures that chose them. Since it was the state legislatures that conservative or hard-money men mainly feared in the 1780's, this provision can hardly have been introduced in the hope of assuring economic conservatism. It was introduced to mollify the states as states. In the senate the new union was a league of preexisting corporate entities. In the house of representatives it rested more directly on the people. Anyone who had the right to vote in his state could vote for a member of the lower house of Congress. In one respect the federal constitution, by its silence, was more democratic in a modern sense than any of the state constitutions. No pecuniary or religious qualification was specified for any office.

The new constitution was a compromise, but that it produced a less popular federal government, less close to the people, than that of the Articles of Confederation, seems actually contrary to the facts. It created a national arena for political controversy. There were now, for the first time, national elections in which voters could dispute over national issues. One result was the rise, on a national scale, of the Jeffersonian democratic movement in the 1790's.

The Progress of
Constitutional Theory Between
the Declaration of Independence
and the Meeting of
the Philadelphia Convention

EDWARD S. CORWIN

One of the paradoxes of the "spontaneous outbreak of constitution-making" during the Revolutionary era, as Hannah Arendt phrases it, was the failure to clearly distinguish between the sovereignty of the people and the sovereignty of the government established by the sovereign people. Just as the methodology of constitution making evolved during the period from 1776 to 1787, as Professor Palmer has pointed out, so too did thinking about other aspects of constitutional theory evolve during that period. Indeed, debates about the meaning of republican government flourished with as much vigor during the thirteen years after independence in the thirteen states as had the controversy over constitutional issues in the thirteen colonies during the thirteen years before independence. One of the most perceptive accounts of the progress of constitutional theory between the Declaration of Independence and the meeting of the Constitutional Convention is Professor Corwin's article, which lists four constructive ideas that emerged between 1776 and 1787: 1) the growing distinction between judicial power and legislative power in the dispensation of justice; 2) the increasing emphasis on the idea of a higher law and of judicial review; 3) the translation of the Articles of Confederation into such a higher law in relation to acts of state legis-

Edward S. Corwin, "The Progress of Constitutional Theory Between the Declaration of Independence and the Meeting of the Philadelphia Convention," *American Historical Review*, 30 (April 1925), pp. 511–536. Reprinted by permission.

latures; and 4) the identification of the inadequacy of powers at the national level with the faulty organization of government at the state level as a *single* problem of republican government.

CRITICS OF GLADSTONE'S FAMOUS APHORISM ON THE CONSTITUtion seem often to assume that he supposed the members of the Philadelphia Convention to have emptied their minds of all experience upon their arrival in the convention city. The assumption is an entirely gratuitous one. Unquestionably the problems before the Convention were suggested by the experience of its members and were not posed *ex thesi.* But the fact remains, nevertheless, that the solutions which the Convention supplied to those problems not infrequently owed far more to the theoretical prepossessions of its members than they did to tested institutions.

For Americans hardly less than for Frenchmen the period of the Constitution was "an age of rationalism", whereby is intended not a blind ignoring of the lessons of experience, but confidence in the ability of reason, working in the light of experience, to divert the unreflective course of events into beneficial channels; and in no respect was man more the master of his destiny than in that of statecraft. Surely if any man of the time may be regarded as representative of the sober, unimaginative intelligence of America, it was Washington, in whose "Circular Letter addresssed to the Governors", of June 8, 1783, occurs the following passage:

> The foundation of our empire was not laid in the gloomy age of ignorance and superstition; but at an epocha when the rights of mankind were better understood and more clearly defined, than at any other period. The researches of the human mind after social happiness have been carried to a great extent; the treasures of knowledge acquired by the labors of philosophers, sages, and legislators, through a long succession of years, are laid open for our use, and their collected wisdom may be happily applied in the establishment of our forms of government. . . . At this auspicious period, the United States came into existence as a nation; and, if their citizens should not be completely free and happy, the fault will be entirely their own.

The same sense of command over its resources of political wisdom appears again and again in the debates of the Convention, in the pages of the *Federalist,* and in writings of contemporaries.

Nor does the economic interpretation of history . . . detract greatly from the significance of such facts. No one denies that the concern felt by the Fathers for the rights of property and contract contributed immensely to impart to American constitutional law its strong bias in favor of these rights from the outset, but the concession only serves to throw certain still unanswered questions into a higher relief. For, what warrant had these men for translating any of their interests as *rights;* and why did they adopt the precise means which they did to advance their interests or secure their rights—in other words, why did they choose the precise system set up by the Constitution to do the work which they put upon it? Questions of this nature are altogether incapable of answer by any theory of human motive standing by itself. As Sir Henry Maine has phrased it: "Nothing in law springs entirely from a sense of convenience. There are always certain ideas existing antecedently on which the sense of convenience works, and of which it can do no more than form some new combination; and to find these ideas", he adds, "is exactly the problem."

I

A colloquy which occurred between Madison and Sherman of Connecticut in the early days of the Philadelphia Convention as to its purposes affords an excellent preface to the more particular intention of this paper. "The object of the Union", Sherman had declared, "were few", defense, domestic good order, treaties, the regulation of foreign commerce, revenue. Though a conspicuous omission from this enumeration is of any mention of commerce among the states and its regulation, it was not this omission which drew Madison's fire:

> He differed from the member from Connecticut in thinking the objectives mentioned to be all the principal ones that required a National Government. Those were certainly important and necessary objects; but he combined with them the necessity, of providing more effectually for the security of private rights, and the steady dispensation of Justice. Interferences with these were evils which had more perhaps than any thing else, produced this convention. Was it to be supposed that republican liberty could long exist under the abuses of it practiced in some of the States?

These views were heartily chorused by other members: the faulty organization of government within the states, threatening as it did, not alone the Union, but republican government itself, furnished the Convention with a problem of transcendent, even world-wide importance.

In short, the task before the Convention arose by no means exclusively from the inadequacies of the Articles of Confederation for "the exigencies of the Union"; of at least equal urgency were the questions which were thrust upon its attention by the shortcomings of the state governments for their purposes. Indeed, from the point of view of this particular study the latter phase of the Convention's task is, if anything, the more significant one, both because it brings us into contact at the outset with the most persistent problem of American constitutional law—that which has arisen from the existence of a multiplicity of local legislatures with indefinite powers; and also because it was to the solution of this phase of its problem that the Convention brought its "political science" most immediately to bear.

The singular juxtaposition in the Revolutionary state constitutions of legislative supremacy and the doctrine of natural rights need not detain us here. In the words of a contemporary critic of those constitutions: Although their authors "understood perfectly the principles of liberty", yet most of them "were ignorant of the forms and combinations of power in republics."[1] Madison's protest, on the other hand, against "interferences with the steady dispensation of justice" had reference to something more subtle—to what, in fact, was far less a structural than a functional defect in these early instruments of government. That the majority of the Revolutionary constitutions recorded recognition of the principles of separation of power is, of course, well known. What is not so generally understood is that the recognition was verbal merely, for the reason that the material terms in which it was couched still remained undefined; and that this was true in particular of "legislative power" in relations to "judicial power".

It is pertinent in this connection to compare the statement by a modern authority of what is law to-day with actual practice contemporaneous with the framing of the Constitution of the United States. "The legislature", writes Sutherland in his work on *Statutory Construction,*

> may prescribe rules of decision which will govern future cases. . . . But it has no power to administer judicial relief—it can not decide cases nor direct how existing cases or controversies shall be decided by the courts; it can not interfere by subsequent acts with final judgments of the courts. It can not set aside, annul, or modify such judgments, nor grant or order new trials, nor direct what judgment shall be entered or relief given. No declaratory act, that is, one professing to enact what the law now is or was at any past time, can affect any existing rights or controversies.

Turn now to the operation of the principle of the separation of powers in a typical instance in 1787. The New Hampshire constitution of 1784

[1] Niles, *Principles and Acts of the Revolution,* p. 234; from an address by Dr. Benjamin Rush delivered at Philadelphia on July 4, 1787, before members of the Convention and others. The address testifies throughout to the importance of the governmental situation in the states as a problem before the Convention.

contained the declaration that "in the government of this State, the three essential powers thereof, to wit, the legislative, executive and judicial, ought to be kept as separate and independent of each other as the nature of a free government will admit or as is consistent with the chain of connection that binds the whole fabric of the constitution in one indissoluble bond of union or amity". Notwithstanding which the laws of New Hampshire for the years 1784–1792 are replete with entries showing that throughout this period the state legislature freely vacated judicial proceedings, suspended judicial actions, annulled or modified judgments, cancelled executions, reopened controversies, authorized appeals, granted exemptions from the standing law, expounded the law for pending cases, and even determined the merits of disputes.[2] Nor do such practices seem to have been more aggravated in New Hampshire than in several other states. Certainly they were widespread, and they were evidently possible in any of the states under the views then obtaining of "legislative power".

Neither is the explanation of such views far to seek. Coke's fusion of what we should to-day distinguish as "legislative" and "judicial" powers in the case of the "High Court of Parliament" represented the teaching of the highest of all legal authorities before Blackstone appeared on the sceen. What is equally important, the Cokian doctrine corresponded exactly to the contemporary necessities of many of the colonies in the earlier days of their existence. Thus, owing to the death not only of courts and lawyers, but even of a recognized code of law, bodies like the Massachusetts General Court had thrust upon them at first a far greater bulk of judicial and administrative work, in to-day's sense of these terms, than of lawmaking proper, while conversely such judges as existed in these early days performed administrative as well as judicial functions, very much as had been the case with the earliest itinerant judges in England. By the middle of the eighteenth century, it is true, a distinct improvement had taken place in these regards. Regularly organized systems of courts now existed in all the colonies. A bar trained in the common law was rapidly arising. Royal governors sometimes disallowed enactments interfering with the usual course of justice in the ordinary courts, on grounds anticipatory of modern doctrine. Then, however, came the outbreak of the Revolution, and with it a reversion to more primitive practices and ideas, traceable in the first instance to the collapse of the royal judicial establishment, but

2 See *Laws of New Hampshire,* ed. Batchellor, V. *passim.* Some of the less usual items are those on pp. 21, 66, 89, 90–91, 110–111, 125–126, 130–131, 167–168, 243, 320–321, 334–335, 363, 395–396, 400–401, 404–406, 411–412, 417–418, 455–456, 485, 499, 522. The volume is crowded with acts "restoring" a defeated or defaulting party "to his law", "any usage, custom, or law to the contrary notwithstanding".

later to the desire to take a short course with enemies of the new régime, against whom, first and last, every state in the Union appears to have enacted bills of pains and penalties of greater or less severity. Furthermore, it should be observed that, owing to a popular prejudice, certain of the states—notably New York and Massachusetts—at first withheld equity powers from their courts altogether, while several others granted them but sparingly. The result was fairly to compel the legislature to intervene in many instances with "special legislation", disallowing fraudulent transactions, curing defective titles, authorizing urgent sales of property, and the like. Between legislation of this species and outright interferences with the remedial law itself there was often little to distinguish.

That, therefore, the vague doctrine of the separation of powers should at first have been interpreted and applied in the light of this history is not astonishing. This, as we have seen, left legislative power without definition on its side toward judicial power, except as the power of the supreme organ of the state, which meant, however, the withholding from judicial power of that which, to the modern way of thinking, is its highest attribute—to wit, power of deciding with finality. Nothing could be more instructive in this connection than some sentences from Jefferson's *Notes on Virginia,* dating from about 1781. Pointing out that the Virginia constitution of 1776 incorporated the principle of the separation of powers, Jefferson proceeds to expound this principle in a way which leaves it meaning little more than a caution against plurality of offices. "No person shall exercise the powers of more than one of them [the three departments] at the same time", are his words. But even more significant is the following passage:

> If, [it runs] the legislature assumes executive and judiciary powers, no opposition is likely to be made; nor, if made, can it be effectual; because in that case they may put their proceedings into the form of an act of assembly, which will render them obligatory on the other branches. They have, accordingly, in many instances, decided rights which should have been left to judiciary controversy; and the direction of the executive, during the whole time of their session, is becoming habitual and familiar.

The concept of legislative power here expressed is obviously a purely formal one: "legislative power" is any power which the legislative organ may choose to exercise by resort to the ordinary parliamentary processes.

And not less striking is the recital which Hamilton gives in *Federalist,* number 81, of certain objections by opponents of the Constitution to the powers of the Supreme Court:

The authority of the Supreme Court of the United States, which is to be a separate and independent body, will be superior to that of the legislature. The power of construing the laws according to the *spirit* of the Constitution will enable that court to mould them into whatever shape it may think proper; especially as its decisions will not be in any manner subject to the revision or correction of the legislative body. This is as unprecedented as it is dangerous. . . . The Parliament of Great Britain, and the legislatures of the several States, can at any time rectify, by law, the exceptionable decisions of their respective courts. But the errors and usurpations of the Supreme Court of the United States will be uncontrollable and remediless.

Hamilton's answer to all this was simply that "the theory neither of the British, nor the State constitutions, authorizes the revisal of a judicial sentence by a legislative act", that "the impropriety of the thing" even in the case of the United States Constitution rested not on any distinctive provision thereof, but "on the general principles of law and reason"; that a legislature could not, "without exceeding its province . . . reverse a determination once made in a particular case," though it might "prescribe a new rule for future cases"; and that this principle applied "in all its consequences, exactly in the same manner and extent, to the State governments as to the national government". This answer, for which is cited only the authority of Montesquieu, is conclusive from the standpoint of modern constitutional doctrine; but its contradiction of the views and practices which were prevalent in 1787 is manifest.

II

Finally, the structural and funtcional shortcomings of the early state constitutions played directly into the hands of both popular and doctrinal tendencies which distinctly menaced what Madison called "the security of private rights". Throughout the Revolution the Blackstonian doctrine of "legislative omnipotence" was in the ascendant. Marshall read Blackstone and so did Iredell—to what effect later developments were to make clear. And even more radical doctrine was abroad. One Benjamin Hichborn's assertion, in a speech delivered in Boston in 1777, that civil liberty was "not a government by laws", but a "power existing in the people at large" "to alter or annihilate both the mode and essence of any former government" "for any cause or for no cause at all, but their own sovereign pleasure" voiced an extension to the right of revolution hitherto unheard of outside the pages of Rousseau; and even so good a republican as John

Adams was disturbed at manifestations of social ferment which he traced to a new spirit of equality.

The sharp edge of "legislative omnipotence" did not pause with the Tories who, as enemies of the state, were perhaps beyond the pale of the Constitution. Everywhere legislative assemblies, energized by the reforming impulse of the period, were led to attempt results which, even when they lay within the proper field of lawmaking, we should to-day regard as requiring constitutional amendments to effect them. Virginia, as Bancroft writes, used her "right of original and complete legislation to abolish the privileges of primogeniture, cut off entails, forbid the slave-trade, and establish the principle of freedom in religion as the inherent and inalienable possession of spiritual beings"; while elsewhere the liberal forces of the hour assailed the vested interest of negro slavery more directly. Vermont, Massachusetts, and New Hampshire ridded themselves of slavery by constitutional amendment or in consequence of judicial construction of the Constitution. In Pennsylvania, Rhode Island, and Connecticut, on the other hand, gradual emancipation was brought about by ordinary legislative enactment. Yet the cause of reform did not have it all its own way. When a similar measure was proposed in New Jersey, it drew forth a protest on constitutional grounds which is remarkable in its anticipation of later doctrines.

But it was not reform, nor even special legislation, which early affixed to the state legislature a stigma of which as an institution it has never even yet quite ridded itself. The legislation just reviewed belonged for the most part to the period of the war and was the work of a society which, the Tory element apart, was politically unified and acknowledged an easily ascertainable leadership. Once, however, hostilities were past and the pressure alike of a common peril and a common enthusiasm removed, the republican lute began to show rifts. The most evident line of cleavage at first was that between seaboard and back country; but this presently became coincident to a large extent with a much more ominous division into creditors and debtors. That class of farmer-debtors which now began to align itself with the demagogues in the state legislatures, in opposition to the mercantile-creditor class, was experiencing the usual grievance of agriculturists after a war, that of shouldering the burden of the return to normalcy. But the point of view of the creditor class may not be justly ignored either. By their provincial policies with respect to commerce the state legislatures had already seriously impaired legitimate interests of this class, and they now proceeded to attack what under the standing law were its unchallengeable rights. In each of the thirteen states a "rag money" party appeared, which in seven states triumphed outright, while in several others it came near doing so. Nor was payment even in

paper currency always the creditor's lot, for besides rag-money measures
and tender laws, or in lieu of them, statutes suspending all actions upon
debts were enacted, payment of debts in kind was authorized, and even
payment in land.

It is a frequent maxim of policy that things must be permitted to grow
worse before their betterment can be attempted to advantage. The paper-
money craze at least proved serviceable in invigorating the criticism
which had begun even earlier of the existing state governments. One
such critic was Jefferson, who in his *Notes on Virginia* bitterly assailed
the Virginia constitution of 1776 for having produced a concentration
of power in the legislative assembly which answered to "precisely the
definition of despotic government". Nor did it make any difference, he
continued, that such powers were vested in a numerous body "chosen
by ourselves"; "one hundred and seventy-three despots" were "as oppressive as one"; and "an elective despotism was not the government we fought
for, but one which should not only be founded on free principles, but in
which the powers of government should be so divided and balanced
among several bodies of magistracy, as that no one could transcend their
legal limits, without being effectually checked and restrained by the
others".

And this was also the point of view of the Pennsylvania Council of
Censors, in their celebrated report of 1784. Extending through some
thirty finely printed pages, this document listed many examples, "selected",
we are told, "from a multitude", of legislative violations of the state
constitution and bill of rights. Several of the measures so stigmatized
were of a general nature, but those for which the censors reserved their
severest strictures were acts involving the rights of named parties. Thus
fines had been remitted, judicially established claims disallowed, verdicts
of juries set aside, the property of one given to another, defective titles
secured, marriages dissolved, particular persons held in execution of debt
released—and all by a species of legislative activity which had been explicitly condemned both by "the illustrious Montesquieu" and "the great
Locke".

Two years later came the early volumes of John Adams's *Defence of
the Constitutions,* in answer to M. Turgot's criticism that the American
constitutions represented "an unreasonable imitation of the usages of
England". In reality the work was much less a "defence" than an exhorta-
tion to constitutional reform in other states along the lines which Massachusetts had already taken under Adams's own guidance. A new and
significant note, however, appears in this work. In his earlier writings
Adams had assumed with Montesquieu that the great source of danger to
liberty lay in the selfishness and ambition of the governors themselves.

But with the lesson of the paper-money agitation before him, he now gives warning of the danger to which republics, when they have become populous and overcrowded and the inevitable doom of poverty has appeared in their midst, are peculiarly exposed from the rise of parties. "Misarrangements now made", he writes, "will have great, extensive, and distant consequences; and we are now employed, how little soever we may think of it, in making establishments which will effect the happiness of a hundred millions of inhabitants at a time, in a period not very distant."

Copies of the *Defence* reached the United States early in 1787, and were circulated among the members of the Philadelphia Convention, reviving and freshening belief in "political science" and particularly in the teachings of Montesquieu. Yet in one respect at least the idea of reform for which Adams's work stood and that which the Convention represented were poles apart. For while the former still illustrated the opinion that constitutional reform was a purely local problem, the Convention represented the triumph of the idea that reform to be effective must be national in scope and must embrace the entire American constitutional system in a single coherent programme. That such a programme could have been elaborated without the signal contribution to it of the effort for local reform is, on the other hand, altogether improbable.

III

It was Walter Bagehot's opinion that Americans were prone to give credit to the Constitution which was more justly due themselves. "The men of Massachusetts", he declared, "could work *any* constitution." What had evidently impressed him was the American habit of supplying shortcomings in the Constitution by construction rather than outright amendment. Yet for construction to do really effective work, it must have elbow-room and a handle to take hold of; and at least the merit of having afforded these can not be denied the Constitution.

Nor were the early state constitutions entirely lacking in invitation to this American aptitude for documentary exegesis, which had its origin, one suspects, in an earlier taste of theological disquisition. The executive veto, which was the practical nub of all Adams's preachments, was brought about, to be sure, through specific provision being made for it in the written constitution, and to so good purpose that it is to be found to-day in nearly every constitution in the country. The other suggested remedy of critics of "the legislative vortex", on the contrary, was introduced solely by the processes of interpretation and without the slightest textual alteration being made in the constitutions involved. This was judicial review. Thus while the executive veto and judicial review have a common explanation in the political necessity which they were devised to meet, the manner in which they were respectively articulated to the American constitutional system was widely and for us most significantly divergent. The executive veto was and remains mere matter of fact without the slightest further interest for us; judicial review is both a practice and a *doctrine,* and in the latter aspect especially is of immediate interest.

As a practice judicial review made its initial appearance in independent America in 1780, in the case of Holmes *v.* Walton, in which the supreme court of New Jersey refused to carry out an act of the legislature providing for the trial of a designated class of offenders by a jury of six, whereas, the court held, the state constitution contemplated the common-law jury of twelve. Although the opinion of the court apparently was never published, the force of the example may have been considerable. From this time on the notion crops up sporadically in other jurisdictions, at intervals of about two years, in a series of dicta and rulings which—thanks in no small part to popular misapprehension as to their precise bearings—brought the idea before the Philadelphia Convention. And meantime the main premises of the *doctrine* of judicial review—the principles whereby it came to be annexed to the written constitution—had been worked out.

First and last, many and various arguments have been offered to prove that judicial review is implied in the very nature of a written constitution, some of them manifestly insufficient for the purpose; though that is not to say that they may not have assisted in securing general acceptance of the institution. "Superstitions believed are, in their effect, truths"; and it has accordingly happened more than once that the actual influence of an idea has been out of all proportion to its logical or scientific merits. These more or less spurious proofs of judicial review, however, we here pass by without further consideration, in order to come at once to what, on both historical and logical grounds, may be termed the true doctrine of judicial review. This embraces three propositions: First, that the Constitution is supreme; second, that it is law, in the sense of a rule enforceable by courts; and third, that judicial interpretations of the standing law are final, at least for the cases in the decision of which they are pronounced. Let us consider the two latter propositions somewhat further.

The claim of the Constitution to be considered *law* may rest on either one of two grounds, depending on whether "law" be regarded as an unfolding of the divine order of things or as an expression of human will—as an act of knowledge (or revelation) or an act of power. Considered from the former point of view—which is that of Locke and other exponents of the law of nature—the claim of the Constitution to be obeyed is due simply to its content, to the principles which it incorporates because of their intrinsic sanctity; considered from the latter point of view—that of Hobbes and the "positive school of jurisprudence"—its claim to obedience is due to its source in a sovereign will—that of the people. Actually both views have been taken at different times, but that judicial review originally owed more to the former than to the latter conception seems fairly clear.

Of all the so-called "precedents" for judicial review antecedent to the Convention of 1787, the one which called forth the most elaborate argument on theoretical grounds and which produced the most evident impression on the membership of the Convention, was the Rhode Island case of Trevett v. Weeden, which was decided early in 1786. The [chief] feature of the case . . . [it involved paper money] is the argument which it evoked against the act on the part of the attorney for defendant, James Varnum. In developing the theory of a law superior to legislative enactments, Varnum appealed indifferently to the Rhode Island charter, "general principles", "invariable custom", "Magna Carta", "fundamental law", "the law of nature", "the law of God"; asserting with reference to the last, that "all men, judges included", were bound by it "in preference to any human laws". In short, Varnum, going directly back to the Cokian tradition, built his argument for judicial review on the loose connotation of the word "law" still obtaining in the eighteenth century, especially among American readers of Coke and Locke—to say nothing of the host of writers on the Law of Nations. Nor is the conduciveness of such an argument to judicial review open to conjecture. In the first place, it kept alive, even after the fires of revolution had cooled, the notion that the claim of law to obedience consists in its intrinsic excellence rather than its origin. Again, it made rational the notion of a hierarchy of laws in which the will of merely human legislators might on occasion be required to assume a subordinate place. Lastly, by the same token, it made rational the notion of judges pitting knowledge against sheer legislative self-assertion.

Contrariwise, the Blackstonian concept of legislative sovereignty was calculated to frustrate judicial review not only by attributing to the legislature an uncontrollable authority, but also by pressing forward the so-called "positive" conception of law and the differentiation of legal from moral obligation which this impels. Fortunately, in the notion of popular sovereignty the means of checkmating the notion of legislative sovereignty was available. For, once it became possible to attribute to the people at large a lawmaking, rather than a merely constituent, capacity, the Constitution exchanged its primary character as a statement of sacrosanct principles for that of the expressed will of the highest lawmaking power on earth.[3]

But to produce judicial review, the notion of the Constitution as law must be accompanied by the principle of the finality of judicial constructions of the law, which obviously rests upon a definition of the respective rôles of "legislative" and "judicial" power in relation to the standing law. In other words, judicial review raised from the other side of the line the same problem as did "legislative interferences with the dispensation of justice"; and, in fact, it can be shown that the solution of the two problems proceeded in many jurisdictions *pari passu.* The whole subject is one which demands rather ample consideration.

Although the functional differentiation of the three powers of government, first hinted in Aristotle's *Politics,* necessarily preceded their organic distribution to some extent, it is not essential for our purpose to trace either process further back than to Coke's repeated insistence in his *Institutes* that "the King hath wholly left matters of Judicature according to his laws to his Judges". In these words, it is not too much to say, the royal prerogative, which had long lain fallow in this respect, was thrust forever from the province of the courts. One of these same courts, on the other hand, was "the High Court of Parliament"; and Coke nowhere suggests that "the power of judicature" which he attributes to Parliament is to be distinguished from the power which Parliament ordinarily exercised in "proceeding by bill". Far different is the case of Locke. His declaration that "the legislative or supreme authority cannot assume to itself a power to rule by extemporary arbitrary decrees, but is bound to dispense justice and decide the rights of the subject by promulgated standing laws and known authorized judges" represents progress towards a "material" as against a merely "formal" definition of legislative power, both in the total exclusion which it effects of the legislative body from the business of judging and also in the ideal which it lays down of statute law. Noteworthy, too, from the same point of view is Montesquieu's characterization of the judges as "but the mouthpieces of the law", accompanied, as it is, by the assertion that the mergence of "the judiciary power" with "the legislative" would render the judge "a legislator" vested with arbitrary power over the life and liberty of the subject.

---

[3] Compare in this connection Luther Martin's "Genuine Information", in Farrand's *Records,* III. 230, with Hamilton's argument for judicial review in *Federalist,* no. 78, and Marshall's opinion in Marbury *v.* Madison, 1 Cranch 129. The former regards political authority as a *cessio* from the people to the government which "never devolves back to them" except in events amounting to a dissolution of government. The latter regard it as a revocable *translatio* to agents by a principal who is by no means bound to act through agents.

As usual, Blackstone's contribution is somewhat more difficult to assess. He adopts without qualification the views just quoted from Locke and Montesquieu, and he urges that "all laws should be made to commence *in futuro*". Yet the very illustration he furnishes of his definition of "municipal law" as "a rule . . . permanent, uniform, and universal" violates this precept radically, since it shows that in his estimation the *ex post facto* operation of a rule, however undesirable in itself, does not affect its title to be regarded as "law". Nor, in fact, does it occur to him, in assigning to Parliament power to "expound" the law, to distinguish those instances in which the exercise of this power would mark an intrusion upon judicial freedom of decision, while this sweeping attribution to Parliament of jurisdiction over "all mischiefs and grievances, operations and remedies that transcend the ordinary course of the laws"—a matter evidently to be judged of by Parliament itself—lands us again in the Cokian bog from from which we set out.

The differentiation of legislative and judicial power, upon which judicial review pivots, appears to have been immediately due, not to any definition of legislative *power,* but to a definition of judicial *duty* in relation to the standing law and especially to the law of decided cases. In the opening sentence of Bacon's Essay on Judicature one reads: "Judges ought to remember that their office is *'jus dicere'* and not *'jus dare';* to interpret law, and not to make or give law"—words which have been reiterated many times as embodying the doctrine of *stare decisis.* Coke employs different language, but his thought is not essentially different: "judges discern by law what is just"; the law "the golden metwand whereby all men's causes are justly and evenly measured". He also notes the artificiality of the law's "reason and judgment", and pays full tribute to the burden of study and experience "before that a man can attain to the cognizance of it". Judicial duty is thus matched with judicial aptitude—the judges are the experts of the law—or, in the words of Blackstone, its "living oracles", sworn to determine, not according to their own private judgment, "but according to the known laws and customs of the land; not delegated to pronounce a new law, but to maintain and expound the old one".

In brief, it is the duty of judges to conserve the law, not to change it, a task for which their learning pre-eminently fits them. Yet a mystery remains to clear up; for how came this *duty* of subordination to the law to be transmuted into a claim of exclusive *power* in relation to it—the power of interpreting it with final force and effect? By the doctrine of the separation of powers, the outstanding prerogatives of each department are no doubt its peculiar possession; but still that does not explain why in the final apportionment of territory between the legislative and judicial departments in the United States, the function of law-interpretation fell to the latter. The fact is that we here confront *the* act of creation —or perhaps it would be better to say, act of prestidigitation—attending the elaboration of the doctrine of judicial review; and what is more, we know the authors of it—or some of them.

In his argument in the case of Trevett *v.* Weeden, Varnum put the question: "Have the judges a power to repeal, to amend, to alter, or to make new laws?" and then proceeded to answer it thus; "God forbid! In that case they would be legislators. . . . But the judiciary have the sole power of judging of laws . . . and can not admit any act of the legislatures as law against the Constitution." And to the same effect is the defense which James Iredell penned of the North Carolina supreme court's decision in Bayard *v.* Singleton, while Davie, his associate in the case, was in attendance upon the Convention at Philadelphia.

> The duty of that [the judicial] department [he wrote] I conceive in all cases is to decide according to the laws of the State. It will not be denied, I suppose, that the constitution is a law of the State, as well as an act of Assembly, with this difference only, that it is the *fundamental* law, and unalterable by the legislature, which derives all its power from it. . . . The judges, therefore, must take care at their peril, that every act of Assembly they presume to enforce is warranted by the constitution, since if it is not, they act without lawful authority.

Nor is this a power which may be exercised by ministerial officers, "for if the power of judging rests with the courts their decision is final".

Here are all the premises of the doctrine of judicial review either explicitly stated or clearly implied: the superiority of the Constitution to statute law—the case of the common law had still to be dealt with; its quality as law knowable by judges in their official capacity and applicable by them to cases; the exclusion of "legislative power" from the ancient field of parliamentary power in law-interpretation, except in circumstances in which the law is subject to legislative amendment. The classical version of the doctrine of judicial review in *Federalist,* number 78, improves upon the statement of these premises but adds nothing essential to them.

IV

We turn now to that phase of the problem which confronted the Philadelphia Convention in consequence of the insufficiencies of the government established by the Articles of Confederation. And at the outset let it be remarked that with all their defects, and serious as these were, the Articles none the less performed two services of great moment: they kept the idea of union vital during the period when the feeling of national unity was at its lowest ebb; and they accorded formal recognition that the great powers of war and foreign relations were intrinsically national in character. Those two most dramatic and interesting functions belonged to the general government from the first and became the central magnet to which other powers necessarily gravitated.

The essential defect of the Articles of Confederation, as has been so often pointed out, consisted in the fact that the government established by them operated not upon the individual citizens of the United States but upon the states in their corporate capacity—that, in brief, it was not a government at all, but rather the central agency of an alliance. As a consequence, on the one hand, even the powers theoretically belonging to the Congress of the Confederation were practically unenforceable; while, on the other hand, the theoretical scope of its authority was unduly narrow. Inasmuch as taxes are collectible from individuals, Congress could not levy them; inasmuch as commerce is an affair of individuals, Congress could not regulate it; and its treaties had not at first the force of laws, since to have given them that operation would again have been to impinge upon individuals directly and not through the mediation of the state legislatures. Furthermore, the powers withheld from Congress remained with the states—which is to say, *with their legislatures.* The evil thence resulting was thus a double one. Not only was a common policy impracticable in fields where it was most evidently necessary, but also the local legislatures had it in their power to embroil both the country as a whole with foreign nations and its constituent parts with each other. So the weakness of the Confederation played directly into the hands of the chief defect of government within the states themselves—an excessive concentration of power in the hands of the legislative department.

The endeavors which were made to render the Articles of Confederation a workable instrument of government proceeded, naturally, along the two lines of amendment and construction. In theory the Articles were amendable; but owing to the requirement that amendments had to be ratified by all the states, in practice they were not so. Recourse, therefore, had early to be had to the other method, and eventually with fruitful results.

Yet the possibilities of constitutional construction, too, were at the outset seriously curtailed by the transmutation of the Blackstonian teaching into the dogma of state sovereignty. Fortunately, the notion of American nationality, which the early fervors of the Revolution had evoked into something like articulate expression, did not altogether lack a supporting interest. This consisted in the determination of the states with definite western boundaries to convert the territory between the Alleghenies and the Mississippi into a national domain. Their spokesman accordingly advanced the argument that the royal title to this region had devolved, in consequence of the Revolution, not upon the states with "sea-to-sea" charters, but upon the American people as a whole—a premise of infinite possibilities, as soon appeared.

On the very last day of 1781 Congress passed the act incorporating the Bank of North America. Not only was there no clause of the Articles which authorized Congress to create corporations, but the second article specifically stipulated that "each State retains its sovereignty, freedom, and independence, and every power, jurisdiction, and right which is not by the Confederation expressly delegated to the United States in Congress assembled". Quite naturally, the validity of the charter was challenged, whereupon its defense was undertaken by James Wilson. The article just quoted Wilson swept aside at the outset as entirely irrelevant to the question. Inasmuch, said he, as no state could claim or exercise "any power or act of sovereignty extending over all the other States or any of them", it followed that the power to "incorpoate a bank commensurate to the United States" was "not an act of sovereignty or a power . . . which by the second Article . . . must be expressly delegated to Congress in order to be possessed by that body". Congress's power, in fact, rested on other premises.

> To many purposes [he continued] the United States are to be considered as one undivided nation; and as possessed of all the rights and powers, and properties by the law of nations incident to such. Whenever an object occurs to the direction of which no particular state is competent, the management of it must of necessity belong to the United States in Congress assembled.

In short, from the very fact of its exercise on a national scale a power ceased to be one claimable by a state. The reflection is suggested that if the Articles of Confederation had continued subject to this canon of construction, they might easily have come to support an even greater structure of derived powers than the Constitution of the United States does at this moment.

The question, however, upon which the permanently fruitful efforts of constitutional construction were at this time brought to bear was that of treaty enforcement; and while the story is not a new one, its full significance seems not to have been altogether appreciated. The starting-point is furnished by the complaints which the British government began lodging with Congress very shortly after the making of the peace treaty that the state legislatures were putting impediments in the way of British creditors and were renewing confiscations of Loyalist property contrary to Articles IV. and VI., respectively, of the treaty.

Now it should be observed that the immediate beneficiaries of these articles were certain classes of *private persons,* whose claims, moreover, were such as would ordinarily have to be asserted against other individuals *in court.* If, therefore, it could only be assured that the state courts would accord such claims proper recognition and enforcement, the obligation of the United States as a government, under the treaty, would be performed and the complaints of the other party to the treaty must thereupon cease. But how could this be assured? The answer was suggested by the current vague connotation of the word "law" and the current endeavor to find in "judicial power" a check upon legislative power in the states.

Nor can there be any doubt as to who first formulated this solution. It was Alexander Hamilton in his argument before a municipal court in New York City in the case of Rutgers *v.* Waddington in 1784, practically contemporaneously with the British protests above referred to. The case involved a recent enactment of the state legislature creating a right of action for trespass against Tory occupants of premises in favor of owners who had fled the city during the British possession. In his capacity as Waddington's attorney, Hamilton assailed the act as contrary to principles of the law of nations, to the treaty of peace, which he asserted implied an amnesty, and the Articles of Confederation, and as, therefore, void. Only the manuscript notes of his argument are extant, but these sufficiently indicate its bearing for our purpose:

> Congress have made a treaty [they read in part]. A breach of that would be a breach of their constitutional authority. . . . as well a County may alter the laws of the State as the State those of the Confederation. . . . While Confed. exists its cons. Autho. paramount. But how are Judges to decide? Ans.: Cons. giving Jud. Power only in prize causes in all others Judges of each State must of necessity be judges of United States. And the law of each State must adopt the laws of Congress. Though in relation to its own Citizens local laws might govern, yet in relation to foreigners those of United States must prevail. It must be conceded Leg. of one State cannot repeal law of United States. All must be construed to Stand together.

There is a striking parallel between the cases of Rutgers *v.* Waddington and Trevett *v.* Weeden, and especially between the subsequent fate of Hamilton's argument in the one and Varnum's in the other. In each case the court concerned decided adversely to the party relying upon the statute before it, but did so on grounds which avoided its committing itself on the issue of judicial review. In each case, nevertheless, the exponents of Blackstonian absolutism raised loud protests in behalf of the threatened legislative authority, with the results of spreading the impression that the judges had met the issue squarely. Yet since what the judges had met the issue squarely. Yet since what the judges had said hardly bore out this impression, interested attention was naturally directed in turn to the franker and more extensive claims of counsel; and while Varnum was spreading his argument broadcast as a pamphlet, Hamilton was reiterating his views in his "Letters from Phocion".

Of the various repercussions from Hamilton's argument in Rutgers v. Waddington the most important is the report which John Jay—a fellow New Yorker—rendered to Congress as secretary for foreign affairs, in October, 1786, on the subject of state violations of treaties. The salient passage of this document reads as follows:

> Your Secretary considers the thirteen independent sovereign states as having, by express delegation of power, formed and vested in Congress a perfect though limited sovereignty for the general and national purposes specified in the confederation. In this sovereignty they cannot severally participate (except by their delegates) or have concurrent jurisdiction. . . . When therefore a treaty is constitutionally made, ratified and published by Congress, it immediately becomes binding on the whole nation, and superadded to the laws of the land, without the intervention, consent or fiat of state legislatures.

It was therefore, Jay argued, the duty of the state judiciaries in cases between private individuals "respecting the meaning of a treaty", to give it full enforcement in harmony with "the rules and maxims established by the laws of nations for the interpretation of treaties". He accordingly recommended that Congress formally deny the right of the state legislatures to enact laws construing "a national treaty" or impeding its operation "in any manner", that it avows its opinion that all acts on the statute books repugnant to the treaty of peace should be at once repealed, and that it urge the repeal to be in general terms which would leave it with the local judiciaries to decide all cases arising under the treaty according to the intent thereof "anything in the said acts . . . to the contrary notwithstanding".

The following March Congress adopted the resolutions which Jay had proposed, without a dissenting vote, and in April, within a month of the date set for the assembling of the Philadelphia Convention, transmitted them to the state legislatures, by the majority of which they were promptly complied with. Nor is the theory on which such repeals were based doubtful. We find it stated in the declaration of the North Carolina supreme court in the above-mentioned case of Bayard v. Singleton, which was decided the very month that the Convention came together, that "the Articles of Confederation are a part of the law of the land unrepealable by any act of the general assembly".

From all this to Article VI. of the Constitution is manifestly only a step, though an important one. The supremacy which Jay's plan assured the national treaties is in Article VI. but part and parcel of national supremacy in all its phases; but this broader supremacy is still guaranteed by being brought to bear upon individuals, in contrast to states, through the intervention in the first instance often of the state courts. Thus the solution provided of the question of treaty enforcement, whereby the cause of national supremacy was linked with that of judicial review, clearly foreshadowed the ultimate character of the national government as a government acting upon individuals in the main rather than upon the states. Logically, national power operative through courts is a deduction from a government over individuals; chronologically, the order of ideas was the reverse.

V

The theory that the Articles of Confederation were for some purposes law, directly cognizable by courts, entirely transformed the character of the Confederation so far forth, and must sooner or later have suggested the idea of its entire transformation into a real government. Nor was judicial review the only possible source of such a suggestion. As Madison points out in the *Federalist,* "in cases of capture; of piracy; of the post-office; of coins, weights, and measures; of trade with the Indians; of claims under grants of land by different States; and, above all, in the case of trials by courts-martial in the army and navy", the government of the Confederation acted immediately on individuals from the first. Again, proposals which were laid at various times before the states for conferring a customs revenue on Congress, though none was ever finally ratified, served to bring the same idea before the people, as also did the proposals which never reached the states from Congress to endow the latter with "the sole and exclusive" power over foreign and interstate trade.

But even earlier the suggestion of a "continental conference" for the purpose of framing a "Continental Charter" akin to Magna Carta had been propounded in that famous issue of *Common Sense* in which the signal was given for independence itself. It would be the task of such a body, wrote Paine, to fix "the number and manner of choosing members of Congress and members of assembly", and to draw "the line of business and jurisdiction between them (always remembering that our strength is continental and not provincial)". Such a charter would also secure "freedom and property to all men", and indeed, would fill the place of monarchy iteslf in the new state. "That we may not appear to be defective even in earthly honors, let a day be solemnly set apart for proclaiming the charter; let it be brought forth placed on the divine law, the word of God; let a crown be placed thereon, by which the world may know that so far we approve monarchy that in America the law is King."

In this singular mixture of sense and fantasy, so characteristic of its author, are adumbrated a national constitutional convention, the dual plan of our federal system, a national bill of rights, and "worship of the Constitution"; and this was some months before the earliest state constitution and nearly four years before Hamilton's proposal, in his letter to Duane of September 3, 1780, of "a solid, coercive Union".

But the great essential precursor to the success of all such proposals was the consolidation of a sufficient interest transcending state lines, and this was slow in forming. It was eventually brought about in three ways: first, through the abuse by the states of their powers over commerce; secondly, through the rise of the question—in which Washington was especially interested—of opening up communications with the West; thirdly, on account of the sharp fear which was aroused among property owners everywhere by the Shays Rebellion. The last was the really decisive factor. The call for a constitutional convention which had emanated from Annapolis in the autumn of 1786 was heeded by only three states, Virginia, New Jersey, Pennsylvania, and was ignored by Congress; but the call which Congress itself issued in the following February under the stimulus imparted by the uprising in Massachusetts was responded to by nine states in due course—New Hampshire being the last on account of the late date of the assembling of its legislature. Testimony from private sources is to the same effect; it shows how the Massachusetts uprising completed the work of the paper-money craze in convincing men that constitutional reform had ceased to be a merely local problem.

In this connection a paper prepared by Madison in April, 1787, and entitled "Vices of the Political System of the United States", becomes of great interest both for its content and because of the leading part later taken by its author in the work of the Convention. The title itself is significant: "the Political System of the United States" is *one,* and therefore the problem of its reform in all its branches is a single problem; and the argument itself bears out this prognosis. The defects of the Confederation are first considered: the failure of the states to comply with the requisitions of Congress, their encroachments on the central authority, their violations of the treaties of the United States and the Law of Nations, their trespasses on the rights of each other, their want of concert in matters of common interest, the lack of a coercive power in the government of the Confederation, the lack of a popular ratification of the Articles—all these are noted. Then in the midst of this catalogue appears a hitherto unheard-of specification: "want of guaranty to the States of their constitutions and laws against internal violence"—an obvious deduction from the Shays Rebellion.

It is, however, for the legislative evils which he finds within the states individually that Madison reserves his strongest words of condemnation. "As far as laws are necessary", he writes, "to mark with precision the duties of those who are to obey them, and to take from those who are to administer them a discretion which might be abused, their number is the price of liberty. As far as laws exceed this limit, they are a nuisance; a nuisance of the most pestilent kind." Yet "try the Codes of the several States by this test, and what a luxuriancy of legislation do they present. The short period of independency has filled as many pages as the century which preceded it". Nor was this multiplicity of laws the greatest evil—worse was their mutability, a clear mark "of vicious legislation"; and worst of all their injustice, which brought "into question the fundamental principle of republican Government, that the majority who rule in such governments are the safest Guardians both of public Good and private rights".

Indeed Madison proceeded to argue, in effect, that majority rule was more or less of a superstition. No doubt the evils just recounted were traceable in part to the individual selfishness of the representatives of the people; but their chief cause lay in a much more stubborn fact—the natural arrangement of society.

All civilized societies [he wrote] are divided into different interests and factions, as they happen to be creditors or debtors—rich or poor—husbandmen, merchants or manufacturers—members of different religious sects—followers of different political leaders—inhabitants of different districts—owners of different kinds of property, etc., etc. In republican Government the majority however composed, ultimately give the law. Whenever therefore an apparent interest or common passion unites a majority what is to restrain them from unjust violations of the rights and interests of the minority, or of individuals?

Merely moral or persuasive remedies Madison found to be useless when addressed to political selfishness—which itself never lacks a moral excuse—nor does he once refer to the teachings of Montesquieu, for the reason, it may be surmised, that the model constitution of the Union by this test had broken down at the very moment of crisis. One device, nevertheless, remained untried: the enlargement of the geographical sphere of government. For the advantage of a large republic over a small one, Madison insisted, was this: owing, on the one hand, to the greater variety of interests scattered through it, and, on the other, to the natural barrier of distance, a dangerous coalescence of factions became much more difficult. "As a limited monarchy tempers the evils of an absolute one; so an extensive Republic meliorates the administration of a small Republic."

And how precisely was this remedy to be applied in the case of the United States? In the paper before us, Madison seems to imply the belief that the states ought to surrender all their powers to the national government, but his letters make it plain that this was not his programme. Rather, the powers of the central government should be greatly enlarged, and it should be converted into a real government, operative upon individuals and vested with all the coercive powers of government; then this enlarged and strengthened government, which on account of the territorial extent of its constituency would with difficulty fall a prey to faction, should be set as a check upon the exercise by the state governments of the considerable powers which must still remain with them. "The national government" must "have a negative in all cases whatsoever on the legislative acts of the states", he wrote, like that of the King in colonial days. This was "the least possible abridgment of the State sovereignties". "The happy effect" of such an arrangement would be "its control on the internal vicissitudes of State policy and the aggressions of interested majorities on the rights of minorities and individuals". Thus was the Balance of Power, which Montesquieu had borrowed from the stock teachings of the eighteenth-century diplomacy, to transform it into a maxim of free constitutions, projected into the midway field of federal government.

Every constitutional system gives rise, in relation to the interests of the people whom it is designed to serve, to certain characteristic and persistent problems. The most persistent problem of the American constitutional system arises from the fact that to a multitude of state legislatures are assigned many of the most important powers of government over the individual. Originally, indeed, the bias in favor of local autonomy so overweighted the American constitutional system in that direction that it broke down entirely, both within the states, where the basic rights of property and contract were seriously infringed, and throughout the nation at large, because from the central government essential powers had been withheld.

In the solution of the problems thence resulting, four important constructive ideas were successively brought forward in the years immediately preceding the Philadelphia Convention, all of them reflecting the doctrine of the separation of powers or the attendant notion of a check and balance in government. The abuses resulting from the hitherto undifferentiated character of "legislative power" were met by the idea that it was something intrinsically distinct from "judicial power", and that therefore it was exceeded when it interfered with the dispensation of justice through the ordinary courts. Then building upon this result, the finality of judicial determinations was represented as extending to the interpretation of the standing law, a proposition which, when brought into association with the notion of a higher law, yielded the initial form of the doctrine of judicial review. Meantime, the idea was being advanced that the Articles of Confederation were, in relation to acts of the local legislatures, just such a higher law, thus suggesting a sanction for the acts of the Confederation which in principle entirely transformed its character. Finally, from Madison, who from the first interested himself in every phase of the rising movement for constitutional reform both in his own state and the country at large, came the idea that the problem of providing adequate safeguards for private rights and adequate powers for a national government was one and the same problem, inasmuch as a strengthened national government could be made a make-weight against the swollen prerogatives of the state legislatures. It remained for the Constitutional Convention, however, while it accepted Madison's main idea, to apply it through the agency of judicial review. Nor can it be doubted that this determination was assisted by a growing comprehension in the Convention of the *doctrine* of judicial review.

The Transformation
of Republican Thought

GORDON S. WOOD

The progress of constitutional theory in the decade following independence had transformed republican thought by the time that state ratification conventions met to debate the fate of the federal Constitution. The crucial question turned on the role of the public in a republic, the relationship of the representatives to the represented, and inevitably focused attention on the need to separate the strands of popular sovereignty which had been merged during the Revolution with those of legislative sovereignty and state sovereignty. In his massive study of *The Creation of the American Republic*, Gordon S. Wood does on a grand scale what Corwin did in his pioneering article nearly forty-five years earlier, tracing the evolution of constitutional theory between 1776 and 1787 and portraying the Constitution as the climax of the American Revolution. The Americans of the Revolutionary generation had perfected "The American Science of Politics," he writes, breaking through "the conceptions of political theory that had imprisoned men's minds for centuries" and brilliantly reconstructing "the framework for a new republican polity, a reconstruction that radically changed the future of politics," one that "would 'decide forever the fate of republican government.'"

THE PROBLEM OF SOVEREIGNTY WAS NOT SOLVED BY THE DEClaration of Independence. It continued to be the most important theoretical question of politics throughout the following decade, the ultimate abstract principle to which nearly all argument were sooner

Gordon S. Wood, *The Creation of the American Republic, 1776–1787* (Chapel Hill, University of North Carolina Press, 1969), pp. 354, 355, 360, 361–362, 372–374, 376, 381, 382–384, 385, 387–389, 409–413, 425–426, 430–438, 463–467. Reprinted by permission of University of North Carolina Press and the Institute of Early American History and Culture.

or later reduced. Curiously, however, sovereignty was not as explosive and as wide-ranging an issue in the formation of the American's confederation as might have been expected from the experience of the debate of the previous decade.

With Independence it became obvious that the Continental Congress, not really a governmental body and created simply out of the exigency of events in 1774, needed some more solid basis; the congressional delegates immediately began working on an agreement that would more permanently connect the new states in a central union. But the creation of these Articles of Confederation sparked no extensive exploration into the problems of politics. Throughout the 1770's there was remarkably little discussion in the press or pamphlets of the nature of the union being formed. What debate there was was largely confined within the walls of Congress and was very limited and intellectually insignificant in comparison with the exciting and sweeping debates over the formation of the state constitutions—a graphic indication of the relative importance Americans attributed to their central and state governments. The principle of sovereignty was not probed and analyzed by Americans in 1776–77 the way it had been in the sixties, because whatever the limitations the Confederation may have placed in fact on the individual sovereignty of the states, few believed that their union in any theoretical sense contravened that sovereignty. . . . [The Confederation] was not, as Ezra Stiles remarked in 1783, meant to be "a body in which resides authoritative sovereignty; for there is no real cession of dominion, no surrender or transfer of sovereignty to the national council, as each state in the confederacy is an independent sovereignty.". . .

Beginning in the early 1780's there were some Americans, increasingly concerned with the weakness of the confederacy, who sought by every possible means to strengthen Congress, by direct amendment, by broad interpretation of the Articles, or even by military force and dictatorship. Only with the multiplication of these proposals for reform was the problem of sovereignty as it related to the Confederation seriously and widely confronted; but the issue was decided even before it was raised. Despite all of their fulminations against "the present futile and senseless confederation" and their frantic denials of "the *Complete Sovereignty of each State*," the advocates of a stronger central government could not escape from the basic confederate nature of the union and the principle of sovereignty. "There was in nature no middle way between a federal and a corporate union," opponents of centralization repeatedly retorted. "Each party to the confederation must possess a sovereignty, for without that they are no longer States, and while they possess a sovereignty, that sovereignty must be independent: For a dependent sovereignty is nonsense.". . .

As vigorous as these efforts to increase the strength of the central government in the early eighties were, they were not at the heart of the problems of politics in the Confederation period. It was the exigencies of the financial and war situation in 1780, more than the logic of Hamilton's *Continentalist* essays, that had prompted what nearly successful attempts there were to add a limited taxing power to Congress. And with the coming of peace the temporary ascendancy of those "who think continentally" rapidly declined and the chances of reforming the Confederation piecemeal with them. Simply to assert, as one writer in 1783 did, that Congress was "a tribunal to which all subordinate powers must appeal, and whose decision is conclusive and compulsory," or to urge, as Pelatiah Webster did in the same year, that the states part with as much of their sovereignty as necessary for an effectual central government was to fly in the face of the realities of American politics in the 1780's. With peace Americans were now more eager than ever before "to oppose all encroachments of the American Congress upon the sovereignty and jurisdiction of the separate states." The states had become increasingly jealous of their power and in fact through their handling of public lands and public debts were fast moving to absorb the major political and economic groups, creating a vested interest in state sovereignty. It had become obvious from the early eighties that no substantial reform of the Confederation was possible as long as each state retained "the idea of an uncontrollable sovereignty . . . over its internal police."

Ironically, however, it was the very "JEALOUSY OF POWER" so much deplored by the proponents of centralization that was to be the eventual source of their success. The most significant political developments of these years lay not in the attempts by a dynamic minority of nationalists to weaken the idea of the sovereignty of the states from above, that is, by adding powers to Congress. Rather they lay in the widespread attacks on the idea of state sovereignty from below, that is, by the repeated and intensifying denials by various groups that the state legislatures adequately spoke for the people. Sovereignty was still the issue, but in the struggles between the legislatures and the people-at-large the state governments were put on the defensive as they had not been with the Congress. In the contest between the states and the Congress the ideological momentum of the Revolution lay with the states; but in the contest between the people and the state governments it decidedly lay with the people.

"It is a Maxim," proclaimed the Massachusetts General Court in January 1776, "that, in every Government, there must exist, Somewhere, a Supreme, Sovereign, absolute, and uncontroulable Power; But this Power resides, always in the body of the People, and it never was, or can be delegated, to one Man, or a few." In one sense this was a traditional utterance, for no one doubted, even most Tories, that all power ultimately resided in the people. But it was in another intensely real sense that many Americans in the years after 1776 were to interpret the sovereignty of the people. It was to become no vague abstraction of political science to which all could pay lip service. The trite theory of popular sovereignty gained a verity in American hands that European radicals with all of their talk of all power in the people had scarcely considered imaginable except at those rare times of revolution. "Civil liberty" became for Americans "not 'a government of laws,' made agreeable to charters, bills of rights or compacts, but a power existing in the people at large, at any time, for any cause, or for no cause, but their own sovereign pleasure, to alter or annihilate both the mode and essence of any former government, and adopt a new one in its stead." American liberty seemed in fact to have made revolution perpetual and civil disorder legitimate. . . .

THE TRANSFERRAL OF SOVEREIGNTY

It was inevitable that the orthodox notion of sovereignty, the most important doctrine of eighteenth-century political science, would be thrust in the way of these radical constitutional developments; for this denigration of the legislature's authority, this "reservation of any power in the hands of the people" in order to "interfere with the power of the Legislature to consult the public interest, and prevent its exercise," more directly violated the concept of sovereignty than did any of the Americans' efforts prior to 1787 to erect or strengthen the Confederation. "Sovereignty . . . ," went the conventional doctrine, "consists in the understanding and will of the political society," which admittedly was originally in the people. When the government was formed, however, the people vested the sovereignty "where and in what manner" they pleased; "he or they to whom it is delegated is the sovereign, and is thus vested with the political understanding and will of the people, for their good and advantage solely." Since "the power of making rules or laws to govern or protect the society is the essence of sovereignty," the legislatures of the states had become the sovereign powers in America. There thus could be no power in the states existing outside of the legislatures, because "this sovereignty can never be a subordinate power, or be amenable to any other power."

Hence beginning in the late seventies and continuing on through the eighties opponents of all of these radical extensions of Whiggism—the mobbing and electioneering, the proliferation of conventions, the broadened use of instructions, the acute actualization of representation—repeatedly fell back upon this doctrine of sovereignty as the final, best rebuttal they could offer. "The idea of Committees forming County Conventions, and these County Conventions advising State Conventions to act in opposition to, or in conformity with General Court, the supreme authority of the State, . . . the supposition of two different powers in a State assuming the right of controling the people," seemed to the people of Worcester, Massachusetts, "to be intirely inconsistent with the best and most established maxims of government," forming "that great political solecism imperium in imperio, a head within a head." In every state, legislative authority was "placed in an assembly, that is annually and fully chosen by the people." These representative assemblies, as those alarmed by the growing disrespect of legislative actions repeated over and over, were no distant Parliament; they were the people's own elected representatives, in whom the sovereignty had been deposited. "The people resign their own authority to their representatives—the acts of these deputies are in effect the acts of the people. . . . It is as wrong to refuse obedience to the laws made by our *representatives,* as it would be to break laws made by *ourselves.*" If a law was bad, then the people could elect new deputies to repeal it; "but while it is a law, it is the act and will of the sovereign power and ought to be obeyed." As every good republican should know, "the Legislature have an undoubted right to make the interest of the State forego that of individuals, and that our duty is to acquiesce." The representative legislature must be "considered as the greatest power on earth," since *"there cannot be two wills in the same public body."* The resort to binding instructions from local districts formented by "a *directing* club or committee" would prove to be "a dangeerous Jesuitical imperium in imperio" and make the legislature "as a *body* contemptible." The concept of sovereignty was as essential to a republic as to any state. "This kind of sovereignty is the *power that enacts laws,"* which in every state was "lodged in the *General Assembly."* The people retained elective powers, but "the deliberative powers" of lawmaking belonged to the sovereign legislature. "A right to *instruct* the sovereignty places the *deliberative power in the people,* and brings everything back to that chaos which existed before the compact." The point was, as Benjamin Rush said in 1787 summing up the arguments of those resisting this popular radicalism, "the people of America have mistaken the meaning of the word sovereignty." "It is often said that 'the sovereign and all other power is seated *in* the people.' This idea is unhappily expressed. It should be—'all power is derived *from* the people.' They possess it only on the days of their elections. After this, it is the property of their rulers, nor can they exercise it or resume it, unless it is abused."

But this common distinction "between power being *derived* from the people, and being *seated* in the people" was rapidly being dissolved in the years after Independence, as radical writers "in the transition from monarchy to a republic" expanded and indeed "bastardized" the principles of the Revolution. The people, it was argued, "must not only retain the right of delegating, but of resuming power, at stated periods, if they will be free. . . . If power sufficient to controul the Officers of Government is *not seated* in the people," then the Revolution had been meaningless. "Who have we . . . besides the people? and if they are not to be trusted with the care of their own interests who can?" The Americans, it was claimed at the outset by the freeholders of Augusta County, Virginia, were "neither guided, nor will ever be influenced by that slavish maxim in politicks, 'that whatever is enacted by that body of men in whom the supreme power of the state is vested must in all cases be implicitly obeyed.'" Those who iterated such a view, realizing the dangerous logic of it, could "disclaim the construction . . . and the application some have made of it" and disavowed the anarchy it could induce. Yet Americans, being good Whigs, could never deny the sentiment itself: "Is it possible," asked the Augusta freeholders, "that they should *believe* the contrary?" Yet a decade later men were still compelled to contend "that the boasted *omnipotence* of the Legislature is but a gingle of words, and literally understood is but little short of blasphemy. . . . If there is *no* bound to the Legislature, we are no longer in a free country, but governed by an oligarchial tyranny."

Many thus found themselves by the 1780's increasingly pressed to determine these bounds and to distinguish between lawful and unlawful resistance to legislative authority. . . .

The search for this remedy—a way to control and restrict the elected representatives in their power—dominated the politics and constitutionalism of the Confederation period. Yet the devices to limit legislative omnipotence being discovered or implemented in these years—the idea of a written constitution as fundamental law, the resort to special constituting bodies, and the actualization of representation through the growing use of instructions and local residence requirements—were all products of the very breakdown of confidence between people and representatives and the atmosphere of suspicion and jealousy so much condemned. It seemed that once it was conceded that the legislature did not possess the full power of the people to do anything it wished for the good of the state, then there could be no logical way of restraining the slippage of nearly all authority away from the legislature to the people-at-large.

No one saw this more clearly, no one grasped more fully the interconnectedness of all the political and constitutional developments of the 1780's, than did Noah Webster, writing in 1787–88 as "Giles Hickory" in an extraordinary series of articles published in his own *American Magazine*. . . .

Again and again throughout all of his rambling criticisms of America's recent constitutional developments Webster kept coming back to this question of the representativeness of the people in their assemblies: "Whether, in a free State, there ought to be any distinction between the powers of the people or electors, and the powers of the Representatives in the Legislature." All of Webster's attacks on the right of instructions, on unalterable constitutions, and on special constitutional conventions, were eventually grounded on his conviction, the basic conviction of orthodox eighteenth-century political science, that *"the Legislature has all the power, of all the people,"* and that there could be in no state "a pretended power pramount to the legislature." Representation should not be actual or partial; "the powers of a Legislature should be co-extensive with those of the people," for "the collective body of Representatives is the collective sense and authority of the people." There could thus be "no power residing in the State at large, which does not reside in the legislature." If some power was withheld from the representatives and left with the people-at-large, then the way was opened to a full denial of legislative power. "Unless the Legislature is the supreme power, and invested with *all* the authority of the State, its acts are not laws, obligatory upon the whole State." The principle of sovereignty required that if the legislature had an "unlimited power to do *right*" for the state, then it must also have "an unlimited power to do *wrong*." There was no other choice. If the representation of the people in the legislature was not full and "virtual," then, as Webster saw as acutely as anyone, the various state legislatures were in theory no more sovereign, no more lawmaking bodies, than was the Confederation Congress.

However "repugnant to the principles received by my countrymen and recognized by some of the state constitutions" Webster's sentiments were, the logic of his central argument was compelling—the same logic that the British had used against the Americans in the late sixties and early seventies: there must be in every state a supreme, absolute, indivisible, sovereign power. If the Americans in the 1780's were forced to choose between their legislatures and the people-at-large as the repository of this sovereignty, just as they had been forced in the early seventies to choose between Parliament and their legislatures, there could be no doubt now as there had been no doubt then where they would place the final supreme power. "For," as one Connecticut town declared in 1783, "there is an original, underived and incommunicable authority and supremacy, in the collective body of the people, to whom all delegated power must submit, and from whom there is no appeal." Rather than disavow the powerful conception of sovereignty when confronted with it, many now, as earlier, chose to relocate it. If sovereignty had to reside somewhere in the state—and the best political science of the eighteenth century said it did—then many Americans concluded that it must reside only in the people-at-large. The legislatures could never be sovereign; no set of men, representatives or not, could "set themselves up against the general voice of the people." "The community, however represented, ought to remain the supreme authority and ultimate judicature." In the people alone "that plenary power rests and abides which all agree should rest somewhere."

To someone steeped in British legal thought this explicit retention of legal sovereignty in the people was preposterous. It could only signify a repudiation of the concept and an eventual breakdown of all governmental order. But developments in America since 1776 had infused an extraordinary meaning into the idea of the sovereignty of the people. The Americans were not simply making the people a nebulous and unsubstantial source of all political authority. The new conception of a constitution, the development of extralegal conventions, the reliance on instructions, the participation of the people in politics out-of-doors, the clarification of the nature of representation, the never-ending appeals to the people by competing public officials—all gave coherence and reality, even a legal reality, to the hackneyed phrase, the sovereignty of the people.

THE DISEMBODIMENT OF GOVERNMENT

Transferring sovereignty from the legislative bodies to the people-at-large outside of all governmental institutions represented far more than simply an intellectual shift of a political conception. It had consequences and implications that were at first only vaguely perceived, but when sparked into illumination by debates and the logic of arguments became confusing and often frightening indications of the changes Americans were making in their inherited political theory. By weakening the representativeness of the people in the legislatures through the resort to conventions, instructions, and other out-of-doors action, by expressing as much fear and suspicion of their elected representatives as of their senators and governors, the Americans were fundamentally unsettling the traditional understanding of how the people in a republic were to participate in the government. The logic of the principles of the Revolution was being spun out with such rapidity in these years, impelled by the strongest kinds of polemical pressures and political and social circumstances, that most scarcely sensed the enormity of the intellectual changes they were participating in. All that had begun in the 1760's with the debate with England was now being brought to a head. A series of tiny, piecemeal changes in thought, no one of which seemed immensely consequential, was preparing Americans for a revolution in their conceptions of law, constitutionalism, and politics.

If the people were not actually voicing their will in the representative assemblies, then no law enacted by the legislatures could be considered fully binding. Some almost immediately in the 1780's began drawing that conclusion, arguing that it was "impossible" for the representatives "to impose an irrevocable act contrary to the majority of the people, from whom they received their power." Horrified opponents retorted that this made the people "not subject to law" and indeed destroyed the idea of law itself. "If an act of a representative is not the act of his constituents, it is nothing; it is only the act of an individual—of Tom, Dick, or Harry." For some this was precisely what the laws in the 1780's seemed to be: acts of mistrusted individuals that were in the nature of temporary recommendations to the people, standing only so far as "the vote of the community does not oppose." And such communal opposition, as the proliferation of committees and conventions demonstrated, was even considered by some to be legitimate. No legislature, said a New Jerseyite, could ignore the voice of the people out-of-doors, for "the plain definition of republican government is that every elector has a voice in every law which is made to govern him the same as if he personally sat in council." The state legislatures, it was claimed, contained no more of the inherent power of the American people than the British Parliament ever had. With the repeated complaints in the press and pamphlets that the legislatures were violating the bounds of justice and all that made law what it was, the people were increasingly advised from the 1770's on through the eighties never to accept that "plausible nonsense 'that nothing is beyond the reach of the Supreme Legislature.'" With the resort to conventions and extra-legislative organizations it was now realistically possible to deny "that the will of the people is properly known from the Representatives." The legislators must realize that they merely possessed "a trust from the people for their good, and in several instances so far from possessing an absolute power, they ought to acknowledge that they have no power at all." Representation of the people could therefore never be full and inclusive. "It is a vain and weak argument," wrote Thomas Tudor Tucker of South Carolina in 1784, "that, the legislature being the representatives of the people, the act of the former is therefore always to be considered as the act of the latter. They are the representatives of the people for certain purposes only, not to all intents and purposes whatever." The significance for men's understanding of law of this change in the conception of representation was immense. If law made by a legislature was not really a reflection of the will of the people, not the command of a superior sovereign, but only the act of the people's suspected agents, then some sanction other than consent would have to be emphasized in order to make law obligatory.

The implications of these changes in the nature of the people's role in the government were as important for men's understanding of politics as they were for their understanding of law. They were in fact tending not only to a radical redistribution of the powers of society within the government but to a total destruction of these powers and a shattering of the categories of government that had dominated Western thinking for centuries. Already by the middle eighties the senates in several states were being regarded as a kind of double representation of the people with disturbing but not always clearly perceived consequences for the theory of mixed government. . . .

The use of binding instructions and the growing sense that the representative was merely a limited agent or spokesman for the local interests of his constituents in the decade after Independence ate away the independent authority of the representative and distorted, even destroyed, the traditional character of representation. Evidently the people could never be fully embodied in their houses of representatives; sovereignty and the ultimate power to make law, as the extra-legislative devices developing in this period illustrated, remained with the collective people. The logic of these developments was to take the people out of the government altogether, and to blur the previous distinction among representatives, senators, and magistrates. Once the supposed representatives of the people (the democratic elements) in the lower houses of the legislature were regarded with the same suspicion and uneasiness as the traditional rulers and upper houses (the monarchical and aristocratic elements) had been (representation was after all, said one Virginian, "at best, but a species of aristocracy"), it became a much simpler matter to view the rulers and senators in the same light as the supposed representatives were viewed. Once the mutuality of interests between representatives and people that made representation what it was to most eighteenth-century Englishmen was broken down by the American atmosphere of suspicion and jealousy, the only criterion of representation left was election, which helps explain the Americans' increasing concern with the right to vote as a measure of representation. With election or simply the derivation of authority from the people becoming the sole basis and measure of representation, the several branches of the government began to seem indistinguishable. All elected officials could be considered as kinds of representatives of the people, as equally trusted or mistrusted agents of the people. "In our republican government," the people could now be told, "not only our *Deputies,* but our *Governor* and *Council* may in a good sense be esteemed our representatives, as they are annually chosen by you, to manage our public affairs." After all, "who have we in America but the people? Members of congress, of assemblies, or councils, are still a part of the people. The honours do not take them out of the aggregate body." It was not unreasonable now to argue that "the principle for Representation" should be extended "throughout every public body" so that all elected, hence representative, officials—senators or others—should be elected in proportion to the population, the logic of which it has taken us nearly two centuries to realize. "In a free state," wrote Thomas Tudor Tucker of South Carolina in 1784, "every officer, from the Governor to the constable, is, so far as the powers of his office extend, as truly the representative of the people, as a member of the legislature; and his act, within the appointed limitation, is the act of the people; for he is their agent, and derives his authority from them."

The people no longer actually shared in a part of the government (as, for example, the people of England participated in their government through the House of Commons), but they remained outside the entire government, watching, controlling, pulling the strings for all their agents in every branch or part of the government. They embraced the whole government, and no branch or part could speak with the complete authority of the people. Indeed, not even all parts of the government collectively incorporated the full powers of the people. "With us it would be an absurd surrender of liberty to delegate full powers to any set of men whatever." Conventions, assemblies, senates, magistracy were all agents of the people for certain limited purposes. Only such a conception of representation made sense of the developments of the Confederation period—the use of instructions, the electioneering, and the extra-legislative organizations, in particular the special constituting conventions creating a superior law ratifiable by the people themselves in their sovereign capacity and hence unalterable by the people's provisional agents in the legislatures. "Delegates may be sent to a convention with powers, under certain restrictions, to frame a constitution. Delegates are sent to the General Assembly with powers, under certain restrictions prescribed . . . by a previously established compact or constitution, to make salutary laws." Yet neither the convention nor the assembly possessed the total authority of the people. "If either one or the other should exceed the powers vested in them, their act is no longer the act of their constituents." The power of the people outside of the government was always absolute and untrammeled; that of their various delegates in the government could never be.

These were revolutionary ideas that had unfolded rapidly in the decade after Independence, but not deliberately or evenly. Men were always only half aware of where their thought was going, for these new ideas about politics were not the products of extended reasoned analysis but were rather numerous responses of different Americans to a swiftly changing reality, of men involved in endless polemics compelled to contort and draw out from the prevailing assumptions the latent logic few had foreseen. Rarely before 1787 were these new thoughts comprehended by anyone as a whole. They were bits and pieces thrown up by the necessities of argument and condition, without broad design or significance. But if crystalized by sufficient pressures they could result in a mosaic of an entirely new conception of politics to those who would attempt to describe it. . . .

DEMOCRATIC DESPOTISM

In the 1780's the Americans' inveterate suspicion and jealousy of political power, once concentrated almost exclusively on the Crown and its agents, was transferred to the various state legislatures. Where once the magistracy had seemed to be the sole source of tyranny, now the legislatures through the Revolutionary state constitutions had become the institutions to be most feared. American "prejudices against the Executive," said James Wilson in 1787, "resulted from a misapplication of the adage that the parliament was the pallidium of liberty. Where the Executive was really formidable, *King* and *Tyrant,* were naturally associated in the minds of the people." But where the executive was weak, as in the American constitutions, "*legislature* and *tyranny* . . . were most properly associated." Increasingly, from the outset of the Revolution on through the next decade, the legislatures, although presumably embodying the people's will, were talked of in terms indistinguishable from those formerly used to describe the magistracy. "If it is possible for the legislature to be influenced by avarice and ambition and by either of these extremes to *betray* their country, and abuse the people . . . , then would the state be in danger of being ruined by their *Representatives.*" As the supposedly representative legislatures drifted away from the people, men more and more spoke of the legislators' being just other kinds of rulers, liable to the same temptations and abuses rulers through history had shown—all of which made comprehensible the intensifying desire to make the representatives more dependent on the opinion of their constituents and the increasing invocations of "the collective body of the people" to set against the legislatures.

Yet there were some Americans who perceived that the problems of the 1780's were not due to the drifting and unrepresentative character of the legislatures, but were rather due to the legislatures' very representativeness. The distresses of the period, in other words, did not arise because the people-at-large had been forsaken by their legislatures, "but because their transient and indigested sentiments have been too implicitly adopted." The evils and vices of state legislation, said James Madison, were not based, as some said, on the temporary deceit of a few designing men who were perverting their representative authority for their own selfish ends. Such vices actually sprang from the emergent nature of American society, and therefore brought "into question the fundamental principle of republican Government, that the majority who rule in such governments are the safest Guardians both of public Good and private rights." "According to Republican Theory," said James Madison, "Right and power being both vested in the majority, are held to be synonimous." But was this truly the case? asked Madison in a brilliant series of letters and essays, describing clearly and cogently what he thought was happening to the traditional assumptions of Whig constitutionalism. "Wherever the real power in a Government lies," he told Jefferson, "there is the danger of oppression. In our Governments the real power lies in the majority of the Community, and the invasion of private rights is chiefly to be apprehended, not from acts of Government contrary to the sense of its constituents, but from acts in which the Government is the mere instrument of the major number of the constituents." The people, it seemed, were as capable of despotism as any prince; public liberty was no guarantee after all of private liberty. At the beginning of the Revolution, wrote Madison, Americans obviously had not perceived this danger to the private rights of property from public liberty. "In all the Governments which were considered as beacons to republican patriots and lawgivers, the rights of persons were subjected to those of property"; throughout history the poor had always been sacrificed to the rich. In 1776 Americans had assumed that their society was unique—so egalitarian that both rights coincided, so different that "a provision for the rights of persons was supposed to include of itself those of property." And Americans naturally inferred, said Madison, "from the tendency of republican laws"—like the abolition of primogeniture and entail—"that these different interests would be more and more identified." But alas! "experience and investigation" had eventually taught Madison that America was not different from other societies, that equality of condition was a chimera. Only a minority, said Madison, "can be interested in preserving the rights of property." Yet what could be done? In 1786 a New Jersey critic of this majoritarian tyranny had argued that there were occasions when the legislature must ignore the voice of its constituents. "A virtuous legislature will not, cannot listen to any proposition, however popular, that came within the description of being *unjust,* impolitic or unnecessary." "Then we are not a republican government," was the formidable reply, "for the evident signification thereof is that the people (the majority of the people) bear rule, and it is for them to determine whether a proposition is *unjust, impolitic,* and *unnecessary* or not."

Americans thus experienced in the 1780's not merely a crisis of authority—licentiousness leading to anarchy—which was a comprehensible abuse of republican liberty, but also a serious shattering of older ways of examining politics and a fundamental questioning of majority rule that threatened to shake the foundations of their republican experiments. It was extremely difficult, however, for most Americans to grasp what was happening and fit it into their accepted paradigm of politics. Most commentators were concerned with what they described as the breakdown in governmental authority, the tendency of the people to ignore the government and defy the laws by their claims that "a *subordination* to the laws, is always the cant word to enslave the people." "Every man of sense," said Fisher Ames, "must be convinced that our disturbances have arisen more from the want of power than the abuse of it." Yet the pressing constitutional problem was not really the lack of power in the state legislatures but the excess of it—popular despotism. Writers, like Noah Webster, cried out against the evils of the day: "So many legal infractions of sacred right—so many public invasions of private property—so many wanton abuses of legislative powers!" Nevertheless, in almost the same breath, they urged the people to obey their elected legislatures, right or wrong, contending that the only remedy for abuses was new elections. Somehow the people were both licentious and tyrannical, but ironically the remedy for one was the source of evil for the other.

Shays's Rebellion in western Massachusetts was received with excited consternation mingled with relief by many Americans precisely because it was an anticipated and understandable abuse of republican liberty. Liberty had been carried into anarchy and the throwing off of all government—a more comprehensible phenomenon to most American political thinkers than legislative tyranny. The rebels, announced the town of Boston, must obey the majority. "Let the majority be ever so much in the wrong," it was the only remedy for grievances "compatible with the ideas of society and government!" The insurgents, argued a publicist, must rely on their elected representatives for the redress of wrongs: "Can human wisdom devise a more effectual security to our liberties?" So relieved by the rebellion were many social conservatives that some observers believed the Shaysites were fomented by those who wanted to demonstrate the absurdity of republicanism.

Nothing so insidious has been proved, but many social conservatives did see the rebellion as encouraging the move for constitutional reform. It was both a confirmation of their worst fears—hence their horror, and a vindication of their desires for stronger government—hence their relief. It fitted nicely into the traditional pattern of political thinking and thus cleared the air of much of the confusion which had hung over the 1780's. Yet Shays's Rebellion was irrelevant to the major constitutional difficulty experienced in the Confederation period—the problem of legal tyranny, the usurpation of private rights under constitutional cover. Connecticut had no violence like that of Massachusetts, said Noah Webster, "because the Legislature wear the complexion of the people." Only "the temporizing of the legislatures in refusing legal protection to the prosecution of the just rights of creditors," remarked David Ramsay, freed the southern states from similar disturbances. Within a few months, however, observers noted that the Shaysites were trying their strength in another way, "that is," said James Madison, "by endeavoring to give the elections such a turn as may promote their views under the auspices of constitutional forms." Merely subduing the rebels and calling upon them to obey the authority of the legislature did not go to the heart of the Americans' predicament. With "a total change of men" in the legislature, wrote Webster, "there will be, therefore, no further insurrection, because the Legislature will represent the sentiments of the people." Hence some Americans in the 1780's could come to believe that "sedition itself will sometimes make laws."

The classical political spectrum did not make sense to a perceptive and probing mind trying to understand American politics. "It has been remarked," wrote Madison to Jefferson, "that there is a tendency in all Governments to an augmentation of power at the expense of liberty." But for Madison the statement now seemed ill founded. There seemed little danger in the American republics that the tyranny of the rulers would subvert liberty. No doubt, said Madison, governmental power, when it attained a certain degree of energy and independence, went on to expand itself. "But when below that degree, the direct tendency is to further degrees of relaxation, until the abuses of liberty beget a sudden transition to an undue degree of power." Licentiousness, in other words, led not to anarchy, but to a new kind of popular depotism. Only in this sense, said Madison, was the traditional spectrum of power "applicable to the Governments in America." America had little to fear from the traditional abuse of power by the few over the many. "It is much more to be dreaded that the few will be unnecessarily sacrificed to the many.". . . .

THE CONTINUANCE OF HOPE

For all of the expressions of pessimism in the 1780's, it is clear that not all American intellectuals had lost their confidence in the republican experiment. Jefferson, viewing the new republics while standing amidst the pomp and debauchery of Paris, remained calm and sanguine. America—by contrast—still seemed the land of happy frugal yeomen. "With all the defects of our constitutions, whether general or particular, the comparison of our governments with those of Europe are like a comparison of heaven and hell." Send those gentry, he urged, who had forsaken the American republics "here to count the blessings of monarchy." "The best schools for republicanism," Jefferson concluded, "are London, Versailles, Madrid, Vienna, Berlin etc." It was absurd, admonished Benjamin Rush in 1787, for Americans to "cry out, after the experience of three or four years, that we are not proper materials for republican government. Remember, we assumed these forms of government in a hurry, before we were prepared for them." The American Revolution, declared Rush, was not yet over. "We have changed our forms of government, but it remains yet to effect a revolution in our principles, opinions, and manners so as to accommodate them to the forms of government we have adopted." Rush had no doubt of the present vice-ridden character of the American people, but he was sure that the vices could be eradicated. "Let us have patience. Our republican forms of government will in time beget republican opinions and manners. All will end well." Others agreed. Americans were expecting too much too soon. It took time to eliminate ancient prejudices. . . .

CONSTITUTIONAL REFORM

Apparently the Americans of 1776 had not fully understood the science of politics after all. "We were, at the commencement of the late war, but novices in politics," wrote Thomas Tudor Tucker of South Carolina in 1784, "and it is to be wished that we may not now be too indolent to correct our mistakes." After lopping off "the monarchical part" of the English constitution, "we vainly imagined that we had arrived at perfection, and that freedom was established on the broadest and most solid basis that could possibly consist with any social institution. That we have in some points been mistaken, is too evident to be denied." "Although we understood perfectly the principles of Liberty," said Benjamin Rush in 1787, "yet most of us were ignorant of the forms and combinations of power in republics." Looking back, 1776 now seemed to be a very unfavorable time for constitution-making. The war and the threats of invasion had been too unsettling, and hatred of the British had been so intense that Americans "unfortunately refused to copy some things in the administration of justice and power, in the British government, which have made it the admiration and envy of the world." Americans soon began telling themselves that their early constitutions were "hasty productions on the spur of exigency," ill adapted to the nature of the society. "Our government should in some degree be suited to our manners and circumstances," John Jay said to Washington early in 1787, "and they, you know, are not strictly democratical." By 1787 it had become a common opinion among many that "the source of all evils of which we complain, and of all those which we apprehend" lay in their "political systems." Indeed, to some the American states possessed "some of the weakest and most inefficient governments . . . that ever nations were afflicted with." There could be no doubt, as Washington put it, that "we have errors to correct." If the American character was not capable of sustaining the popular nature of the Revolutionary constitutions, then the structure of those governments must be changed.

"When by some violent convulsion a revolution has been effected," governments would obviously be unsettled. "Some time must always intervene before new ideas can be received, new forms established, and the machine of government brought back to a regular motion. . . . Defects appear which time only could bring to view; many things require amendment, and some must undergo a total alteration." Yet the ink on the Revolutionary constitutions of 1776 was scarcely dry before defects were appearing and reforms were being proposed. Within even a few months some of those states which had delayed their constitution-making were beginning to entertain doubts about the capacity of their people to maintain extremely popular governments. And it was not long before men in other states which had quickly adopted popular constitutions in 1776 were reconsidering their earlier assumptions. The Pennsylvania Constitution of 1776, it was widely pointed out, had paid no attention "to the ancient habits and customs of the people of Pennsylvania in the distribution of the supreme power of the state. . . . It supposes perfect equality, and equal distribution of property, wisdom and virtue, among the inhabitants of the state." The people of Massachusetts, declared the Essex County Convention in 1776, were in danger of committing similar errors.

Perhaps the people in 1775 had dismissed parts of their old colonial government too brusquely. In New York fear of a government too popular for the society was especially acute in 1776, and some of the gentry were even reluctant to leave the state for the Continental Congress out of fear of surrendering the framing of the constitution to those who would create a government, as Robert Livingston put it, "without that influence that is derived from respect to old families wealth age etc." Everywhere reformation seemed to be in tandem with the formation of the Revolutionary constitutions.

Since the "unsteadiness of the people" was the complaint most commonly made, the kinds of governmental reforms needed soon became obvious. "We have been guarding against an evil that old States are most liable to, *excess of power* in the rulers," said Benjamin Franklin; "but our present danger seems to be *defect of obedience* in the subjects." The liberty of the people in the traditional mixed government must be lessened, and the power of the monarchical and aristocratical elements must be strengthened. In other words, power had to be taken from the houses of representatives and given to the senates and particularly to the governors. "At the commencement of the revolution," Americans were telling themselves in the eighties, "it was supposed that what is called the executive part of a government was the only dangerous part; but we now see that quite as much mischief, if not more, may be done, and as much arbitrary conducted acted, by a legislature." The early state constitutions had rendered government too feeble. "The principal fault," constitutional reformers agreed, "seems to be, a want of energy in the administration of govermnent." In nearly all of the states there were growing demands that the libertarian bias of 1776 be corrected, that the apparent licentiousness of the people be offset by an increase of magisterial power in order to provide for the "execution of the laws that is necessary for the preservation of justice, peace, and internal tranquility."

By the middle eighties Franklin could write to correspondents abroad that whatever faults there were in the Americans' constitutions were being rapidly corrected. "We are, I think, in the right Road of Improvement, for . . . we are daily more and more enlightened." But the reforms were not easily made, for they flew in the face of much of what the American Whigs had learned from their colonial experience under the British monarchy. The problem was conspicuously revealed at the outset in the drafting of the New York Constitution of 1777. The New York constitution-makers, meeting in the spring of 1777, continually found themselves in dilemmas. Torn in two directions—between the inherited dread of magisterial depotism and a fear of popular disorder which was greater than that of any state at that time—the New York Convention was repeatedly obliged to resort to unusual and intricate expedients in order to avoid the extremes. The executive veto, both feared and desired, was eventually transformed into the ingenious Council of Revision, made up of the governor, chancellor, and Supreme Court judges. The power of appointment, the crucial power in the Whig scheme of politics, was the most confused and hotly debated issue; it deadlocked the Convention and was only settled by another unique invention, a Council of Appointment, made up of the governor and four senators chosen by the Assembly, thus resolving the problem of lodging the power of appointment exclusively with either the governor or the legislature. The result was a Constitution in tension—one which members of the same social standing could describe quite differently. For some it savored too much of "the leveling principle," while for others it was "the best system which has as yet been adopted, and possibly as good as the temper of the times would admit of." For constitutional reformers outside of New York, however, the Constitution of 1777, with its strong Senate and its independent governor elected directly by the people for a three-year term, seemed to be a great victory for energy and order. It pointed the direction constitutional reform would take.

It was the Massachusetts Constitution of 1780, adopted by the state after a long and embarrassing delay and the defeat by the towns of one proposed Constitution in 1778, that eventually came to stand for the reconsidered ideal of a *"perfect constitution."* Only the partial limitation on the governor's veto authority and the popular election of the militia officers, said Theophilus Parsons in 1780, marred its perfection. The Constitution seemed to many to have recaptured some of the best elements of the British constitution that had been forgotten in the excitement of 1776. It alone of all the American constitutions had happily found the true mixture. "It in some measure inculcates the doctrine of *equality,* so far as is consistent with the present state of humanity, and tho' it makes *virtue* its principal pillar, it has not rested itself on that single foundation. It inspires with the principles of *honour and dignity,* which attach to its interest a most valuable class of citizens; and like a *despot* it may stamp dread upon those, who can be governed by no other motive." The legislature was balanced between a House of Representatives embodying the people and a Senate of forty whose membership was proportioned to districts in accord with the amount of public taxes paid by the inhabitants. The members of the three branches of the legislature, the House of Representatives, the Senate, and the governor, were qualified by an ascending scale of property-holding and residence. A lengthy bill of rights preceded the Constitution and spelled out the principle of separation of powers in repetitious detail. Although the governor was circumscribed by a Council, selected by both houses from those chosen to be senators, he still represented the most powerful magistrate of all of the states. Like the New York governor, he was elected directly by the people. But unlike the New York governor, the Massachusetts chief magistrate could alone veto all acts of the legislature, except those repassed by a two-thirds majority of both houses. Together with the Council, the governor was granted much of the power his royal predecessor had held, in particular the power to appoint the judicial and leading civil officers, and was given a fixed salary so that "the governor should not be under the undue influence of any of the members of the general court, by a dependence on them for his support."

The Massachusetts Constitution of 1780 not only had a direct influence on the New Hampshire Constitution adopted in 1784 but it seemed to many in the 1780's to climax the second wave of state constitutional construction. In its structure at least, it came to represent much of what reformers in other states desired for their own constitutions—a strengthening of the governor at the expense of the legislature, particularly the lower house. The executive power, as the New Hampshire Convention of 1781 declared in defense of its proposed Constitution, had become "the active principle in all governments: It is the soul, and without it the body-politic is but a dead corpse." The governor, as Jefferson's draft in the early eighties for a new Virginia Constitution stated, must be granted those powers "which are necessary to execute the laws (and administer the government) and which are not in their nature either legislative or judiciary," their precise extent being "left to reason." Reformers sought to center magisterial responsibility in the governors by making the executive councils more advisory than they were in the early Revolutionary constitutions. They also sought to make the governors less dependent on the legislatures, especially in election. Election of the governors by the legislature, said Madison, "not only tends to faction intrigue and corruption, but leaves the Executive under the influence of an improper obligation to that department." Election by the people-at-large, as in New York and Massachusetts, or by some system of indirect election, "or indeed by the people through any other channel than their legislative representatives, seems to be far preferable." Critics of the early constitutions now saw that vesting the power of appointment to offices, so much feared in 1776, in the legislatures destroyed "all responsibility" and created "a perpetual source of faction and corruption." Election of the militia officers by the soldiers rather than magisterial appointment from above "not only renders every superior officer dependent on his inferior, but opens a dangerous avenue to division, discord and animosity in every corps." It now seemed unquestionable that the governor should participate in legislation through some sort of revisionary power, such as a council of revision as in New York, or through a limited veto as in Massachusetts, if there were to be "a check to precipitate, to unjust, and to unconstitutional laws."

Since it was the power of the houses of representatives in particular that had to be checked, the constitutional reformers urged that the upper branches of the legislatures be made more stable, if they were, as Madison said, "to withstand the occasional impetuosities of the more numerous branch." This meant longer terms for senators and some distinct means of qualification which would "supply the defect of knowledge and experience incident to the other branch." Jefferson in his proposal of 1783 for a new Virginia Constitution favored an indirect method of electing senators and the elimination of all restrictions on the senate's power to originate or amend any bill. Only a strong senate, the Virginia reformers believed, could "maintain that system and steadiness in public affairs without which no Government can prosper or be respectable." The judiciary as well must be freed of all dependence on any branch of the government. Only appointment by the governors during good behavior would make the judges "*wholly* independent of the Assembly—of the Council—nay more, of the people." And to ensure that the best men be maintained in office, rotation, which had been such a cardinal principle in 1776, was now openly attacked as leading to instability and confusion. Although even the reactionary *Essex Result* had admitted a need for rotating the governor in 1778, by 1780 the members of the Massachusetts Convention wanted no restrictions on the governor's tenure.

While the magisterial power was to be invigorated, the authority of the legislatures, which, as many now saw, had become "wholly undefined and unlimited, so that neither the people know the extent of their privileges, nor the legislatures the bounds of their power," was to be correspondingly reduced. In his draft for a new Virginia Constitution Jefferson explicitly denied the legislature "the power to infringe this constitution," "to abridge the civil rights of any person on account of his religious beliefs," and to pass certain specified acts, including bills of attainder and *ex post facto* laws. The constitutions themselves, reformers argued, must be made more fundamental, drawn directly by the people and thus rendered unalterable by ordinary legislatures. But higher laws and executive vetoes were not enough. If unjust and foolish laws were to be prevented from even being enacted, the character of the lower houses themselves must be changed, largely, the reformers argued, by decreasing the number of the members by as much as one-half. A smaller house, it was claimed, would be more orderly and energetic and more devoted to the public good. The New Hampshire Convention of 1781 even went so far as to propose a system of indirect election for a fifty-member House of Representatives. The mode of "being twice sifted," the Convention declared, would result in a higher proportion of suitable legislators.

Because these proposals for constitutional reform attempted to reverse the democratic tendencies of the early constitutions, that is, because they sought to lessen the power of the representatives of the people in the legislatures, and conversely to strengthen the magisterial power, they were bitterly resisted, on the very formidable ground that such reforms were antagonistic to the spirit of 1776 and all that the Revolution was politically about. The constitutional changes, like those embodied in the Massachusetts Constitution of 1780, it was charged, "will introduce (at Least) as Many Evils as Could have Been feared from the British power in Case They had Succeeded in Their first attempts against This Continent." It seemed to many that the proposed reforms were but insidious devices to return to the aristocratic and monarchical tones of the former colonial governments. To enhance the rulers' power and to diminish the power of the houses of representatives was precisely what British officials had attempted on the eve of the Revolution. Americans had been indoctrinated too long in the Whig fear of governmental power to consent readily to its aggrandizement at the expense of liberty. . . .

Yet the changes in constitutionalism that were advocated in the years after Independence never seemed quite as unpopular or as unwhiggish as opponents made them out to be. For the Americans' ideas of what constituted governmental power and what constituted popular liberty were not frozen in 1776. Indeed, as has been seen, they were constantly in flux, continually adapting and adjusting to ever-shifting political and social circumstances. Involved in the midst of these changes and contributing to them, the constitutional reformers soon found themselves developing arguments against the construction of the early state constitutions that seemed to be elaborations and extensions rather than repudiations of what Americans had fought for. All of the developments in political thought taking place in the decade after 1776—the changes in the character of representation, in the nature of the senate and the magistracy, in the conception of a constitution and the institution of a convention, in the growing discrepancy between the power of the people out-of-doors and their delegates in the legislatures—all of these developments were both furthered and used by those who in the late seventies and early eighties sought to amend the state constitutions drafted in 1776. By the 1780's such had been the evolution of political ideas that it was no longer self-evident, as it would have been a decade earlier, that the Massachusetts Constitution of 1780 was less popular, less libertarian, less democratic, than the Pennsylvania Constitution of 1776.

THE ABANDONMENT OF THE STATES

As vigorously as the constitutional reforms of the states were urged and adopted in the 1780's they never seemed sufficient. Despite the remedies embodied in the New York, Massachusetts, and New Hampshire constitutions and the probability of reform in the other states, the disillusionment with American politics in the 1780's only grew more intense. Although some could admit that "many of the state constitutions we have chosen, are truly excellent," possessing in theory the necessary powers to act vigorously, it seemed increasingly evident that such powers were not being implemented. In the politics of the various states "it often happens, that those who are appointed to manage the affairs of the State, are extremely averse to exercise those powers with which they are invested. . . . While they feel themselves so frequently dependent on the breath of the people for a continuance in their elevated stations, many will . . . court the favour of the multitude and basely violate the most solemn obligations rather than hazard their own popularity." Only by shifting the arena of reform to the federal level, it seemed, could the evils of American politics be finally remedied. "It is very extraordinary . . . ," some were saying as early as 1783, "that so much pains have been taken to form and organize the constitutions of the several individual governments, and so little has been taken, in that which respects the whole nation of America, and which is superiorly important, that all our greatness, and our greatest concerns rest upon it." While some like Charles Carroll of Maryland were still convinced as late as 1787 that "a Reform of our State Constitutions or Governments should accompany, if not precede the reformations of the federal Government," most reformers by that date were looking to some sort of modification of the structure of the central government as the best, and perhaps the only, answer to America's problems.

The central government had never been entirely ignored. Right from the beginning of the war a continental-minded minority centered in the middle Atlantic states had sought to strengthen the authority of the Confederation at the expense of the states. By the early eighties the nationalist program of men like Robert Morris and Alexander Hamilton had gathered a substantial amount of support from various groups. The war was dragging on, and the value of the paper money issued to finance it was sinking fast. The attempts of the states to prevent the depreciation of currency by legal-tender laws, price-fixing, and anti-monopoly legislation only aggravated discontent among business interests. Both the army and the public creditors of the Confederation were clamoring for help. It

seemed for a moment in 1780–81 that the weakness of the central government was actually threatening the victory against Britain. Yet despite such
pressure even the nationalists' proposals for a limited federal impost and
a restricted congressional commercial power could not overcome the
Revolution's commitment to the separate sovereignty of the states. And
with the end of the war and the reassertion of state authority, expressed
most explicitly in the states' absorption of the congressional debt, the
nationalist program rapidly dissipated. The reputation of Robert Morris,
as the superintendent of finance, became clouded with suspicion. The
army grumbled but disbanded, and most of the nationalist delegates in
Congress completed their three-year terms and retired. By the middle
eighties Congress had virtually collapsed. The danger of the Union's falling to pieces, however great, meant little in the face of most Americans'
deeply rooted mistrust of central power. As urgent as the need for some
sort of revision of the Articles had become by 1785, many creditors and
merchants like Theodore Sedgwick, Stephen Higginson, and the entire
Massachusetts delegation in Congress still hesitated to subject the Confederation to "a *chance of alteration*" for fear of giving "birth to new
hopes of an aristocratical faction which every community possesses." In
the opinion of the Massachusetts delegates there were too many Americans
with "artfully laid, and vigorously pursued" plans afoot which aimed at
transforming "our republican Governments into balefull Aristocracies."
In the end it was not pressure from above, from the manifest debility of
the Confederation, that provided the main impulse for the Federalist
movement of 1787; it was rather pressure from below, from the problems
of politics within the separate states themselves, that eventually made
constitutional reform of the central government possible.

By early 1787 with the experience of Shays's rebellion and its aftermath
Sedgwick, Higginson, and other New England men like them had altered
their thinking and reinterpreted their fears. Not only the fact of the rebellion itself but the eventual victory of the rebels at the polls brought
the contradictions of American politics to a head, dramatically clarifying
what was taking place in nearly all the states. Urging the people to obey
the laws of their state governments as a cure for the anarchical excesses
of the period seemed to be backfiring, resulting in evils even worse than
licentiousness. If the elected representatives in the state legislatures were
likely, as they increasingly seemed to be, "to establish iniquity by Law,"
then obedience to these unjust laws was no solution to the evils of the
day. Orators and writers, struggling with the consequences, admitted, on
the one hand, that legislators in the enactment of "private views" could
be "tyrannical" and warned that "statutes contradictory and inconsistent
are to be expected, and even such as might invert the order of things, and

substitute vice, in the room of virtue." Yet, on the other hand, they realized at the same time that the need for authority and "our social obligations require us to be subject to laws which we may think very inconvenient." Although the legislatures were daily committing acts of "injustice" and were violating "the most simple ties of common honesty," still "while we pretend to be governed by our Representatives in General Court assembled, let not each man foolishly assume the reins of government, and attempt to enforce his sentiments against the majority." State governments, however well structured, no longer seemed capable of creating virtuous laws and citizens. Had not the Massachusetts Constitution of 1780, asked Thomas Dawes in a Fourth of July oration of 1787, been acclaimed as the model of political perfection? "But if our constitution is the perfect law of liberty, whence those mighty animosities which have so lately distracted the bosom of peace, and stained the first pages of our history with civil blood?" Actually, said Dawes, in an opinion that others had reached by this time, the structure of the Massachusetts Constitution was not at fault. "Our sufferings have arisen from a *deeper fountain* than the deficiency of a single constitution." Even if Massachusetts had possessed a more perfect and more exalted government, its citizens, declared Dawes, would continue to experience evils, "should our *National Independence* remain deprived of its proper *federal authority*." "In vain," said Stephen Higginson in 1787, "must be all our exertions to brace up our own Government without we have a better federal System than the present."

By 1786–87 the reconstruction of the central government had become the focal point of most of the reform sentiment that had earlier been concentrated on the states. The continental-minded of the early eighties now found their efforts to invigorate the national government reinforced by the support of hitherto suspicious state-minded men. What had formerly been considered advisable for the functioning of the Confederation was fast becoming essential for the future of republicanism itself. It was no longer simply a matter of cementing the union or of satisfying the demands of particular creditor, mercantile, or army interests. The ability of America to sustain any sort of republican government seemed to be the issue. As long as the revision of the Articles was based solely on the need to solve specific problems of finance, commerce, and foreign policy, its support was erratic and fearful. But once men grasped, as they increasingly did in the middle eighties, that reform of the national government was the best means of remedying the evils caused by the state governments, then the revision of the Articles of Confederation assumed an impetus and an importance that it had not had a few years earlier. The desire for reform of the states now came together with national reform opinion to create a new and powerful force. As Benjamin Rush told Richard Price in June of 1787, "the same enthusiasm *now* pervades all classes in favor of *government* that actuated us in favor of *liberty* in the years 1774 and 1775, with this difference, that we·are more *united* in the former than we were in the latter pursuit."

The move for a stronger national government thus became something more than a response to the obvious weaknesses of the Articles of Confederation. It became as well an answer to the problems of the state governments. It was "the vile State governments," rather than simply the feebleness of the Confederation, that were the real "sources of pollution," preventing America from "being a nation." It was "the corruption and mutability of the Legislative Councils of the States," the "evils operating in the States," that actually led to the overhauling of the federal government in 1787. These vices coming out of the state governments, said Madison, "so frequent and so flagrant as to alarm the most stedfast friends of Republicanism, . . . contributed more to that uneasiness which produced the Convention, and prepared the public mind for a general reform, than those which accrued to our national character and interest from the inadequacy of the Confederation to its immediate objects." The federal Constitution became the culmination of a decade's efforts by Americans to readjust their constitutional structures to fit what Hamilton called "the commercial character of America" and what Jay called "manners and circumstances" that were "not strictly democratical." The calling of the Philadelphia Convention in 1787 was the climax of the process of rethinking that had begun with the reformation of the state constitutions in the late seventies and early eighties, a final step "taken from the fullest conviction that there was not a better, perhaps no other, which could be adopted in this crisis of our public affairs." The federal Convention, Americans told themselves repeatedly, was to frame a constitution that would "decide forever the fate of republican government."

THE FEDERAL CONSTITUTION

The Founding Fathers:
A Case Study
in Democratic Politics

JOHN P. ROCHE

In any government based on popular sovereignty, political leaders must constantly seek popular approval. Starting with that basic idea, Professor Roche analyzes the Constitutional Convention "as a case study in democratic politics," stressing the Founding Fathers' "collective experience as professional politicians in a democratic society." Portraying the founders as spokesmen of "a new and compelling credo: *American* nationalism," he notes that "the *only* weapon in the Constitutionalist arsenal was an effective mobilization of public opinion." "The result," Roche concludes, "was a Constitution which the people, in fact, by democratic processes, did accept, and a new and far better national government was established."

As a secondary theme, Roche develops the idea of the Convention as a *"nationalist* reform caucus," labeling the Constitution as a "patchwork" of compromises, "a makeshift affair," rather than an "apotheosis of 'constitutionalism.'" But the radical reconstruction of the American constitutional system in accordance with the popular political procedures of the day seems clearly to be not only a "vivid demonstration of effective democratic political action," as Roche says, but also a significant achievement for institutionalizing constitutional change and establishing political and constitutional principles. As James Wilson, one of the founders, observed, "this revolution principle—that the sovereign power residing in the people, they may change their constitution and government whenever they please—is not a principle of discord, rancour, or war; it is a principle of melioration, contentment, and peace." It was "the great panacea," he noted in the ratification debates, "of human politics." And Douglas Adair, one of the most penetrating of constitutional scholars,

John P. Roche, "The Founding Fathers: A Reform Caucus in Action," *American Political Science Review*, 55 (1961), 799–816. Reprinted by permission.

noted in a major interpretive article in the *Huntington Library Quarterly* ("That Politics May Be Reduced to a Science," 20 [1957], 343–360), the framers were engaged in a "genuinely 'scientific' attempt" to discover "the 'constant and universal principles' of any republican government is regard to liberty, justice, and stability."

OVER THE LAST CENTURY AND A HALF, THE WORK OF THE CONstitutional Convention and the motives of the Founding Fathers have been analyzed under a number of different ideological auspices. To one generation of historians, the hand of God was moving in the assembly; under a later dispensation, the dialectic (at various levels of philosophical sophistication) replaced the Deity: "relationships of production" moved into the niche previously reserved for Love of Country. Thus, in counterpoint to the Zeitgeist, the Framers have undergone miraculous metamorphoses: at one time acclaimed as liberals and bold social engineers, today they appear in the guise of sound Burkean conservatives, men who in our time would subscribe to *Fortune,* look to Walter Lippmann for political theory, and chuckle patronizingly at the antics of Barry Goldwater. The implicit assumption is that if James Madison were among us, he would be President of the Ford Foundation, while Alexander Hamilton would chair the Committee for Economic Development.

The "Fathers" have been admitted to our best circles; the revolutionary ferocity which confiscated all Tory property in reach and populated New Brunswick with outlaws has been converted by the "Miltown School" of American historians into a benign dedication to "consensus" and "prescriptive rights." The Daughters of the American Revolution have, through the ministrations of Professors Boorstin, Hartz, and Rossiter, at last found ancestors worthy of their descendants. It is not my purpose here to argue that the "Fathers" were, in fact, radical revolutionaries; that proposition has been brilliantly demonstrated by Robert R. Palmer in his *Age of the Democratic Revolution.* My concern is with the further position that not only were they revolutionaries; they were also democrats. Indeed, in my view, there is one fundamental truth about the Founding Fathers that *every* generation of Zeitgeisters has done its best to obscure: they were first and foremost superb democratic politicians. I suspect that in a contemporary setting, James Madison would be Speaker of the House of Representatives and Hamilton would be the *éminence grise* dominating (*pace* Theodore Sorenson or . . . [H. Kissinger]) the Executive Office of the President. They were, with their colleagues, *political men*—not metaphysicians, disembodied conservatives or Agents of History—and as recent research into the nature of American politics in the 1780's confirms, they were committed (perhaps willy-nilly) to working within the democratic framework, within a universe of public approval. Charles Beard *and* the filiopietists to the contrary notwithstanding, the Philadelphia Convention was not a College of Cardinals or a council of Platonic guardians working within a manipulative, predemocratic framework; it was a *nationalist* reform caucus which had to operate with great delicacy and skill in a political cosmos full of enemies to achieve the one definitive goal—popular approbation.

Perhaps the time has come, to borrow Walton Hamilton's fine phrase, to raise the Framers from immortality to mortality, to give them credit for their magnificent demonstration of the art of democratic politics. The point must be reemphasized; they *made* history, and did it within the limits of consensus. There was nothing inevitable about the future in 1787; the *Zeitgeist,* that fine Hegelian technique of begging causal questions, could be discerned only in retrospect. What they did was to hammer out a pragmatic compromise which would both bolster the "national interest" and be acceptable to the people. What inspiration they got came from their collective experience as professional politicians in a democratic society. As John Dickinson put it to his fellow delegates on August 13th: "Experience must be our guide. Reason may mislead us."

In this context, let us examine the problems they confronted and the solutions they evolved. The Convention has been described picturesquely as a counterrevolutionary junta and the Constitution as a *coup d'état,* but this has been accomplished by withdrawing the whole history of the movement for constitutional reform from its true context. No doubt the goals of the constitutional elite were "subversive" to the existing political order, but it is overlooked that their subversion could have succeeded only if the people of the United States endorsed it by regularized procedures. Indubitably they were "plotting" to establish a much stronger central government than existed under the Articles, but only in the sense in which one could argue equally well that John F. Kennedy was, from 1956 to 1960, "plotting" to become President. In short, on the fundamental *procedural* level, the Constitutionalists had to work according to the prevailing rules of the game. Whether they liked it or not is a topic for spiritualists—and is irrelevant: one may be quite certain that had Washington agreed to play the De Gaulle (as the Cincinnati once urged), Hamilton would willingly have held his horse, but such fertile speculation in no way alters the actual context in which events took place.

I

When the Constitutionalists went forth to subvert the Confederation, they utilized the mechanisms of political legitimacy. And the roadblocks which confronted them were formidable. At the same time, they were endowed with certain potent political assets. The history of the United States from 1786 to 1790 was largely one of a masterful employment of political expertise by the Constitutionalists as against bumbling, erratic behavior by the opponents of reform. Effectively, the Constitutionalists had to induce the states, by democratic techniques of coercion, to emasculate themselves. To be specific, if New York had refused to join the new Union, the project was doomed; yet before New York was safely in, the reluctant state legislature had *sua sponte* to take the following steps: (1) agree to send delegates to the Philadelphia Convention; (2) provide maintenance for these delegates (these were distinct stages: New Hampshire was early in naming delegates, but did not provide for their maintenance until July); (3) set up the special *ad hoc* convention to decide on ratification; and (4) concede to the decision of the *ad hoc* convention that New York should participate. New York admittedly was a tricky state, with a strong interest in a *status quo* which permitted her to exploit New Jersey and Connecticut, but the same legal hurdles existed in every state. And at the risk of becoming boring, it must be reiterated that the *only* weapon in the Constitutionalist arsenal was an effective mobilization of public opinion.

The group which undertook this struggle was an interesting amalgam of a few dedicated nationalists with the self-interested spokesmen of various parochial bailiwicks. The Georgians, for example, wanted a strong central authority to provide military protection for their huge, underpopulated state against the Creek Confederacy; Jerseymen and Connecticuters wanted to escape from economic bondage to New York; the Virginians hoped to establish a system which would give that great state its rightful place in the councils of the republic. The dominant figures in the politics of these states therefore co-operated in the call for the Convention. In other states, the thrust toward national reform was taken up by opposition groups who added the "national interest" to their weapons system; in Pennsylvania, for instance, the group fighting to revise the Constitution of 1776 came out foursquare behind the Constitutionalists, and in New York, Hamilton and the Schuyler ambience took the same tack against George Clinton. There was, of course, a large element of personality in the affair: there is reason to suspect that Patrick Henry's opposition to the Convention and the Constitution was founded on his conviction that

Jefferson was behind both, and a close study of local politics elsewhere surely reveal that others supported the Constitution for the simple (and politically quite sufficient) reason that the "wrong" people were against it.

To say this is not to suggest that the Constitution rested on a foundation of impure or base motives. It is rather to argue that in politics there are no immaculate conceptions and that in the drive for a stronger general government, motives of all sorts played a part. Few men in the history of mankind have espoused a view of the "common good" or "public interest" that militated against their private status; even Plato with all his reverence for disembodied reason managed to put philosophers on top of the pile. Thus it is not surprising that a number of diversified private interests joined to push the nationalist public interest; what would have been surprising was the absence of such a pragmatic united front. And the fact remains that, however motivated, these men did demonstrate a willingness to compromise their parochial interests in behalf of an ideal which took shape before their eyes and under their ministrations.

As Stanley Elkins and Eric McKitrick have suggested in a perceptive essay, what distinguished the leaders of the Constitutionalist caucus from their enemies was a "Continental" approach to political, economic, and military issues. To the extent that they shared an institutional base of operations, it was the Continental Congress (thirty-nine of the delegates to the Federal Convention had served in Congress), and this was hardly a locale which inspired respect for the state governments. Robert de Jouvenal observed French politics half a century ago and noted that a revolutionary deputy had more in common with a nonrevolutionary deputy than he had with a revolutionary nondeputy; similarly one can surmise that membership in the Congress under the Articles of Confederation worked to establish a Continental frame of reference, that a congressman from Pennsylvania and one from South Carolina would share a universe of discourse which provided them with a conceptual common denominator *vis à vis* their respective state legislatures. This was particularly true with respect to external affairs: the average state legislator was probably about as concerned with foreign policy then as he is today, but congressmen were constantly forced to take the broad view of American prestige, were compelled to listen to the reports of Secretary John Jay and to the dispatches and pleas from their frustrated envoys in Britain, France, and Spain. From considerations such as these, a "Continental" ideology developed which seems to have demanded a revision of our domestic institutions primarily on the ground that only by invigorating our general government could we assume our rightful place in the international arena. Indeed, an argument with great force—particularly since Washington was its incarnation—urged that our very survival in the

Hobbesian jungle of world politics depended upon a reordering and strengthening of our national sovereignty.

Note that I am not endorsing the "Critical Period" thesis; on the contrary, Merrill Jensen seems to me quite sound in his view that for most Americans, engaged as they were in self-sustaining agriculture, the "Critical Period" was not particularly critical. In fact, the great achievement of the Constitutionalists was their ultimate success in convincing the elected representatives of a majority of the white male population that change was imperative. A small group of political leaders with a Continental vision and essentially a consciousness of the United States' *international* impotence, provided the matrix of the movement. To their standard other leaders rallied with their own parallel ambitions. Their great assets were (1) the presence in their caucus of the one authentic American "father figure," George Washington, whose prestige was enormous, (2) the energy and talent of their leadership (in which one must include the towering intellectuals of this time, John Adams and Thomas Jefferson, despite their absence abroad); and their communications "network," which was far superior to anything on the opposition side, (3) the preemptive skill which made "their" issue The Issue and kept the locally oriented opposition permanently on the defensive; and (4) the subjective consideration that these men were spokesmen of a new and compelling credo: *American* nationalism, that ill-defined but nonetheless potent sense of collective purpose that emerged from the American Revolution.

Despite great institutional handicaps, the Constitutionalists managed in the mid-1780's to mount an offensive which gained momentum as years went by. Their greatest problem was lethargy, and paradoxically, the number of barriers in their path may have proved an advantage in the long run. Beginning with the initial battle to get the Constitutional Convention called and delegates appointed, they could never relax, never let up the pressure. In practical terms, this meant that the local "organizations" created by the Constitutionalists were perpetually in movement building up their cadres for the next fight. (The word "organization" has to be used with great caution: a political organization in the United States —as in contemporary England—generally consisted of a magnate and his following, or a coalition of magnates. This did not necessarily mean that it was "undemocratic" or "aristocratic," in the Aristotelian sense of the word: while a few magnates such as the Livingstons could draft their followings, most exercised their leadership without coercion on the basis of popular endorsement. The absence of organized opposition did not imply the impossibility of competition any more than low public participation in elections necessarily indicated an undemocratic suffrage.)

The Constitutionalists got the jump on the "opposition" (a collective noun: oppositions would be more correct) at the outset with the demand for a Convention. Their opponents were caught in an old political trap: they were not being asked to approve any specific program of reform, but only to endorse a meeting to discuss and recommend needed reforms. If they took a hard line at the first stage, they were put in the position of glorifying the *status quo* and of denying the need for *any* changes. Moreover, the Constitutionalists could go to the people with a persuasive argument for "fair play"—"How can you condemn reform before you know precisely what is involved?" Since the state legislatures obviously would have the final say on any proposals that might emerge from the Convention, the Constitutionalists were merely reasonable men asking for a chance. Besides, since they did not make any concrete proposals at that stage, they were in a position to capitalize on every sort of generalized discontent with the Confederation.

Perhaps because of their poor intelligence system, perhaps because of overconfidence generated by the failure of all previous efforts to alter the Articles, the opposition awoke too late to the dangers that confronted them in 1787. Not only did the Constitutionalists manage to get every state but Rhode Island (where politics was enlivened by a party system reminiscent of the "Blues" and the "Greens" in the Byzantine Empire) to appoint delegates to Philadelphia, but when the results were in, it appeared that they dominated the delegations. Given the apathy of the opposition, this was a natural phenomenon: in an ideologically non-polarized political atmosphere, those who get appointed to a special committee are likely to be the men who supported the movement for its creation. Even George Clinton, who seems to have been the first opposition leader to awake to the possibility of trouble, could not prevent the New York Legislature from appointing Alexander Hamilton—though he did have the foresight to send two of his henchmen to dominate the delegation. Incidentally, much has been made of the fact that the delegates to Philadelphia were not elected by the people; some have adduced this fact as evidence of the "undemocratic" character of the gathering. But put in the context of the time, this argument is wholly specious: the central government under the Articles was considered a creature of the component states; and in all the states but Rhode Island, Connecticut, and New Hampshire, members of the national Congress were chosen by state legislatures. This was not a consequence of elitism or fear of the mob; it was a logical extension of states'-rights doctrine to guarantee that the national institution did not end-run the state legislatures and make direct contact with the people.

II

With delegations safely named, the focus shifted to Philadelphia. While waiting for a quorum to assemble, James Madison got busy and drafted the so-called Randolph or Virginia Plan with the aid of the Virginia delegation. This was a political masterstroke. Its consequence was that once business got under way, the framework of discussion was established on Madison's terms. There was no interminable argument over agenda; instead the delegates took the Virginia Resolutions—"just for purposes of discussion"—as their point of departure. And along with Madison's proposals, many of which were buried in the course of the summer, went his major premise: a new start on a Constitution rather than piecemeal amendment. This was not necessarily revolutionary—a little exegesis could demonstrate that a new Constitution might be formulated as "amendments" to the Articles of Confederation—but Madison's proposal that this "lump sum" amendment go into effect after approval by nine states (the Articles required unanimous state approval for any amendment) was thoroughly subversive.

Standard treatments of the Convention divide the delegates into "nationalists" and "states'-righters," with various improvised shadings ("moderate nationalists," and so on), but these are *a posteriori* categories which obfuscate more than they clarify. What is striking to one who analyzes the Convention as a case study in democratic politics is the lack of clear-cut ideological divisions in the Convention. Indeed, I submit that the evidence —Madison's *Notes,* the correspondence of the delegates, and debates on ratification—indicates that this was a remarkably homogeneous body on the ideological level. Yates and Lansing, Clinton's two chaperons for Hamilton, left in disgust on July 10th. (Is there anything more tedious than sitting through endless disputes on matters one deems fundamentally misconceived? It takes an iron will to spend a hot summer as an ideological *agent provocateur.*) Luther Martin, Maryland's bibulous narcissist, left on September 4th in a huff when he discovered that others did not share his self-esteem; others went home for personal reasons. But the hard core of delegates accepted a grinding regimen throughout the attrition of a Philadelphia summer precisely because they shared the Constitutionalist goal.

Basic differences of opinion emerged, of course, but these were not ideological; they were *structural*. If the so-called "states'-rights" group had not accepted the fundamental purposes of the Convention, they could simply have pulled out and by doing so have aborted the whole enterprise. Instead of bolting, they returned day after day to argue and to compromise.

An interesting symbol of this basic homogeneity was the initial agreement on secrecy: these professional politicians did not want to become prisoners of publicity; they wanted to retain that freedom of maneuver which is possible only when men are not forced to take public stands in the preliminary stages of negotiation. There was no legal means of binding the tongues of the delegates: at any stage in the game a delegate with basic principled objections to the emerging project could have taken the stump (as Luther Martin did after his exit) and denounced the Convention to the skies. Yet Madison did not even inform Thomas Jefferson in Paris of the course of the deliberations, and available correspondence indicates that the delegates generally observed the injunction. Secrecy is certainly uncharacteristic of any assembly marked by strong ideological polarization. This was noted at the time: the *New York Daily Advertiser*, August 14, 1787, commented that the ". . . profound secrecy hitherto observed by the Convention [we consider] a happy omen, as it demonstrates that the spirit of party on any great and essential point cannot have arisen to any height."

Commentators on the Constitution who have read *The Federalist* in lieu of reading the actual debates have credited the Fathers with the invention of a sublime concept called "Federalism." Unfortunately, *The Federalist* is probative evidence for only one proposition: that Hamilton and Madison were inspired propagandists with a genius for retrospective symmetry. Federalism, as the theory is generally defined, was an improvisation which was later promoted into a political theory. Experts on "Federalism" should take to heart the advice of David Hume, who warned in his *Of the Rise and Progress of the Arts and Sciences* that ". . . there is no subject in which we must proceed with more caution than in [history], lest we assign causes which never existed and reduce what is merely contingent to stable and universal principles." In any event, the final balance in the Constitution between the states and the nation must have come as a great disappointment to Madison, while Hamilton's unitary views are too well known to need elucidation.

It is indeed astonishing how those who have glibly designated James Madison the "father" of Federalism have overlooked the solid body of fact which indicates that he shared Hamilton's quest for a unitary central government. To be specific, they have avoided examining the clear import of the Madison-Virginia Plan, and have disregarded Madison's dogged inch-by-inch retreat from the bastions of centralization. The Virginia Plan envisioned a unitary national government effectively freed from and dominant over the states. The lower house of the national legislature was to be elected directly by the people of the states with membership proportional to population. The upper house was to be selected by the lower, and the two chambers would elect the executive and choose the judges. The national government would be thus cut completely loose from the states.

The structure of the general government was freed from state control in a truly radical fashion, but the scope of the authority of the national sovereign as Madison initially formulated it was breathtaking—it was a formulation worthy of the Sage of Malmesbury himself. The national legislature was to be empowered to disallow the acts of state legislatures, and the central government was vested, in addition to the powers of the nation under the Articles of Confederation, with plenary authority wherever ". . . the separate States are incompetent or in which the harmony of the United States may be interrupted by the exercise of individual legislation." Finally, just to lock the door against state intrusion, the national Congress was to be given the power to use military force on recalcitrant states. This was Madison's "model" of an ideal national government, though it later received little publicity in *The Federalist*.

The interesting thing was the reaction of the Convention to this militant program for a strong autonomous central government. Some delegates were startled, some obviously leery of so comprehensive a project of reform, but nobody set off any fireworks and nobody walked out. Moreover, in the two weeks that followed, the Virginia Plan received substantial endorsement *en principe*; the initial temper of the gathering can be deduced from the approval "without debate or dissent," on May 31st, of the Sixth Resolution, which granted Congress the authority to disallow state legislation ". . . contravening *in its opinion* the Articles of Union." Indeed, an amendment was included to bar states from contravening national treaties.

The Virginia Plan may therefore be considered, in ideological terms, as the delegates' Utopia, but as the discussions continued and became more specific, many of those present began to have second thoughts. After all, they were not residents of Utopia or guardians in Plato's Republic who could simply impose a philosophical ideal on subordinate strata of the population. They were practical politicians in a democratic society, and no matter what their private dreams might be, they had to take home an acceptable package and defend it—and their own political futures— against predictable attack. On June 14th the breaking point between dream and reality took place. Apparently realizing that under the Virginia Plan, Massachusetts, Virginia, and Pennsylvania could virtually dominate the national government—and probably appreciating that to sell this program to the "folks back home" would be impossible—the delegates from the small states dug in their heels and demanded time for a consideration of alternatives. One gets a graphic sense of the inner politics from

John Dickinson's reproach to Madison: "You see the consequences of pushing things too far. Some of the members from the small States wish for two branches in the General Legislature and are friends to a good National Government; but we would sooner submit to a foreign power than . . . be deprived of an equality of suffrage in both branches of the Legislature, and thereby be thrown under the domination of the large States."

The bare outline of the *Journal* entry for Tuesday, June 14th, is suggestive to anyone with extensive experience in deliberative bodies. "It was moved by Mr. Patterson [*sic,* Paterson's name was one of those consistently misspelled by Madison and everybody else] seconded by Mr. Randolph that the further consideration of the report from the Committee of the whole House [endorsing the Virginia Plan] be postponed til tomorrow, and before the question for postponement was taken. It was moved by Mr. Randolph seconded by Mr. Patterson that the House adjourn." The House adjourned by obvious prearrangement of the two principals: since the preceding Saturday when David Brearley and Paterson of New Jersey had announced their fundamental discontent with the representational features of the Virginia Plan, the informal pressure had certainly been building up to slow down the steamroller. Doubtless there were extended arguments at the Indian Queen between Madison and Paterson, the latter insisting that events were moving rapidly toward a probably disastrous conclusion, toward a political suicide pact. Now the process of accommodation was put into action smoothly—and wisely, given the character and strength of the doubters. Madison had the votes, but this was one of those situations where the enforcement of mechanical majoritarianism could easily have destroyed the objectives of the majority: the Constitutionalists were in quest of a qualitative as well as quantitative consensus. This was hardly from deference to local Quaker custom; it was a political imperative if they were to attain ratification.

III

According to the standard script, at this point the "states'-rights" group intervened in force behind the New Jersey Plan, which has been characteristically portrayed as a reversion to the *status quo* under the Articles of Confederation with but minor modifications. A careful examination of the evidence indicates that only in a marginal sense is this an accurate description. It is true that the New Jersey Plan put the states back into the institutional picture, but one could argue that to do so was a recognition of political reality rather than an affirmation of states' rights. A serious case can be made that the advocates of the New Jersey Plan, far from being ideological addicts of states' rights, intended to substitute for the Virginia Plan a system which would both retain strong national power and have a chance of adoption in the states. The leading spokesman for the project asserted quite clearly that his views were based more on counsels of expediency than on principle; said Paterson on June 16th: "I came here not to speak my own sentiments, but the sentiments of those who sent me. Our object is not such a Governmt. as may be best in itself, but such a one as our Constituents have authorized us to prepare, and as they will approve." This is Madison's version; in Yates's transcription, there is a crucial sentence following the remarks above: "I believe that a little practical virtue is to be preferred to the finest theoretical principles, which cannot be carried into effect." In his preliminary speech on June 9th, Paterson had stated ". . . to the public mind we must accommodate ourselves," and in his notes for this and his later effort as well, the emphasis is the same. The *structure* of government under the Articles should be retained:

> 2. Because its accord with the Sentiments of the People
> [Proof:] 1. Coms. [Commissions from state legislatures defining the jurisdiction of the delegates]
> 2. News-papers—Political Barometer. Jersey never would have sent Delegates under first [Virginia] Plan—
> Not here to sport Opinions of my own. Wt. [What] can be done. A little practical Virtue preferrable to Theory.

This was a defense of political acumen, not of states' rights. In fact, Paterson's notes of his speech can easily be construed as an argument for attaining the substantive objectives of the Virginia Plan by a sound political route, that is, pouring the new wine into the old bottles. With a shrewd eye, Paterson queried:

> Will the Operation and Force of the [central] Govt. depend upon the mode of Representn.—No—it will depend upon the Quantum of Power lodged in the leg. ex. and judy. Departments—Give [the existing] Congress the same Powers that you intend to give the two Branches, [under the Virginia Plan] and I apprehend they will act with as much Propriety and more Energy. . . .

In other words, the advocates of the New Jersey Plan concentrated their fire on what they held to be the *political liabilities* of the Virginia Plan— which were matters of institutional structure—rather than on the proposed scope of national authority. Indeed, the Supremacy Cause of the Constitution first saw the light of day in Paterson's Sixth Resolution; the New

Jersey Plan contemplated the use of military force to secure compliance with national law; and finally Paterson made clear his view that under either the Virginia or the New Jersey systems, the general government would ". . . act on individuals and not on states." From the states'-rights viewpoint, this was heresy: the fundament of that doctrine was the proposition that any central government had as its constituents the states, not the people, and could reach the people only through the agency of the state government.

Paterson then reopened the agenda of the Convention, but he did so within a distinctly nationalist framework. Paterson's position was one of favoring a strong central government in principle, but opposing one which in fact *put the big states in the saddle*. (The Virginia Plan, for all its abstract merits, did very well by Virginia.) As evidence for this speculation, there is a curious and intriguing proposal among Paterson's preliminary drafts of the New Jersey Plan:

> Whereas it is necessary in Order to form the People of the U.S. of America in to a Nation, that the States should be consolidated, by which means all the Citizens thereof will become equally intitled to and will equally participate in the same Privileges and Rights . . . it is therefore resolved, that all the Lands contained within the Limits of each state individually, and of the U.S. generally be considered as constituting one Body or Mass, and be divided into thirteen or more integral parts.

> Resolved, That such Divisions or integral Parts shall be styled Districts.

This makes it sound as though Paterson was prepared to accept a strong unified central government along the lines of the Virginia Plan if the existing states were eliminated. He may have got the idea from his New Jersey colleague Judge David Brearley, who on June 9th had commented that the only remedy to the dilemma over representation was ". . . that a map of the U.S. be spread out, that all the existing boundaries be erased, and that a new partition of the whole be made into 13 equal parts." According to Yates, Brearley added at this point, ". . . then a government on the present [Virginia Plan] system will be just."

This proposition was never pushed—it was patently unrealistic—but one can appreciate its purpose: it would have separated the men from the boys in the large-state delegations. How attached would the Virginians have been to their reform principles if Virginia were to disappear as a component geographical unit (the largest) for representational purposes? Up to this point, the Virginians had been in the happy position of supporting high ideals with that inner confidence born of knowledge that the "public interest" they endorsed would nourish their private interest.

Worse, they had shown little willingness to compromise. Now the delegates from the small states announced that they were unprepared to be
offered up as sacrificial victims to a "national interest" which reflected
Virginia's parochial ambition. Caustic Charles Pinckney was not far off
when he remarked sardonically that ". . . the whole [conflict] comes to
this: Give N. Jersey an equal vote, and she will dismiss her scruples, and
concur in the Natil. system." What he rather unfairly did not add was that
the Jersey delegates were not free agents who could adhere to their
private convictions; they had to take back, sponsor, and risk their reputa-
tions on the reforms approved by the Convention—and in New Jersey,
not in Virginia.

Paterson spoke on Saturday, and one can surmise that over the weekend
there was a good deal of consultation, argument, and caucusing among the
delegates. One member at least prepared a full-length address: on Monday,
Alexander Hamilton, previously mute, rose and delivered a six-hour oration. It was a remarkably apolitical speech; the gist of his position was
that *both* the Virginia and New Jersey plans were inadequately centralist,
and he detailed a reform program which was reminiscent of the Pro-
tectorate under the Cromwellian *Instrument of Government* of 1653. It
has been suggested that Hamilton did this in the best political tradition
to emphasize the moderate character of the Virginia Plan, to give the
cautious delegates something *really* to worry about; but this interpretation
seems somehow too clever, particularly since the sentiments Hamilton expressed happened to be completely consistent with those he privately—
and sometimes publicly—expressed throughout his life. He wanted, to
take a striking phrase from a letter to George Washington, a "strong well
mounted government"; in essence, the Hamilton Plan contemplated an
elected life monarch, virtually free of public control, on the Hobbesian
ground that only in this fashion could strength and stability be achieved.
The other alternatives, he argued, would put policy-making at the mercy
of the passions of the mob; only if the sovereign was beyond the reach
of selfish influence would it be possible to have government in the interests of the whole community.

From all accounts, this was a masterful and compelling speech, but
(aside from furnishing John Lansing and Luther Martin with ammuni-
tion for later use against the Constitution) it made little impact. Hamilton was simply transmitting on a different wavelength from the rest of
the delegates; the latter adjourned after his great effort, admired his
rhetoric, and then returned to business. It was rather as if they had taken
a day off to attend the opera. Hamilton, never a particularly patient man
or much of a negotiator, stayed for another ten days, and then left, in
considerable disgust, for New York. Although he came back to Phila-

delphia sporadically and attended the last two weeks of the Convention, Hamilton played no part in the laborious task of hammering out the Constitution. His day came later when he led the New York Constitutionalists into the savage imbroglio over ratification—an arena in which his unmatched talent for dirty political infighting may well have won the day. For instance, in the New York Ratifying Convention, Lansing threw back into Hamilton's teeth the sentiments the latter had expressed in his June 18th oration in the Convention. However, having since retreated to the fine defensive positions immortalized in *The Federalist,* the Colonel flatly denied that he had ever been an enemy of the states, or had believed that conflict between states and nation was inexorable! As Madison's authoritative *Notes* did not appear until 1840, and there had been no press coverage, there was no way to verify his assertions, so in the words of the reporter, ". . . a warm personal altercation between [Lansing and Hamilton] engrossed the remainder of the day [June 28, 1788]."

IV

On Tuesday morning, June 19th, the vacation was over. James Madison led off with a long, carefully reasoned speech analyzing the New Jersey Plan which, while intellectually vigorous in its criticisms, was quite conciliatory in mood. "The great difficulty," he observed, "lies in the affair of Representation; and if this could be adjusted, all others would be surmountable." (As events were to demonstrate, this diagnosis was correct.) When he finished, a vote was taken on whether to continue with the Virginia Plan as the nucleus for a new constitution: seven states voted "Yes"; New York, New Jersey, and Delaware voted "No"; and Maryland, whose position often depended on which delegates happened to be on the floor, divided. Paterson, it seems, lost decisively; yet in a fundamental sense he and his allies had achieved their purpose: from that day onward, it could never be forgotten that the state governments loomed ominously in the background and that no verbal incantations could exorcise their power. Moreover, nobody bolted the convention: Paterson and his colleagues took their defeat in stride and set to work to modify the Virginia Plan, particularly with respect to its provisions on representation in the National Legislature. Indeed, they won an immediate rhetorical bonus; when Oliver Ellsworth of Connecticut rose to move that the word "national" be expunged from the Third Virginia Resolution ("Resolved that a *national* Government ought to be established consisting of a *supreme* Legislative, Executive and Judiciary"), Randolph agreed, and the motion passed unanimously. The process of compromise had begun.

For the next two weeks, the delegates circled around the problem of legislative representation. The Connecticut delegation appears to have evolved a possible compromise quite early in the debates, but the Virginians and particularly Madison (unaware that he would later be acclaimed as the prophet of "Federalism") fought obdurately against providing for equal representation of states in the second chamber. There was a good deal of acrimony, and at one point Benjamin Franklin—of all people—proposed the institution of a daily prayer; practical politicians in the gathering, however, were meditating more on the merits of a good committee than on the utility of divine intervention. On July 2nd, the ice began to break when through a number of fortuitous events—and one that seems deliberate—the majority against equality of representation was converted into a dead tie. The Convention had reached the stage where it was "ripe" for a solution (presumably all the therapeutic speeches had been made), and the South Carolinians proposed a committee. Madison and James Wilson wanted none of it, but with only Pennsylvania dissenting, the body voted to establish a working party on the problem of representation.

The members of this committee, one from each state, were elected by the delegates—and a very interesting committee it was. Despite the fact that the Virginia Plan had held majority support up to that date, neither Madison nor Randolph was selected (Mason was the Virginian), and Baldwin of Georgia, whose shift in position had resulted in the tie, was chosen. From the composition, it was clear that this was not to be a "fighting" committee: the emphasis in membership was on what might be described as "second-level political entrepreneurs." On the basis of the discussions up to that time, only Luther Martin of Maryland could be described as a "bitter-ender." Admittedly, some divination enters into this sort of analysis, but one does get a sense of the mood of the delegates from these choices—including the interesting selection of Benjamin Franklin, despite his age and intellectual wobbliness, over the brilliant and incisive Wilson or the sharp, polemical Gouverneur Morris, to represent Pennsylvania. His passion for conciliation was more valuable at this juncture than Wilson's logical genius, or Morris's acerbic wit.

There is a common rumor that the Framers divided their time between philosophical discussions of government and reading the classics in political theory. Perhaps this is as good a time as any to note that their concerns were highly practical, that they spent little time canvassing abstractions. A number of them had some acquaintance with the history of political theory (probably gained from reading John Adams's monumental compilation *A Defence of the Constitutions of Government,* the first volume of which appeared in 1786), and it was a poor rhetorician indeed who could not cite Locke, Montesquieu, or Harrington *in support* of a desired goal. Yet up to this point in the deliberations, no one had expounded a defense of states' rights or the "separation of powers" on anything resembling a theoretical basis. It should be reiterated that the Madison model had no room either for the states or for the "separation of powers": effectively *all* governmental power was vested in the national legislature. The merits of Montesquieu did not turn up until *The Federalist*; and although a perverse argument could be made that Madison's ideal was truly in the tradition of John Locke's *Second Treatise of Government,* the Locke whom the American rebels treated as an honorary president was a pluralistic defender of vested rights, not of parliamentary supremacy.

It would be tedious to continue a blow-by-blow analysis of the work of the delegates; the critical fight was over representation of the states, and once the Connecticut Compromise was adopted, on July 17th, the Convention was over the hump. Madison, James Wilson, and Gouverneur Morris of New York (who was there representing Pennsylvania!) fought the compromise all the way in a last-ditch effort to get a unitary state with parliamentary supremacy. But their allies deserted them, and they demonstrated after their defeat the essentially opportunist character of their objections—using "opportunist" here in a nonpejorative sense, to indicate a willingness to swallow their objections and get on with the business. Moreover, once the compromise had carried (by five states to four, with one state divided), its advocates threw themselves vigorously into the job of strengthening the general government's substantive powers —as might have been predicted, indeed, from Paterson's early statements. It nourishes an increased respect for Madison's devotion to the art of politics, to realize that this dogged fighter could sit down six months later and prepare essays for *The Federalist* in contradiction to his basic convictions about the true course the Convention should have taken.

V

Two tricky issues will serve to illustrate the later process of accommodation. The first was the institutional position of the executive. Madison argued for an executive chosen by the National Legislature, and on May 29th this had been adopted with a provision that after his seven-year term was concluded, the chief magistrate should not be eligible for re-election. In late July this was reopened, and for a week the matter was argued from several different points of view. A good deal of desultory speechmaking ensued, but the gist of the problem was the opposition from two sources to election by the legislature. One group felt that the states should have a hand in the process; another small but influential circle urged direct election by the people, election by state governors, by electors chosen by state legislatures, by the National Legislature (James Wilson, perhaps ironically, proposed at one point that an electoral college be chosen by lot from the National Legislature!), and there was some resemblance to three-dimensional chess in the dispute because of the presence of two other variables, length of tenure and re-eligibility. Finally, after opening, reopening, and re-reopening the debate, the thorny problem was consigned to a committee for resolution.

The Brearley Committee on Postponed Matters was a superb aggregation of talent, and its compromise on the executive was a masterpiece of political improvisation. (The Electoral College, its creation, however, had little in its favor as an *institution*—as the delegates well appreciated.) The point of departure for all discussion about the Presidency in the Convention was that in immediate terms, the problem was nonexistent; in other words, everybody present knew that under any system devised, George Washington would be President. Thus they were dealing in the future tense, and to a body of working politicians the merits of the Brearley proposal were obvious: everybody got a piece of cake. (Or, to put it more academically, each viewpoint could leave the Convention and argue to its constituents that it had *really* won the day.) First, the state legislatures had the right to determine the mode of selection of the electors; second, the small states received a bonus in the Electoral College in the form of a guaranteed minimum of three votes, while the big states got acceptance of the principle of proportional power; third, if the state legislatures agreed (as six did in the first presidential election), the people could be involved directly in the choice of electors; and finally, if no candidate received a majority in the College, the right of decision passed on to the National Legislature, with each state exercising equal strength. (In the Brearley recommendation, the election went to the Senate, but a motion from the floor substituted the House; this was accepted on the ground that the Senate already had enough authority over the executive in its treaty and appointment powers.)

This compromise was almost too good to be true, and the Framers snapped it up with little debate or controversy. No one seemed to think well of the College as an *institution*; indeed, what evidence there is suggests that there was an assumption that once Washington had finished his tenure as President, the electors would cease to produce majorities and that the Chief Executive would usually be chosen in the House. George Mason observed casually that the selection would be made in the House nineteen times in twenty, and no one seriously disputed this point. The vital aspect of the Electoral College was that it got the Convention over the hurdle and protected everybody's interests. The future was left to cope with the problem of what to do with this Rube Goldberg mechanism.

In short, the Framers did not in their wisdom endow the United States with a College of Cardinals—the Electoral College was neither an exercise in applied Platonism nor an experiment in indirect government based on elitist distrust of the masses. It was merely a jerry-rigged improvisation which has subsequently been endowed with a high theoretical content. When an elector from Oklahoma in 1960 refused to cast his vote for Nixon (naming Byrd and Goldwater instead) on the ground that the Founding Fathers intended him to exercise his great independent wisdom, he was indulging in historical fantasy. If one were to indulge in counterfantasy, he would be tempted to suggest that the Fathers would be startled to find the College still in operation—and perhaps even dismayed at their descendants' lack of judgment or inventiveness.

The second issue on which some substantial practical bargaining took place was slavery. The morality of slavery was, by design, not at issue; but in its other concrete aspects, slavery colored the arguments over taxation, commerce, and representation. The "Three-Fifths Compromise," that three-fifths of the slaves would be counted both for representation and for purposes of direct taxation (which was drawn from the past— it was a formula of Madison's utilized by Congress in 1783 to establish the basis of state contributions to the Confederation treasury), had allayed some northern fears about southern over-representation (no one then foresaw the trivial role that direct taxation would play in later federal financial policy), but doubts still remained. The Southerners, on the other hand, were afraid that congressional control over commerce would lead to the exclusion of slaves or to their excessive taxation as imports. Moreover, the Southerners were disturbed over "navigation acts," that is, tariffs, or special legislation providing, for example, the exports be carried only in American ships; as a section depending upon exports, they wanted protection from the potential voracity of their commercial brethren of the eastern states. To achieve this end, Mason and others urged that the Constitution include a proviso that navigation and commercial laws should require a two-thirds vote in Congress.

These problems came to a head in late August and, as usual, were handed to a committee in the hope that, in Gouverneur Morris's words, ". . . these things may form a bargain among the Northern and Southern states." The committee reported its measures of reconciliation on August 25th, and on August 29th the package was wrapped up and delivered. What occurred can best be described in George Mason's dour version (he anticipated Calhoun in his conviction that permitting navigation acts to pass by majority vote would put the South in economic bondage to the North—it was mainly on this ground that he refused to sign the Constitution):

> The Constitution as agreed to till a fortnight before the Convention rose was such a good one as he would have set his hand and heart to. . . . [Until that time] The 3 New England States were constantly with us in all questions . . . so that it was these three States with the 5 Southern ones against Pennsylvania, Jersey and Delaware. With respect to the importation of slaves, [decision-making] was left to Congress. This disturbed the two Southernmost States who knew that Congress would immediately suppress the importation of slaves. Those two States therefore struck up a bargain with the three New England States. If they would join to admit slaves for some years, the two Southern-most States would join in changing the clause which required the 2/3 of the Legislature in any vote [on navigation acts]. It was done.

On the floor of the Convention there was a virtual love feast on this happy occasion. Charles Pinckney, of South Carolina, attempted to overturn the committee's decision, when the compromise was reported to the Convention, by insisting that the South needed protection from the imperialism of the northern states. But his southern colleagues were not prepared to rock the boat, and General C. C. Pinckney arose to spread oil on the suddenly ruffled waters; he admitted that:

> It was in the true interest of the S[outhern] States to have no regulation of commerce; but considering the loss brought on the commerce of the Eastern States by the Revolution, their liberal conduct towards the views of South Carolina [on the regulation of the slave trade] and the interests the weak Southn. States had in being united with the strong Eastern states, he thought it proper that no fetters should be imposed on the power of making commercial regulations; *and that his constituents, though prejudiced against the Eastern States, would be reconciled to this liberality.* He had himself prejudices agst the Eastern States before he came here, but would acknowledge that he had found them as liberal and candid as any men whatever. [Italics added]

Pierce Butler took the same tack, essentially arguing that he was not too happy about the possible consequences but that a deal was a deal. Many southern leaders were later—in the wake of the "Tariff of Abominations" —to rue this day of reconciliation; Calhoun's *A Disquisition on Government* was little more than an extension of the argument in the Convention against permitting a congressional majority to enact navigation acts.

VI

Drawing on their vast collective political experience, utilizing every weapon in the politician's arsenal, looking constantly over their shoulders at their constituents, the delegates put together a Constitution. It was a makeshift affair; some sticky issues (for example, the qualification of voters) they ducked entirely; others they mastered with that ancient instrument of political sagacity, studied ambiguity (for example, citizenship), and some they just overlooked. In this last category, I suspect, fell the matter of the power of the federal courts to determine the constitutionality of acts of Congress. When the judicial article was formulated (Article III of the Constitution), deliberations were still in the stage where the legislature was endowed with broad power under the Randolph formulation, authority which by its own terms was scarcely amenable to judicial review. In essence, courts could hardly determine when ". . . the separate States are incompetent or . . . the harmony of the United States may be interrupted"; the National Legislature, as critics pointed out, was free to define its own jurisdiction. Later the definition of legislative authority was changed into the form we know, a series of stipulated powers, *but the delegates never seriously reexamined the jurisdiction of the judiciary under this new limited formulation.* All arguments on the intention of the Framers in this matter are thus deductive and *a posteriori,* though some obviously make more sense than others.

The Framers were busy and distinguished men, anxious to get back to their families, their positions, and their constituents, not members of the French Academy devoting a lifetime to a dictionary. They were trying to do an important job, and do it in such fashion that their handiwork would be acceptable to very diverse constituencies. No one was rhapsodic about the final document, but it was a beginning, a move in the right direction, and one they had reason to believe the people would endorse. In addition, since they had modified the impossible amendment provisions of the Articles (the requirement of unanimity which could always be frustrated by "Rogues Island") to one demanding approval by only three-quarters of the states, they seemed confident that gaps in the fabric which experience would reveal could be rewoven without undue difficulty.

So with a neat phrase introduced by Benjamin Franklin (but devised by Gouverneur Morris) which made their decision sound unanimous, and an inspired benediction by the Old Doctor urging doubters to doubt their own infallibility, the Constitution was accepted and signed. Curiously, Edmund Randolph, who had played so vital a role throughout, refused to sign, as did his fellow Virginian George Mason and Elbridge Gerry of

Massachusetts. Randolph's behavior was eccentric, to say the least—his excuses for refusing his signature have a factitious ring even at this late date; the best explanation seems to be that he was afraid that the Constitution would prove to be a liability in Virginia politics, where Patrick Henry was burning up the countryside with impassioned denunciations. Presumably, Randolph wanted to check the temper of the populace before he risked his reputation, and perhaps his job, in a fight with both Henry and Richard Henry Lee. Events lend some justification to this speculation: after much temporizing and use of the conditional subjunctive tense, Randolph endorsed ratification in Virginia and ended by getting the best of both worlds.

Madison, despite his reservations about the Constitution, was the campaign manager in ratification. His first task was to get the Congress in New York to light its own funeral pyre by approving the "amendments" to the Articles and sending them on to the state legislatures. Above all, momentum had to be maintained. The anti-Constitutionalists, now thoroughly alarmed and no novices in politics, realized that their best tactic was attrition rather than direct opposition. Thus they settled on a position expressing qualified approval but calling for a second Convention to remedy various defects (the one with the most demagogic appeal was the lack of a Bill of Rights). Madison knew that to accede to this demand would be equivalent to losing the battle, nor would he agree to conditional approval (despite wavering even by Hamilton). This was an all-or-nothing proposition: national salvation or national impotence with no intermediate positions possible. Unable to get congressional approval, he settled for second best: a unanimous resolution of Congress transmitting the Constitution to the states for whatever action they saw fit to take. The opponents then moved from New York and the Congress, where they had attempted to attach amendments and conditions, to the states for the final battle.

At first the campaign for ratification went beautifully: within eight months after the delegates set their names to the document, eight states had ratified. Only in Massachusetts had the result been close (187–168). Theoretically, a ratification by one more state convention would set the new government in motion, but in fact until Virginia and New York acceded to the new Union, the latter was fiction. New Hampshire was the next to ratify; Rhode Island was involved in its characteristic political convulsions (the legislature there sent the Constitution out to the towns for decision by popular vote and it got lost among a series of local issues); North Carolina's convention did not meet until July, and then postponed a final decision. This is hardly the place for an extensive analysis of the conventions of New York and Virginia. Suffice it to say that the Constitutionalists clearly outmaneuvered their opponents, forced them into impossible political positions, and won both states narrowly. The Virginia Convention could serve as a classic study in effective floor management: Patrick Henry had to be contained, and a reading of the debates discloses a standard two-stage technique. Henry would give a four- or five-hour speech denouncing some section of the Constitution on every conceivable ground (the federal district, he averred at one point, would become a haven for convicts escaping from state authority!). When Henry subsided, "Mr. Lee of Westmoreland" would rise and poleax him with sardonic invective. (When Henry complained about the militia power, "Lighthorse Harry" really punched below the belt: observing that while the former governor had been sitting in Richmond during the Revolution, *he* had been out in the trenches with the troops and thus felt better qualified to discuss military affairs.) Then the gentlemanly Constitutionalists (Madison, Pendelton, and Marshall) would pick up the matters at issue and examine them in the light of reason.

Indeed, modern Americans who tend to think of James Madison as a rather desiccated character should spend some time with this transcript. Probably Madison put on his most spectacular demonstration of nimble rhetoric in what might be called the "Battle of the Absent Authorities." Patrick Henry in the course of one of his harangues alleged that Jefferson was known to be opposed to Virginia's approving the Constitution. This was clever: Henry hated Jefferson, but was prepared to use any weapon that came to hand. Madison's riposte was superb: First, he said that with all due respect to the great reputation of Jefferson, he was not in the country and therefore could not formulate an adequate judgment; second, no one should utilize the reputation of an outsider—the Virginia Convention was there to think for itself; third, if there were to be recourse to outsiders, the opinions of George Washington should certainly be taken into consideration; and, finally, he knew from privileged personal communications from Jefferson that in fact the latter *strongly favored* the Constitution. To devise an assault route into this rhetorical fortress was literally impossible.

VII

The fight was over; all that remained now was to establish the new frame of government in the spirit of its Framers. And who were better qualified for this task than the Framers themselves? Thus victory for the Constitution meant simultaneous victory for the Constitutionalists; the anti-Constitutionalists either capitulated or vanished into limbo—soon

Patrick Henry would be offered a seat on the Supreme Court and Luther Martin would be known as the Federalist "bull-dog." And, irony of ironies, Alexander Hamilton and James Madison would shortly accumulate a reputation as the formulators of what is often alleged to be our political theory, the concept of "Federalism." Also, on the other side of the ledger, the arguments would soon appear over what the Framers "really meant"; while these disputes have assumed the proportions of a big scholarly business in the last century, they began almost before the ink on the Constitution was dry. One of the best early ones featured Hamilton versus Madison on the scope of presidential power, and other Framers characteristically assumed positions in this and other disputes on the basis of their political convictions.

Probably our greatest difficulty is that we know so much more about what the Framers *should have meant* than they themselves did. We are intimately acquainted with the problems that their Constitution should have been designed to master; in short, we have read the mystery story backward. If we are to get the right "feel" for their time and their circumstances, we must, in Maitland's phrase, ". . . think ourselves back into a twilight." Obviously, no one can pretend completely to escape from the solipsistic web of his own environment, but if the effort is made, it is possible to appreciate the past roughly on its own terms. The first step in this process is to abandon the academic premise that because we can ask a question, there must be an answer.

Thus we can ask what the Framers meant when they gave Congress the power to regulate interstate and foreign commerce, and we emerge, reluctantly perhaps, with the reply that (Professor Crosskey to the contrary notwithstanding) they may not have known what they meant, that there may not have been any semantic consensus. The Convention was not a seminar in analytic philosophy or linguistic analysis. Commerce was *commerce*—and if different interpretations of the word arose, later generations could worry about the problem of definition. The delegates were in a hurry to get a new government established; when definitional arguments arose, they characteristically took refuge in ambiguity. If different men voted for the same proposition for varying reasons, that was politics (and still is); if later generations were unsettled by this lack of precision, that would be their problem.

There was a good deal of definitional pluralism with respect to the problems the delegates did discuss, but when we move to the question of extrapolated intentions we enter the realm of spiritualism. When men in our time, for instance, launch into elaborate talmudic exegesis to demonstrate that federal aid to parochial schools is (or is not) in accord with the intentions of the men who established the Republic and endorsed the

Bill of Rights, they are engaging in historical extrasensory perception. (If one were to join this E.S.P. contingent for a minute, he might suggest that the hard-boiled politicians who wrote the Constitution and Bill of Rights would chuckle scornfully at such an invocation of authority: obviously a politician would chart his course on the intentions of the living, not of the dead, and count the number of Catholics in his constituency.)

The Constitution, then, was not an apotheosis of "constitutionalism," a triumph of architectonic genius; it was a patchwork sewn together under the pressure of both time and events by a group of extremely talented democratic politicians. They refused to attempt the establishment of a strong, centralized sovereignty on the principle of legislative supremacy, for the excellent reason that the people would not accept it. They risked their political fortunes by opposing the established doctrines of state sovereignty because they were convinced that the existing system was leading to national impotence and probably foreign domination. For two years they worked to get a convention established. For over three months, in what must have seemed to the faithful participants an endless process of give-and-take, they reasoned, cajoled, threatened, and bargained amongst themselves. The result was a Constitution which the people, in fact, by democratic processes, did accept, and a new and far better national government was established.

Beginning with the inspired propaganda of Hamilton, Madison, and Jay, the ideological buildup got under way. *The Federalist* had little impact on the ratification of the Constitution, except perhaps in New York, but this volume had enormous influence on the image of the Constitution in the minds of future generations, particularly on historians and political scientists who have an innate fondness for theoretical symmetry. Yet, while the shades of Locke and Montesquieu *may* have been hovering in the background and the delegates *may* have been unconscious instruments of a transcendent *telos,* the careful observer of the day-to-day work of the Convention finds no overarching principles. The "separation of powers" to him seems to be a by-product of suspicion, and "Federalism" he views as a *pis aller,* as the farthest point the delegates felt they could go in the destruction of state power without themselves inviting repudiation.

To conclude, the Constitution was neither a victory for abstract theory nor a great practical success. Well over half a million men had to die on the battlefields of the Civil War before certain constitutional principles could be defined—a baleful consideration which is somehow overlooked in our customary tributes to the farsighted genius of the Framers and to the supposed American talent for "constitutionalism." The Constitution was, however, a vivid demonstration of effective democratic political action, and of the forging of a national elite which literally persuaded its countrymen to hoist themselves by their own boot straps. American pro-consuls would be wise not to translate the Constitution into Japanese, or Swahili, or treat it as a work of semi-Divine origin; but when students of comparative politics examine the process of nation-building in countries newly freed from colonial rule, they may find the American experience instructive as a classic example of the potentialities of a democratic elite.

Republicanism and Democratic Thought in The Federalist: A Reconsideration of the Framers' Intent

MARTIN DIAMOND

By 1787 the Revolutionary generation, which had been raised to praise the mixed constitution in colonial times, was debating the acceptance of a federal Constitution designed to establish an "unmixed and extensive republic," as James Madison labeled it in *The Federalist*. In his analysis of republicanism and democratic thought in *The Federalist*, Martin Diamond argues that the framers of the Constitution not only sought popular approbation of their creation, as Professor Roche suggests in the preceding essay; they also had principles. Convinced that "men cannot act on a political scale so vast as they did without having and employing a view of the politically fundamental," he notes that the framers were firm believers in popular government, deeply dedicated to the proposition that political authority is "derived from the great body of the society, not from . . . [any] favoured class of it." They also believed that there were several forms of popular government, and they distinguished, for analytical purposes, between direct democracy and republican or representative government, which they divided into small and large—or extensive—republics. The novelty of the proposed federal experiment in representative government in 1787, according to Diamond, who paraphrases Madison, "consisted in solving the problems of popular government by means which yet maintain the government 'wholly popular.'"

Martin Diamond, "Democracy and The Federalist: A Reconsideration of the Framers' Intent," *American Political Science Review*, 53 (March 1959), 52–68. Reprinted by permission.

IT HAS BEEN A COMMON TEACHING AMONG MODERN HISTORIANS OF the guiding ideas in the foundation of our government that the Constitution of the United States embodied a reaction against the democratic principles espoused in the Declaration of Independence. This view has largely been accepted by political scientists and has therefore had important consequences for the way American political development has been studied. I shall present here a contrary view of the political theory of the Framers and examine some of its consequences.

What is the relevance of the political thought of the Founding Fathers to an understanding of contemporary problems of liberty and justice? Four possible ways of looking at the Founding Fathers immediately suggest themselves. First, it may be that they possessed wisdom, a set of political principles still inherently adequate, and needing only to be supplemented by skill in their proper contemporary application. Second, it may be that, while Founding Fathers' principles are still sound, they are applicable only to a part of our problems, but not to that part which is peculiarly modern; and thus new principles are needed to be joined together with the old ones. Third, it may be that the Founding Fathers have simply become [obsolete]; they dealt with bygone problems and their principles were relevant only to those old problems. Fourth, they may have been wrong or radically inadequate even for their own time.

Each of these four possible conclusions requires the same foundation: an understanding of the political thought of the Founding Fathers. To decide whether to apply their wisdom, or to add to their wisdom, or to reject it as irrelevant or as unwise, it is absolutely necessary to understand what they said, why they said it, and what they meant by it. At the same time, however, to understand their claim to wisdom is to evaluate it: to know wherein they were wise and wherein they were not, or wherein (and why) their wisdom is unavailing for our problems. Moreover, even if it turns out that our modern problems require new principles for their solution, an excellent way to discover those new principles would be to see what it is about modernity that has outmoded the principles of the Founding Fathers. For example, it is possible that modern developments are themselves partly the outcome of the particular attempt to solve the problem of freedom and justice upon which this country was founded. That is, our modern difficulties may testify to fundamental errors in the thought of the Founding Fathers; and, in the process of discerning those errors, we may discover what better principles would be.

The solution of our contemporary problems requires very great wisdom indeed. And in that fact lies the greatest justification for studying anew the political thought of the Founding Fathers. For that thought remains the finest American thought on political matters. In studying them we may raise ourselves to their level. In achieving their level we may free ourselves from limitations that, ironically, they tend to impose upon us, *i.e.,* insofar as we tend to be creatures of the society they founded. And in so freeing ourselves we may be enabled, if it is necessary, to go beyond their wisdom. The Founding Fathers still loom so large in our life that the contemporary political problem of liberty and justice for Americans could be stated as the need to choose whether to apply their wisdom, amend their wisdom, or reject it. Only an understanding of them will tell us how to choose.

For the reflections on the Fathers which follow, I employ chiefly *The Federalist* as the clue to the political theory upon which rested the founding of the American Republic. That this would be inadequate for a systematic study of the Founding Fathers goes without saying. But it is the one book, "to which," as Jefferson wrote in 1825, "appeal is habitually made by all, and rarely declined or denied by any as evidence of the general opinion of those˙ who framed and of those who accepted the Constitution of the United States, on questions as to its genuine meaning." As such it is the indispensable starting point for systematic study.

I

Our major political problems today are problems of democracy; and, as much as anything else, the *Federalist* papers are a teaching about democracy. The conclusion of one of the most important of these papers states what is also the most important theme in the entire work: the necessity for "a republican remedy for the diseases most incident to republican government."[1] The theme is clearly repeated in a passage where Thomas Jefferson is praised for displaying equally "a fervent attachment to republican government and an enlightened view of the dangerous propensities against which it ought to be guarded."[2] *The Federalist,* thus, stresses its commitment to republican or popular government, but, of course, insists that this must be an enlightened commitment.

But *The Federalist* and the Founding Fathers generally have not been taken at their word. Predominantly, they are understood as being only quasi- or even anti-democrats. Modern American historical writing, at

---

[1] *Federalist,* No. 10, p. 62. All references are to the Modern Library edition, ed. E. M. Earle.
[2] *Federalist,* No. 49, p. 327.

least until very recently, has generally seen the Constitution as some sort of apostasy from, or reaction to, the radically democratic implications of the Declaration of Independence—a reaction that was undone by the great "democratic breakthroughs" of Jeffersoniartism, Jacksonianism, etc. This view, I believe, involves a false understanding of the crucial political issues involved in the founding of the American Republic. Further, it is based implicitly upon a questionable modern approach to democracy and has tended to have the effect, moreover, of relegating the political teaching of the Founding Fathers to the pre-democratic past and thus of making it of no vital concern to moderns. The Founding Fathers themselves repeatedly stressed that their Constitution was wholly consistent with the true principles of republican or popular government. The prevailing modern opinion, in varying degrees and in different ways, rejects that claim. It thus becomes important to understand what was the relation of the Founding Fathers to popular government or democracy.

I have deliberately used interchangeably their terms, "popular government" and "democracy." The Founding Fathers, of course, did not use the terms entirely synonymously and the idea that they were less than democrats has been fortified by the fact that they sometimes defined "democracy" invidiously in comparison with "republic." But this fact does not really justify the opinion. For their basic view was that *popular government was the genus, and democracy and republic were two species* of that genus of government. What distinguished popular government from other genera of government was that in it, political authority is "derived from the great body of the society, not from . . . [any] favoured class of it."[3] With respect to this decisive question, of where political authority is lodged, democracy and republic—as The Federalist uses the terms—differ not in the least. Republics, equally with democracies, may claim to be wholly a form of popular government. This is neither to deny the difference between the two, nor to depreciate the importance The Federalist

---

[3] *Federalist,* No. 39, p. 244. Here Madison speaks explicitly of the republican form of government. But see on the same page how Madison compares the republican form with "every *other popular* government." Regarding the crucial question of the lodgement of political authority, Madison speaks of republic, democracy and popular government interchangeably. Consider that, in the very paper where he distinguishes so precisely between democracies and republics regarding direct versus representative rule, Madison defines his general aim both as a search for "a republican remedy" for republican diseases *and* a remedy that will "preserve the spirit and the form of *popular* government." (p. 58.) Interestingly, on June 6 at the Federal Convention, Madison's phrasing for a similar problem was the search for "the only defense against the inconveniences of democracy consistent with the *democratic* form of government." Madison, *Writings,* ed. G. Hunt, Vol. 3 (G. P. Putnam's Sons, New York, 1902), p. 103. Italics supplied throughout.

attached to the difference; but in *The Federalist's* view, the difference does not relate to the essential principle of popular government. Democracy means in *The Federalist* that form of popular government where the citizens "assemble and administer the government in person." Republics differ in that the people rule through representatives and, of course, in the consequences of that difference. The crucial point is that republics and democracies are equally forms of popular government, but that the one form is vastly preferable to the other because of the substantive consequences of the difference in form. Those historians who consider the Founding Fathers as less than "democrats," miss or reject the Founders' central contention that, while being perfectly faithful to the *principle* of popular government, they had solved the *problem* of popular government.

In what way is the Constitution ordinarily thought to be less democratic than the Declaration? The argument is usually that the former is characterized by fear of the people, by preoccupation with minority interests and rights, and by measures therefore taken against the power of majorities. The Declaration, it is true, does not display these features, but this is no proof of a fundamental difference of principles between the two. Is it not obviously possible that the difference is due only to a difference in the tasks to which the two documents were addressed? And is it not further possible that the democratic principles of the Declaration are not only compatible with the prophylactic measures of the Constitution, but actually imply them?

The Declaration of Independence formulates two criteria for judging whether any government is good, or indeed legitimate. Good government must rest, procedurally, upon the consent of the governed. Good government, substantively, must do only certain things, *e.g.,* secure certain rights. This may be stated another way by borrowing a phrase from Locke, appropriate enough when discussing the Declaration. That "the people shall be judge" is of the essence of democracy, is its peculiar form or method of proceeding. That the people shall judge rightly is the substantive problem of democracy. But whether the procedure will bring about the substance is problematic. Between the Declaration's two criteria, then, a tension exists: consent can be given or obtained for governmental actions which are not right—at least as the men of 1776 saw the right. (To give an obvious example from their point of view: the people may freely but wrongly vote away the protection due to property.) Thus the Declaration clearly contained, although it did not resolve, a fundamental problem. Solving the problem was not its task; that was the task for the framers of the Constitution. But the man who wrote the Declaration of Independence and the leading men who supported it were perfectly aware of the difficulty, and of the necessity for a "republican remedy."

What the text of the Declaration, taken alone, tells of its meaning may easily be substantiated by the testimony of its author and supporters. Consider only that Jefferson, with no known change of heart at all, said of *The Federalist* that it was "the best commentary on the principles of government which was ever written." Jefferson, it must be remembered, came firmly to recommend the adoption of the Constitution, his criticisms of it having come down only to a proposal for rotation in the Presidency and for the subsequent adoption of a bill of right. I do not, of course, deny the peculiar character of "Jeffersonianism" nor the importance to many things of its proper understanding. I only state here that it is certain that Jefferson, unlike later historians, did not view the Constitution as a retrogression from democracy. Or further, consider that John Adams, now celebrated as America's great conservative, was so enthusiastic about Jefferson's draft of the Declaration as to wish on his own account that hardly a word be changed. And this same Adams, also without any change of heart and without complaint, accepted the Constitution as embodying many of his own views on government.

The idea that the Constitution was a falling back from the fuller democracy of the Declaration thus rests in part upon a false reading of the Declaration as free from the concerns regarding democracy that the framers of the Constitution felt. Perhaps only those would so read it who take for granted a perfect, self-subsisting harmony between consent (equality) and the proper aim of government (justice), or between consent and individual rights (liberty). This asusmption was utterly foreign to the leading men of the Declaration.

II

The Declaration has wrongly been converted into, as it were, a super-democratic document; has the Constitution wrongly been converted in the modern view into an insufficiently democratic document? The only basis for depreciating the democratic character of the Constitution lies in its framers' apprehensive diagnosis of the "diseases," "defects" or "evil propensities" of democracy, and in their remedies. But if what the Founders considered to be defects *are* genuine defects, and if the remedies, without violating the principles of popular government, *are* genuine remedies, then it would be unreasonable to call the Founders anti- or quasi-democrats. Rather, they would be the wise partisans of democracy; a man is not a better democrat but only a foolish democrat if he ignores real defects inherent in popular government. Thus, the question becomes: are there natural defects to democracy and, if there are, what are the best remedies? In part, the Founding Fathers answered this question by employing a traditional mode of political analysis. They believed there were several basic possible regimes, each having several possible forms. Of these possible regimes they believed the best, or at least the best for America, to be popular government, but only if purged of its defects. At any rate, an unpurged popular government they believed to be indefensible. They believed there were several forms of popular government, crucial among these direct democracy and republican—or representative—government (the latter perhaps divisible into two distinct forms, large and small republics). Their constitution and their defense of it constitute an argument for that form of popular government (large republic) in which the "evil propensities" would be weakest or most susceptible of remedy.

The whole of the thought of the Founding Fathers is intelligible and, especially, the evaluation of their claim to be wise partisans of popular government is possible, only if the words *"disease," "defect,"* and *"evil propensity"* are allowed their full force. Unlike modern "value-free" social scientists, the Founding Fathers believed that true knowledge of the good and bad in human conduct was possible, and that they themselves possessed sufficient knowledge to discern the really grave defects of popular government and their proper remedies. The modern relativistic or positivistic theories, implicitly employed by most commentators on the Founding Fathers, deny the possibility of such true knowledge and therefore deny that the Founding Fathers *could* have been actuated by knowledge of the good rather than by passion or interest. (I deliberately employ the language of *Federalist* No. 10. Madison defined faction, in part, as a group "united and actuated by . . . passion, or . . . interest." That is, factions are groups *not*—as presumably the authors of *The Federalist* were —actuated by reason.) How this modern view of the value problem supports the conception of the Constitution as less democratic than the Declaration is clear. The Founding Fathers did in fact seek to prejudice the outcome of democracy; they sought to alter, by certain restraints, the likelihood that the majority would decide certain political issues in bad ways. These restraints the Founders justified as mitigating the natural defects of democracy. But, say the moderns, there are no "bad" political decisions, wrong-in-themselves, from reaching which the majority ought to be restrained. Therefore, ultimately, nothing other than the specific interests of the Founders can explain their zeal in restraining democracy. And inasmuch as the restraints were typically placed on the many in the interest of the propertied, the departure of the Constitution is "anti-democratic" or "thermidorean." In short, according to this view, there cannot be what the Founders claimed to possess, "an *enlightened* view of the dangerous propensities against which [popular government] . . . ought to be guarded," the substantive goodness or badness of such propensities being a matter of opinion or taste on which reason can shed no light.

What are some of the arrangements which have been considered signs of "undemocratic" features of the Constitution? The process by which the Constitution may be amended is often cited in evidence. Everyone is familiar with the arithmetic which shows that a remarkably small minority could prevent passage of a constitutional amendment supported by an overwhelming majority of the people. That is, bare majorities in the thirteen populous states could prevent passage of an amendment desired by overwhelming majorities in the thirty-six most populous states. But let us, for a reason to be made clear in a moment, turn that arithmetic around. Bare majorities in the thirty-seven least populous states can pass amendments against the opposition of overwhelming majorities in the twelve most populous states. And this would mean in actual votes today (and would have meant for the thirteen original states) constitutional amendment by a minority against the opposition of a majority of citizens. My point is simply that, while the amending procedure does involve qualified majorities, the qualification is not of the kind that requires an especially large numerical majority for action.

I suggest that the real aim and practical effect of the complicated amending procedure was not at all to give power to minorities, but to ensure that passage of an amendment would require a *nationally* distributed majority, though one that legally could consist of a bare numerical majority. It was only adventitious that the procedure has the theoretical possibility of a minority blocking (or passing) an amendment. The aim of requiring nationally distributed majorities was, I think, to ensure that no amendment could be passed simply with the support of the few states or sections sufficiently numerous to provide a bare majority. No doubt it was also believed that it would be difficult for such a national majority to form or become effective save for the decent purposes that could command national agreement, and this difficulty was surely deemed a great virtue of the amending process. This is what I think *The Federalist* really means when it praises the amending process and says that "it guards equally against that extreme facility, which would render the Constitution too mutable; and that extreme difficulty, which might perpetuate its discovered faults." All I wish to emphasize here is that the actual method adopted, with respect to the numerical size of majorities, is meant to leave all legal power in the hands of ordinary majorities so long as they are national majorities. The departure from simple majoritianism is, at least, not in an oligarchic or aristocratic direction. In this crucial respect, the amending procedure does conform strictly to the principles of re-publican (popular) government.

Consider next the suffrage question. It has long been assumed as proof of an anti-democratic element in the Constitution that the Founding Fathers depended for the working of their Constitution upon a sub-stantially limited franchise. Just as the Constitution allegedly was ratified by a highly qualified electorate, so too, it is held, was the new government to be based upon a suffrage subject to substantial property qualifications. This view has only recently been seriously challenged, especially by Robert E. Brown, whose detailed researches convince him that the property quali-fications in nearly all the original states were probably so small as to exclude never more than twenty-five per cent, and in most cases as little as only five to ten per cent, of the adult white male population. That is, the property qualifications were not designed to exclude the mass of the poor but only the small proportion which lacked a concrete—however small—stake in society, *i.e.,* primarily the transients or "idlers."

The Constitution, of course, left the suffrage question to the decision of the individual states. What is the implication of that fact for deciding what sort of suffrage the Framers had in mind? The immediately popular branch of the national legislature was to be elected by voters who "shall have the qualifications requisite for electors of the most numerous branch of the State Legislature." The mode of election to the electoral college for the Presidency and to the Senate is also left to "be prescribed in each State by the legislature thereof." At a minimum, it may be stated that the Framers did not themselves attempt to reduce, or prevent the expansion of, the suffrage; that question was left wholly to the states—and these were, ironically, the very hotbeds of post-revolutionary democracy from the rule of which it is familiarly alleged that the Founders sought to escape.[4]

In general, the conclusion seems inescapable that the states had a far broader suffrage than is ordinarily thought, and nothing in the actions of the Framers suggests any expectation or prospect of the reduction of the suffrage. Again, as in the question of the amending process, I suggest that the Constitution represented no departure whatsoever from the demo-

---

[4] Madison must have thought that he had established this point beyond mis-interpretation in *The Federalist,* No. 57. "Who are to be the electors of the federal representatives? Not the rich, more than the poor; not the learned, more than the ignorant; not the haughty heirs of distinguished names, more than the humble sons of obscurity and unpropitious fortune. The electors are to be the great body of the people of the United States. They are to be the same who exercise the right in every State of electing the corresponding branch of the legis-lature of the State." (p. 371.)

cratic standards of the Revolutionary period, or from any democratic standards then generally recognized.[5]

What of the Senate? The organization of the Senate, its term of office and its staggered mode of replacement, its election by state legislatures rather than directly by the people, among other things, have been used to demonstrate the undemocratic character of the Senate as intended by the Framers. Was this not a device to represent property and not people, and was it not intended therefore to be a non-popular element in the government? I suggest, on the contrary, that the really important thing is that the Framers thought they had found a way to protect property *without* representing it. That the Founders intended the Senate to be one of the crucial devices for remedying the defects of democracy is certainly true. But *The Federalist* argues that the Senate, as actually proposed in the Constitution, was calculated to be such a device as would operate only in a way that "will consist . . . with the genuine principles of republican government."[6] I believe that the claim is just.

Rather than viewing the Senate from the perspective of modern experience and opinions, consider how radically democratic the Senate appears when viewed from a pre-modern perspective. The model of a divided legislature that the Founders had most in mind was probably the English Parliament. There the House of Lords was thought to provide some of the beneficial checks upon the popular Commons which it was hoped the Senate would supply in the American Constitution. But the American Senate was to possess none of the qualities which permitted the House of Lords to fulfill its role; *i.e.*, its hereditary basis, or membership upon election by the Crown, or any of its other aristocratic characteristics.[7] Yet the Founding Fathers knew that the advantages of having both a Senate and a House would "be in proportion to the dissimilarity in the genius of the two bodies." What is remarkable is that, in seeking to secure this dissimilarity, they did not in any respect go beyond the limits permitted by the "genuine principles of republican government."

[5] This is not to deny the importance of the existing property qualifications for the understanding of the Founders' political theory. The legal exclusion from the franchise of even a very small portion of the adult population may have enormous significance for the politics and life of a country. This is obvious in the case of a racial, ethnic or religious minority. And the exclusion of otherwise eligible adult males on the grounds of poverty may be equally important. The property qualification clearly praises and rewards certain virtues, implies that the voter must possess certain qualities to warrant his exercise of the franchise, and aims at excluding a "rabble" from the operations of political parties. But important, therefore, as the property qualification was, it does not demonstrate that the Founding Fathers departed radically from the most important aspects of the principle of majority rule.

[6] *Federalist*, No. 62, p. 403.

[7] *Federalist*, No. 63, p. 415.

Not only is this dramatically demonstrated in comparison with the English House of Lords, but also in comparison with all earlier theory regarding the division of the legislative power. The aim of such a division in earlier thought is to secure a balance between the aristocratic and democratic elements of a polity. This is connected with the pre-modern preference for a *mixed* republic, which was rejected by the Founders in favor of a *democratic* republic. And the traditional way to secure this balance or mixture was to give one house or office to the suffrages of the few and one to the suffrages of the many. Nothing of the kind is involved in the American Senate. Indeed, on this issue, so often cited as evidence of the Founders' undemocratic predilections, the very opposite is the case. The Senate is a constitutional device which *par excellence* reveals the strategy of the Founders. They wanted something like the advantages earlier thinkers had seen in a mixed legislative power, but they thought this was possible (and perhaps preferable) without any introduction whatsoever of aristocratic power into their system. What pre-modern thought had seen in an aristocratic senate—wisdom, nobility, manners, religion, etc.—the Founding Fathers converted into stability, enlightened self-interest, a "temperate and respectable body of citizens." The qualities of a senate having thus been altered (involving perhaps comparable changes in the notion of the ends of government), it became possible to secure these advantages through a Senate based wholly upon popular principles. Or so I would characterize a Senate whose membership required no property qualification and which was appointed (or elected in the manner prescribed) by State legislatures which, in their own turn, were elected annually or biennially by a nearly universal manhood suffrage.

The great claim of *The Federalist* is that the Constitution represents the fulfillment of a truly novel experiment, of "a revolution which has no parallel in the annals of society," and which is decisive for the happiness of "the whole human race." And the novelty, I argue, consisted in solving the problems of popular government by means which yet maintain the government "wholly popular."[8] In defending that claim against the idea of the Constitution as a retreat from democracy I have dealt thus far only with the easier task: the demonstration that the constitutional devices and arrangements do not derogate from the legal power of majorities to rule. What remains is to examine the claim that the Constitution did in fact remedy the natural defects of democracy. Before any effort is made in this direction, it may be useful to summarize some of the implications and possible utility of the analysis thus far.

[8] *Federalist*, No. 14, pp. 81, 85.

Above all, the merit of the suggestions I have made, if they are accurate in describing the intention and action of the Founders, is that it makes the Founders available to us for the study of modern problems. I have tried to restore to them their *bona fides* as partisans of democracy. This done, we may take seriously the question whether they were, as they claimed to be, wise partisans of democracy or popular government. If they were partisans of democracy and if the regime they created was decisively democratic, then they speak to us not merely about bygone problems, not from a viewpoint—in this regard—radically different from our own, but as men addressing themselves to problems identical in principle with our own. They are a source from within our own heritage which teaches us the way to put the question to democracy, a way which is rejected by certain prevailing modern ideas. But we cannot avail ourselves of their assistance if we consider American history to be a succession of democratizations which overcame the Founding Fathers' intentions. On that view it is easy to regard them as simply outmoded. If I am right regarding the extent of democracy in their thought and regime, then they are not outmoded by modern events but rather are tested by them. American history, on this view, is not primarily the replacement of a pre-democratic regime by a democratic regime, but is rather a continuing testimony to how the Founding Fathers' democratic regime has worked out in modern circumstances. The whole of our national experience thus becomes a way of judging the Founders' principles, of judging democracy itself, or of pondering the flaws of democracy and the means to its improvement.

III

What was the Founding Fathers' view of the good life? Upon what fundamental theoretical premises did that view of the good life depend? How comprehensive was their understanding of the dangers against which popular government was to be guarded? How efficacious were their remedies and what may have been the anticipated costs of those remedies? These questions are clearly too vast to answer here and now. What follows is only a series of notes which bear upon the problems raised, and which I think may serve as general guides to what it is important to seek in studying the Founding Fathers.

The Federalist does not discuss systematically, as would a theoretical treatise, the question of the ends or purposes of government. That is, it does not deal systematically with philosophical issues. This is not to say that its authors did not have a view in such matters. But what that view was, and what are its implications for the understanding of the Constitution, is a subject on which I find it difficult to speak with confidence. I must still regard as open the question whether the authors of *The Federalist*, or the other leading founders, had themselves fully reflected on these matters, or whether they treated them as settled by thinkers like Locke and Montesquieu, or whether crucial premises in their thought were unreflectively taken for granted. But men cannot act on a political scale so vast as they did without having and employing a view of the politically fundamental; and it is this view which provides the crucial perspective for the understanding of their particular actions and thoughts.

Perhaps the most explicit fundamental utterance of *The Federalist* is the statement regarding

> the great principle of self-preservation . . . the transcendant law of nature and of nature's God, which declares that the safety and happiness of society are the objects at which all political institutions aim, and to which all such institutions must be sacrificed.[9]

But self-preservation, it is made clear, includes more than mere preservation. This passage, which interestingly echoes the Declaration of Independence on the "laws of nature and of nature's God," emphasizes that preservation includes "happiness" as well as "safety." That is, *The Federalist* is aware of and explicitly rejects the kind of regime that would follow from a narrower view of self-preservation. For example, *The Federalist* seems explicitly to be rejecting Hobbes when, in another context, it rejects the view that "nothing less than the chains of despotism can restrain [men] from destroying and devouring one another."[10] But while it rejects the "chains of despotism," *i.e.,* the Hobbesean solution to the problem of self-preservation, it nonetheless seems to accept the Hobbesean statement of the problem. As it were, the primary fears of *The Federalist* are Hobbesean, that is, fears of "foreign war and domestic convulsion." Rejecting a despotic solution, the great aim of *The Federalist* is to supply a liberal and republican solution to the same problem. But while there is a great difference, never to be underestimated, between a liberal and a repressive, a republican and a monarchical solution, it may be that in making the same dangers and their solution *the* desideratum for the structure and functions of government much of the Hobbesean view is preserved.

The main object of *The Federalist* was to urge the necessity of a firm and energetic Union. The utility of such a Union, and therefore the chief ends it will serve, is that it will strengthen the American people against the dangers of "foreign war" and secure them from the dangers of "do-

9 *Federalist*, No. 43, p. 287.
10 *Federalist*, No. 55, p. 365.

mestic convulsion." These functions of government are the most frequently discussed and the most vehemently emphasized in the whole work. To a very great extent, then, *The Federalist* determines the role of government with reference only, or primarily, to the extremes of external and internal danger. It is to avoid the pre-civil forms of these dangers that men form government and it is the civil solution of these dangers which, almost exclusively, determines the legitimate objects of government. But again, *The Federalist* repeatedly emphasizes that a "novel" solution is at hand. The means now exist—and America is uniquely in a position to employ them—for a republican solution which avoids the extremes of tyranny and anarchy. But notice that, on this view, liberalism and republicanism are not the means by which men may ascend to a nobler life; rather they are simply instrumentalities which solve Hobbesean problems in a more moderate manner. It is tempting to suggest that if America is a "Lockean" nation, as is so often asserted, it is true in the very precise sense that Locke's "comfortable preservation" displaces the harshness of the Hobbesean view, while not repudiating that view in general.

To be sure, *The Federalist* does make other explicit statements regarding the ends of government. For example: "Justice is the end of government. It is the end of civil society."[11] But this statement, to the best of my knowledge, is made only once in the entire work; and the context suggests that "justice" means simply "civil rights" which in turn seems to refer primarily to the protection of economic interests. That justice has here this relatively narrow meaning, as compared with traditional philosophical and theological usage, is made more probable when we take account of the crucial statement in *Federalist* No. 10. There the "first object of government" is the protection of the diverse human faculties from which arise the "rights of property" and the unequal distribution of property. The importance of this statement of the function of government is underscored when it is recalled how large a proportion of *The Federalist* deals with the improvements in "commerce" made possible by the new Constitution. For example, in a list of the four "principal objects of federal legislation," three (foreign trade, interstate trade, and taxes) deal explicitly with commerce. The fourth, the militia, also deals with commerce insofar as it largely has to do with the prevention of "domestic convulsion" brought on by economic matters.[12]

The very great emphasis of *The Federalist* on commerce, and on the role of government in nurturing it, may not be at all incompatible with the theme of "happiness" which is the most frequently occurring definition

---

[11] *Federalist,* No. 51, p. 340.
[12] *Federalist,* No. 53, pp. 350–351.

of the "object of government." The most definite statement is the following:

> A good government implies two things: first, fidelity to the object of government, which is the happiness of the people, secondly, a knowledge of the means by which that object can be best obtained.[13]

The Federalist is not very explicit in defining happiness. But there are firm indications that what it had in mind has little in common with traditional philosophical or theological understandings of the term. At one place, *The Federalist* indicates that happiness requires that government "provide for the security, advance the prosperity, [and] support the reputation of the commonwealth."[14] In another, happiness seems to require "our safety, our tranquility, our dignity, our reputation."[15] Part of what these words mean is made clear by the fact that they summarize a lengthy indictment of the Articles of Confederation, the particulars of which deal in nearly every case with commercial shortcomings. Happiness, "a knowledge of the means" to which *The Federalist* openly claims to possess, seems to consist primarily in physical preservation from external and internal danger *and* in the comforts afforded by a commercial society; which comforts are at once the dividends of security and the means to a republican rather than repressive security.

What is striking is the apparent exclusion from the functions of government of a wide range of non-economic tasks traditionally considered the decisive business of government. It is tempting to speculate that this reduction in the tasks of government has something to do with *The Federalist's* defense of popular government. The traditional criticism of popular government was that it gave over the art of government into the hands of the many, which is to say the unwise. It would be a formidable reply to reduce the complexity of the governmental art to dimensions more commensurate with the capacity of the many. I use two statements by Madison, years apart, to illustrate the possibility that he may have had something like this in mind. "There can be no doubt that there are subjects to which the capacities of the bulk of mankind are unequal." But on the other hand, "the confidence of the [Republican party] in the capacity of mankind for self-government"[16] is what distinguished it from

---

[13] *Federalist,* No. 62, p. 404.

[14] *Federalist,* No. 30, p. 186.

[15] *Federalist,* No. 15, p. 88.

[16] Letter to Edmund Randolph, January 10, 1788; letter to William Eustis, May 22, 1823. The letters to Randolph and Eustis were brought to my attention by Ralph Ketcham's article, "Notes on James Madison's Sources for the Tenth Federalist Paper," *Midwest Journal of Political Science,* Vol. 1 (May, 1957).

the Federalist party which distrusted that capacity. The confidence in mankind's capacities would seem to require having removed from government the subjects to which those capacities are unequal.

IV

So far as concerns those ends of government on which *The Federalist* is almost wholly silent, it is reasonable to infer that what the Founders made no provision for they did not rank highly among the legitimate objects of government. Other political theories had ranked highly, as objects of government, the nurturing of a particular religion, education, military courage, civic-spiritedness, moderation, individual excellence in the virtues, etc. On all of these *The Federalist* is either silent, or has in mind only pallid versions of the originals, or even seems to speak with contempt. The founders apparently did not consider it necessary to make special provision for excellence. Did they assume these virtues would flourish without governmental or other explicit provision? Did they consciously sacrifice some of them to other necessities of a stable popular regime—as it were, as the price of their solution to the problem of democracy? Or were these virtues less necessary to a country when it had been properly founded on the basis of the new "science of politics"? In what follows I suggest some possible answers to these questions.

The Founding Fathers are often criticized for an excessive attention to, and reliance upon, mechanical institutional arrangements and for an insufficient attention to "sociological" factors. While a moderate version of this criticism may finally be just, it is nonetheless clear that *The Federalist* pays considerable and shrewd attention to such factors. For example, in *Federalist* No. 51, equal attention is given to the institutional and noninstitutional strengths of the new Constitution. One of these latter is the solution to the "problems of faction." It will be convenient to examine *Federalist* No. 10 where the argument about faction is more fully developed than in No. 51. A close examination of that solution reveals something about *The Federalist's* view of the virtues necessary to the good life.

The problem dealt with in the tenth essay is how "to break and control the violence of faction." "The friend of popular governments never finds himself so much alarmed for their character and fate, as when he contemplates their propensity to this dangerous vice." Faction is, thus, *the* problem of popular government. Now it must be made clear that Madison, the author of this essay, was not here really concerned with the problem of faction generally. He devotes only two sentences in the whole essay to the dangers of *minority* factions. The real problem in a popular government, then, is *majority* faction, or, more precisely, *the* majority faction, *i.e.,* the great mass of the little propertied and unpropertied. This is the only faction that can "execute and mask its violence under the forms of the Constitution." That is, in the American republic the many have the legal power to rule and thus from them can come the greatest harm. Madison interprets that harm fairly narrowly; at least, his overwhelming emphasis is on the classic economic struggle between the rich and the poor which made of ancient democracies "spectacles of turbulence and contention." *The* problem for the friend of popular government is how to avoid the "domestic convulsion" which results when the rich and the poor, the few and the many, as is their wont, are at each others throats. Always before in popular governments the many, armed with political power, invariably precipitated such convulsions. But the friend of popular government must find only "a republican remedy" for this disease which is "most incident to republican government." "To secure the public good and private rights against the danger of . . . [majority] faction, and at the same time to preserve the spirit and the form of popular government, is then the great object to which our inquiries are directed."

Without wrenching Madison's meaning too greatly, the problem may be put crudely this way: Madison gave a beforehand answer to Marx. The whole of the Marxian scheme depends upon the many—having been proletarianized—causing precisely such domestic convulsion and usurpation of property as Madison wished to avoid. Madison believed that in America the many could be diverted from that probable course. How will the many, *the* majority, be prevented from using for the evil purpose of usurping property the legal power which is theirs in a popular regime? "Evidently by one of two [means] only. Either the existence of the same passion or interest in a majority at the same time must be prevented, or the majority, having such co-existent passion or interest, must be rendered, by their number and local situation, unable to concert and carry into effect schemes of oppression." But "we well know that neither moral nor religious motives can be relied on" to do these things. The "circumstance principally" which will solve the problem is the "greater number of citizens and extent of territory which may be brought within the compass" of large republican governments rather than of small direct democracies.

Rather than mutilate Madison, let me complete his thought by quoting the rest of his argument before commenting on it:

> The smaller the society, the fewer probably will be the distinct parties and interests, the more frequently will a majority be found of the same party; and the smaller the number of individuals composing a majority, and the smaller the compass within which they are placed, the more easily will they concert and execute their plans of oppression. Extend

the sphere and you take in a greater variety of parties and interests; you make it less probable that a majority of the whole will have a common motive to invade the rights of other citizens; or if such a common motive exists, it will be more difficult for all who feel it to discover their own strength, and to act in unison with each other.

I want to deal only with what is implied or required by the first of the two means, *i.e.,* preventing the majority from having the same "passion or interest" at the same time. I would argue that this is the more important of the two remedial means afforded by a large republic. If the majority comes to have the same passion or interest and holds to it intensely for a period of only four to six years, it seems certain that it would triumph over the "extent of territory," over the barriers of federalism, and separation of powers, and all the checks and balances of the Constitution. I do not wish to depreciate the importance of those barriers; I believe they have enormous efficacy in stemming the tide Madison feared. But I would argue that their efficacy depends upon a prior weakening of the force applied against them, upon the majority having been fragmented or deflected from its "schemes of oppression." An inflamed Marxian proletariat would not indefinitely be deterred by institutional checks or extent of territory. The crucial point then, as I see it, is the means by which a majority bent upon oppression is prevented from ever forming or becoming firm.

Madison's whole scheme essentially comes down to this. The struggle of classes is to be replaced by a struggle of interests. The class struggle is domestic convulsion; the struggle of interests is a safe, even energizing, struggle which is compatible with or even promotes, the safety and stability of society. But how can this be accomplished? What will prevent the many from thinking of their interest as that of the Many opposed to the Few? Madison, as I see it, implies that nothing can prevent it in a small democratic society where the many are divided into only a few trades and callings: these divisions are insufficient to prevent them from conceiving their lot in common and uniting for oppression. But in a large republic, numerous and powerful divisions will arise among the many to prevent that happening. A host of interests grows up "of necessity in civilized nations, and divide[s] them into different classes, actuated by different sentiments and views." "Civilized nations" clearly means here large, commercial societies. In a large commercial society the interest of the many can be fragmented into many narrower, more limited interests. The mass will not unite as a mass to make extreme demands upon the few, the struggle over which will destroy society; the mass will fragment into relatively small groups, seeking small immediate advantages for their narrow and particular interests.

If the Madisonian solution is essentially as I have described it, it becomes clear that certain things are required for the solution to operate. I only mention several of them. First, the country in which this is to take place will have to be profoundly democratic. That is, all men must be free —and even encouraged—to seek their immediate profit and to associate with others in the process. There must be no rigid class barriers which bar men from the pursuit of immediate interest. Indeed, it is especially the lowly, from whom the most is to be feared, who must feel most sanguine about the prospects of achieving limited and immediate benefits. Second, the gains must be real; that is, the fragmented interests must from time to time achieve real gains, else the scheme would cease to beguile or mollify. But I do not want to develop these themes here. Rather, I want to emphasize only one crucial aspect of Madison's design: that is, the question of the apparently narrow ends of society envisaged by the Founding Fathers. Madison's plan, as I have described it, most assuredly does not rest on the "moral and religious motives" whose efficacy he deprecated. Indeed there is not even the suggestion that the pursuit of interest should be an especially enlightened pursuit. Rather, the problem posed by the dangerous passions and interests of the many is solved primarily by a reliance upon passion and interest themselves. As Tocqueville pointed out, Americans employ the principle of "self-interest rightly understood."

> The principle of self-interest rightly understood is not a lofty one, but it is clear and sure. It does not aim at mighty objects, but it attains . . . all those at which it aims. By its admirable conformity to human weaknesses it easily obtains great dominion; nor is that dominion precarious, since the principle checks one personal interest by another, and uses, to direct the passions, the very same instrument that excites them.

Madison's solution to his problem worked astonishingly well. The danger he wished to avert has been averted and largely for the reasons he gave. But it is possible to question now whether he did not take too narrow a view of what the dangers were. Living today as beneficiaries of his system, we may yet wonder whether he failed to contemplate other equally grave problems of democracy, or whether his remedy for the one disease has had some unfortunate collateral consequences. The Madisonian solution involved a fundamental reliance on ceaseless striving after immediate interest (perhaps now immediate gratification). Tocqueville appreciated that this "permanent agitation . . . is characteristic of a peaceful democracy," one might even say, the price of its peace. And Tocqueville was aware of how great might be the price. "In the midst of this universal tumult, this incessant conflict of jarring interests, this continual striving of men after fortune, where is that calm to be found which is necessary for the deeper combinations of the intellect?"

V

There is, I think, in *The Federalist* a profound distinction made between the qualities necessary for Founders and the qualities necessary for the men who come after. It is a distinction that bears on the question of the Founding Fathers' view of what is required for the good life and on their defense of popular government. Founding requires "an exemption from the pestilential influence of party animosities"; but the subsequent governing of America will depend on precisely those party animosities, moderated in the way I have described. Or again, founding requires that "reason" and not the "passions," "sit in judgment."[17] But, as I have argued, the society once founded will subsequently depend precisely upon the passions, only moderated in their consequences by having been guided into proper channels. The reason of the Founders constructs the system within which the passions of the men who come after may be relied upon.

Founders need a knowledge of the newly improved "science of politics" and a knowledge of the great political alternatives in order to construct a durable regime; while the men who come after need be only legislators who are but interested "advocates and parties to the causes they determine." *The Federalist* speaks, as has often been observed, with harsh realism about the shortcomings of human nature, but, as has not so often observed, none of its strictures can characterize the Founders; they must be free of these shortcomings in order to have had disinterested and true knowledge of political things. While "a nation of philosophers is as little to be expected as the philosophical race of kings wished for by Plato," it is tempting to speculate that *The Federalist* contemplates a kind of philosopher-founder the posthumous duration of whose rule depends upon "that veneration which time bestows on everything," and in particular on a regime well-founded.[18] But once founded, it is a system that has no necessary place and makes no provision for men of the founding kind.

It is clear that not all now regarded as Founding Fathers were thought by the authors of *The Federalist* to belong in that august company. Noting that "it is not a little remarkable" that all previous foundings of regimes were "performed by some individual citizen of pre-eminent wisdom and

---

[17] *Federalist,* No. 37, p. 232; *Federalist,* No. 49, p. 331.
[18] *Federalist,* No. 49, pp. 328, 329.

approved integrity," *The Federalist* comments on the difficulty that must have been experienced when it was attempted to found a regime by the action of an assembly of men.[19] I think it can be shown that *The Federalist* views that assembly, the Federal Convention, as having been subject to all the weaknesses of multitudes of men. The real founders, then, were very few in number, men learned in the new science of politics who seized upon a uniquely propitious moment when their plans were consented to first by a body of respectable men and subsequently, by equally great good fortune, by the body of citizens. As it were, America provided a rare moment when "the prejudices of the community" were on the side of wisdom.[20] Not unnaturally, then, *The Federalist* is extremely reluctant to countenance any re-opening of fundamental questions or delay in ratifying the Constitution.

This circumstance—wisdom meeting with consent—is so rare that "it is impossible for the man of pious reflection not to perceive in it a finger of that Almighty hand."[21] But once consent has been given to the new wisdom, when the government has been properly founded, it will be a durable regime whose perpetuation requires nothing like the wisdom and virtue necessary for its creation. The Founding Fathers' belief that they had created a system of institutions and an arrangement of the passions and interests, that would be durable and self-perpetuating, helps explain their failure to make provision for men of their own kind to come after them. Apparently, it was thought that such men would not be needed.

But does not the intensity and kind of our modern problems seem to require of us a greater degree of reflection and public-spiritedness than the Founders thought sufficient for the men who came after them? One good way to begin that reflection would be to return to their level of thoughtfulness about fundamental political alternatives, so that we may judge for ourselves wisely regarding the profound issues that face us. I know of no better beginning for that thoughtfulness than a full and serious contemplation of the political theory that informed the origin of the Republic, of the thought and intention of those few men who fully grasped what the "assembly of demi-gods" was doing.

---

[19] *Federalist,* No. 38, p. 233.
[20] *Federalist,* No. 49, p. 329.
[21] *Federalist,* No. 38, p. 231.

A Spacious Republic:
From Sovereignty to Federalism

DANIEL J. BOORSTIN

Some of the foundations of American constitutionalism were products of colonial experience in the Old Empire—the idea of federalism, for example. Some owed much to the mother country, but more to the American experience—the concept of popular sovereignty, for instance. And some were almost completely American. The anticolonial "colonial system" embodied in the Northwest Ordinance of 1787 is the classic example, for it broke with the idea of subordinating new territories to older areas, promising instead the right of self-government on the basis of equality with the original states when the population of one of the territories reached 60,000. Under both the temporary territorial governments and the new state constitutions, there was to be freedom of religion, prohibition of slavery, habeas corpus, trial by jury, and the privileges of the common law. The new Constitution, adopted by the Philadelphia Convention two months later, confirmed the admission of new states on the basis of equality with the older ones, establishing what Thomas Jefferson later called an "Empire for Liberty." In the following essay, Professor Boorstin discusses "the novel American machinery for state-making," a "scheme of progressive decolonization" from territorial status to statehood "on an equal footing with the original States in all respects whatever." Though he is critical of the "autocratic colonial rule" authorized for the territorial state, Boorstin nonetheless concludes that "the successful application of this notion of a predictable, gradual, step-by-step progress toward self-government and national involvement is one of the marvels of American history."

Daniel J. Boorstin, *The Americans: The National Experience* (New York, Random House, 1965), pp. 412–413, 417–426. Reprinted by permission.

THE FIRST EFFORTS TO UNITE THE OLD COLONIES UNDER A NEW central authority were not at all in the nature of a new "frame of government" or a constitution. The thirteen sovereign states, each with a government of its own, sought not a central government but (in the phrase of Governor Cooke of Rhode Island) a "Treaty of Confederation," which was not necessarily a permanent alliance, but primarily (some thought, exclusively) a league to wage the war. There is some reason to believe that there was even less national unity after the adoption of the Articles of Confederation than before it.

In its new constitution, a former colony would declare itself a "Sovereign State." Each of the states actually exercised the sort of powers we associate with an independent government. The South Carolina Constitution, for example, expressly asserted the power of the state to make war, conclude peace, enter into treaties, lay embargoes, and maintain an army and navy. Virginia herself ratified the treaty with France, and was so active in foreign affairs that she had to establish a clerkship of foreign correspondence; Governor Patrick Henry sent William Lee abroad to negotiate a loan with the French government. According to Franklin, three separate states of the American confederation were at one time negotiating with France for war aid. There is evidence that states considered the minister sent abroad by the Congress to be not so much a national emissary as a minister who was acting simultaneously on behalf of each of the states individually. States acted as if, in allowing certain functions to be exercised by the Congress, they had not divested themselves of a power to perform similar functions in their own behalf. Thus they organized their own armies, fitted out their own navies, and directed military movements to serve state interests. In the South, the War was conducted in the beginning without the aid of Congress. Each state regulated its own Indian affairs and postal routes. The sovereignty of the states explained why the vote in the Congress of the Confederation was by states and not by individual delegates. That Congress, according to John Adams, was "not a legislative assembly, nor a representative assembly but only a diplomatic assembly.". . .

The generation that made the Federal Constitution was haunted by the suspicion that republican government somehow would not function over a large area. "It is natural for a republic to have only a small territory," Montesquieu had written in his *Spirit of Laws* in 1748, "otherwise it cannot long subsist." And this notion had become a principle of political science. Both John Adams (in his *Defense of the Constitutions of the*

United States, 1787), and Alexander Hamilton (in his speech in the Constitutional Convention, June 18, 1787) drew from history the lesson that the vast extent of the United States made it likely that a durable central government would have to verge on monarchy. Patrick Henry, arguing against ratification of the new Federal Constitution in the Virginia Convention (June 9, 1788), offered this difficulty as axiomatic. "One government," he insisted, "cannot reign over so extensive a country as this is, without absolute despotism." "I call for an example of a great extent of country, governed by one government, or Congress, call it what you will."

The story of the American Revolution, it was said, had been only another illustration of this well-known principle. Had not the British proved unable to adapt their representative government to include far-off America?

But some, less pessimistic, began to imagine that the example which all earlier history could not supply might be found in America. James Madison, for example, in the *Federalist* (Number 10) argued hopefully that a great extent of territory, with its great variety of interests, might actually protect the citizens' rights. "Extend the sphere," Madison explained in a familiar passage, "and you take in a greater variety of parties and interests; you make it less probable that a majority of the whole will have a common motive to invade the rights of other citizens; or if such a common motive exists, it will be more difficult for all who feel it to discover their own strength, and to act in unison with each other. . . . the same advantage which a republic has over a democracy, in controlling the effects of faction, is enjoyed by a large over a small republic—is enjoyed by the Union over the States composing it." Thomas Jefferson, after the turbulent presidential election of 1800–1801 when a tie between him and Aaron Burr in the Electoral College had thrown the decision into the House of Representatives and finally elected him on the thirty-sixth ballot, wrote to Joseph Priestley (March 21, 1801), "We can no longer say there is nothing new under the sun. For this whole chapter in the history of man is new. The great extent of our republic is new." "It furnishes a new proof of the falsehood of Montesquieu's doctrine, that a republic can be preserved only in a small territory. The reverse is the truth. Had our territory been even a third only of what it is, we were gone. But while frenzy and delusion like an epidemic, gained certain parts, the residue remained sound and untouched and held on till their brethen could recover from the temporary delusion; and that circumstance has given me great comfort."

There were, nevertheless, some peculiarly American grounds for pessimism: a secessionist tradition was older even than the Revolution. It was as old as the colonial settlements. The discovery of the New World had made secessions and withdrawals feasible on a continental scale, and American life comprised countless efforts to secede. The Pilgrims were the first outspoken American secessionists. As "separatists" they believed what from an Old World point of view was quite shocking, that men who wanted to live by a purer church could of their own accord separate themselves from their old community and form themselves into a new one. The Pilgrims came to Plymouth only after their effort to separate themselves had been unsuccessful in the Netherlands. In the vast American space, the very idea of "Nonconformity" or of "Toleration" was overshadowed by Separatism and Secessionism.

From the early 17th century till the middle of the 19th century, secession was characteristically American. The colonies expanded and acquired their varied character by secessions. Roger Williams and Anne Hutchinson, separatist heretics, were extruded from Massachusetts Bay and seceded into their own Rhode Island. Thomas Hooker, another separatist, seceded to his Connecticut. Lord Baltimore made it possible for a group of Catholics to secede from English life into a community which, for a while at least, was their own. William Penn provided a separate place of refuge. And so on. Space made all this possible. The Revolution seemed to many at the time to be a triumph of thirteen separate secessionist spirits. In the late 18th and early 19th century, there were westward-moving wagon trains settling new territories and states in a vaguely bounded hinterland, and these too were seceding, after their various secular undogmatic fashions, from the life of the seaboard.

American experience had already shown, then, that the fears of Montesquieu and older political theorists were not without foundation. If a single great republic was to survive here, it would have to find a way of stemming the secessionist tide. Oddly enough, this opportunity was to come through the creation of a new American empire—in Jefferson's phrase, an "Empire for Liberty"—with political arrangements quite similar to those that the American colonists had fought to secede from. The first colonial experience (before the War for Independence) had made an American nation necessary. A second colonial experience (between Independence and the Civil War) would make the nation possible.

The "public domain"—a new American empire controlled now, not from London, but by "the united states in Congress assembled"—became a bond among the states. Without these lands, and the conflicts with foreign powers which they threatened, could a central government have survived between the peace with Britain in 1783 and the convening of the Constitutional Convention in Philadelphia in 1787? What might have happened once the pressure of British attack was removed, once the thirteen separate "Sovereign States" had each started on its own way?

Dreams of this new empire long inspired Jefferson. In 1809, he suggested to President Madison that Napoleon might be willing to let the United States have Cuba. Then, Jefferson went on, by adding Canada, "we should have such an empire for liberty as she has never surveyed since the creation; . . . no constitution was ever before so well calculated as ours for extensive empire and self-government." In the beginning, this new empire was no mere dream, but the very cement of the Union.

Within the next decades, the new central government in America would exercise powers over land and life in a new American empire in which the new colonies were euphemistically called the "public lands" or the "national domain" or the "public domain." This empire was remarkably similar in political structure to that which had driven the earlier American colonies to revolt. The new national government, for example, at first dared to legislate for and to tax this new empire.

In the East, meanwhile, American political institutions would be shaped by this very power and habit of legislating for an ill-defined West. The major measures of the new national government, would, in the vocabulary of an earlier day, have been called measures of imperial control. They were latter-day counterparts of the Proclamation of 1763, the Quebec Act of 1774, and other Acts which disposed of the lives, fortunes, lands, and governments of people far from the central authority in London. Those earlier acts of Parliament were meant to hold an empire together, and bulwark it against foreign enemies. The later acts of the American Congress, such as the Missouri Compromise, the Compromise of 1850, and the Kansas-Nebraska Act of 1854, also imposed decisions from the remote East on people in the West; these decisions were intended to hold together a nation. If the British government had once used Americans as pawns in a world-wide battle for empire, so now the new American government in Washington used Westerners as makeweights between sections of the heavily settled East. . . . The other major pieces of federal legislation—the Land Act of 1796, which provided for rectangular survey; the Land Act of 1820, which required cash for land purchases; the Pre-emption Act of 1830, which gave preference to actual settlers at the time; the Distribution–Pre-emption Act of 1841, which permanently authorized settlement before purchase and which distributed a portion of the proceeds of land-sale to the new states; and the Homestead Act of 1862—these too were eastern measures of control over the acquisition of property and the perfection of land titles in the whole West. Control, or efforts at control, from Washington, dominated Western political problems. Congressional rule was not easily abdicated: the slavery issue added still another reason for direct Congressional responsibility. The rush to settle Kansas by both pro- and antislavery factions and the resulting civil war there (November, 1855, to December, 1856), in which about two hundred were killed, were among the many incidents in the western struggle to satisfy the conditions established by Congress. The Union was held precariously together by this new kind of imperial control.

• • •

The relation of the western territories (soon to comprise the greater number of the states) to the whole new nation showed characteristics of an American political system with institutions of a strongly unionist tendency which would endure into the 20th century. These were the institutions that were to make possible a spacious republic. Who could have predicted that they would be by-products of a secessionist tradition?

Organic Law: a Legal Substitute for Revolution. The novel American machinery for state-making—the basis for an American colonial system —was given classic form in the Northwest Ordinance, adopted by the Congress of the Confederation in July, 1787. This act described a regular set of stages through which a Territory would pass on its way from complete control by Congress to equality as a new State within the Union.

At first, the sparsely populated Territory was to be governed by Congress through its Congressionally-appointed governor, secretary, and three judges. These officials would put together a legal code, borrowing those laws from the original states which they found "best suited to the circumstances of the district." They had autocratic powers, curbed only by the veto of Congress. The next stage was reached "so soon as there shall be five thousand free male inhabitants of full age in the district," when the inhabitants would, if they wished, begin to have a representative government with a two-chamber legislature: a directly elected house of representatives, and a small "legislative council" of five persons, selected by Congress from a list of ten prepared by that house. The governor had veto on all legislation. The two chambers of the Territorial legislature voting together were to elect a delegate, "who shall have a seat in Congress, with a right of debating but not of voting during this temporary government."

Government during these first two stages resembled that under the old British Empire, with Congress standing in place of the Crown and Parliament, with appointed governors, weak legislatures subject to veto by the national legislature, and non-voting commissioners in the national capital. The third and final stage was reached when the free population numbered sixty thousand, at which time the Territory would be admitted as a State. Within the Northwest Territory there were to be "not less than three nor more than five States," all "on an equal footing with the original States in all respects whatever, and shall be at liberty to form a permanent constitution and State government: *Provided,* the constitution and government so to be formed, shall be republican, and in conformity to the principles contained in these articles."

This American colonial system, unlike the British, provided a normal progress from imperial control to self-government. At the final stage, moreover, the outlying territory was to be thoroughly involved in the government of the whole nation. This procedure for state-making had been enacted in the Northwest Ordinance under the Articles of Confederation; it was re-enacted by the First Congress as part of the new Federal system. Its basic principle—predictable procession from autocratic colonial rule to self-government and involution in the nation—became the American way of national growth.

The United States grew politically, then, by recapitulating its colonial experience. By far the larger area of the United States, as it stood in the later 20th century, had once been governed as a colony from the national capital. The colonial experience, lived in an earlier form by each of the thirteen original states, was now relived in a legally formalized version by nearly all the other states that eventually rounded out the nation. If the earlier version had ended in failure from the point of view of the British government in London, the later version would end in success, from the point of view of a transformed American government in Washington.

A half-century after the adoption of the Ordinance of 1787, this scheme of progressive decolonization had become a glorious fixture among American institutions. "It approaches as nearly to absolute perfection," Judge Timothy Walker of Cincinnati, author of the widely read *Introduction to American Law* (1837), declared, "as anything to be found in the legislation of mankind, for after the experience of fifty years it would perhaps be impossible to alter without marring it . . . . it is one of those matchless specimens of sagacious forecast, while even the reckless spirit of innovation would not venture to assail." A full century after the introduction of the scheme, Lord Bryce, in his *American Commonwealth* (1889), conceded that the American scheme of Territorial government had worked well in practice and gave little ground for discontent even to the inhabitants of the Territories themselves.

The successful application of this notion of a predictable, gradual, step-by-step progress toward self-government and national involvement is one of the marvels of American history. The application of the principles of the Northwest Ordinance was not literal nor uniform, but it was general. For example, Ohio's admission as a state in 1803 and Illinois' in 1818, both occurred before their populations reached the specified sixty thousand; while Dakota in 1880, with a population of more than twice the required number, was not seriously considered for statehood, and Utah when admitted in 1896 had contained more than the required number for over thirty years. Political considerations among the existing states were always important and often decisive. Ohio, the first state created from the Northwest Territory, was admitted by a strongly Jeffersonian Congress just in time to help re-elect Jefferson President in 1804.

Before the Civil War, the slavery issue dominated this, as it did other questions. After the struggle over the admission of Missouri as a slave state in 1821, the balance of forces in the national government in Washington depended on the internal history of the Territories. This reversed the flow of forces under the old British Empire, when government in the colonies had been shaped by the accidents of internal politics in London. The existence of a whole continent from which to make political counterweights in the delicate equilibrium between North and South, Free and Slave States, helped keep sectional issues alive. States were admitted and Territories created in pairs: Free and Slave. Even after the Civil War, the Omnibus Bill of 1889 simultaneously admitted four states (North Dakota, South Dakota, Washington, and Montana) so as not to upset the party balance: two were said to be Democratic, the other two Republican.

What is most remarkable is not that the formation of new states was halting, irregular, and influenced by "mother-country" politics, but rather that it worked as well as it did. Two-thirds of a continent was led from colonial rule to self-government within a century and a half. Threats of secession, like that of the Mormons in Utah in 1857, were rare. The system succeeded in preventing what might have been a series of American Wars for Independence in the West.

After an initial period of experimental adjustment to local conditions (for example to French and Spanish traditions in Louisiana), a remarkably standardized system was developed. And despite involvement with such explosive domestic issues as slavery, land pre-emption, banking, and tariff, new Territories were continually created: Arkansas (1819), Florida (1822), Wisconsin (1836), Iowa (1838), Oregon (1848), Minnesota (1849), Utah and New Mexico (1850), and Kansas and Nebraska (1854). By a characteristic American reversal, the point of view of these "colonies" gradually dominated the politics of the "mother country," which now was the eastern third of central North America.

The system of the Northwest Ordinance of 1787 governed substantially, until the last piece of contiguous continental territory was admitted as the State of Arizona in 1912. But after 1861, when slavery and sectional rivalry no longer dominated domestic politics, the creation of new states became slower; Territorial patronage was too useful to be abandoned by Congress simply to satisfy local ambitions for stathood. Between 1867 and 1889 only a single state (Colorado) was admitted, and in the Territories of Dakota, Montana, Utah, New Mexico, and Washington, a whole generation was raised in quasi-colonialism. But the pace of movement along the clearly defined path to self-government was still swift by Old World standards. The direction (as revealed most recently in Alaska, admitted as a state, January 3, 1959, and in Hawaii, admitted August 21, 1959), remained unchanged.

State-making had been reduced to simple, specified procedures. Over a broad continent, "self-government" was created in place after place with perfunctory simplicity. Just as state constitutions in the West were sometimes slavish replicas of eastern models, so too the Organic Acts themselves, which created new western Territories, followed a pattern. The Wisconsin Organic Act of 1836, developing out of similar earlier acts, provided the formula repeated in all later Acts. The will to self-government had now been tamed—another evidence that (in R. R. Palmer's phrase) "revolution had already become domesticated in America."

The American colonial-territorial system, with its plain and easy stages for movement from imperial rule to self-government, was another application of know-how. Like the New England system of manufacturing, it was a plan of organization, in this case summarized in the notion of Organic (Government-organizing) Law. And this too would be a substitute for skill. By this way of mass-producing states, a people could be institutionally transformed from a mere territory, a congeries of transient communities and upstart towns, into a fully equipped representative government, even though they had very little political skill of their own. Much as the Territorial judges with the Governor and the Secretary in the first Organic stage, by a system of interchangeable parts put together their code of laws from pieces ready-made in other parts of the Union, so the later constitution-makers of the western states borrowed ready-made pieces from their predecessors.

A Politics of Accretion: New Political Units. The national history of England, France, Germany, or Italy is a story of unification; the national history of the United States is one of accretion. The United States, from the beginning, grew by adding new areas from a vaguely bounded hinterland. While the national politics of Europe consisted of the adjustment of old entities, the national politics of the United States in its first three-quarters of a century consisted of the creation, adjustment, and interrelations of new entities. This distinction was pregnant for American political life.

In 1790, the nation was confined to the eastern side of the Mississippi River, with most of its population east of the Appalachians. It included some nine hundred thousand square miles organized into a national domain (a Northwest Territory and a Southwest Territory) and thirteen states. By 1861, the nation reached to the Rio Grande and the Pacific, and across the continent up to the forty-ninth parallel, a total of some three million square miles, now organized into over a half-dozen territories and thirty-four states. These simple facts of political arithmetic summed up the primary features of American politics. The political time-table was fanatastically accelerated: between the Congressional creation of a Territory and its admission as a State, there has never been longer than sixty-two years (New Mexico, 62 years; Hawaii 61 years; Arizona, 49 years; Alaska, 47 years; Utah, 46 years), and the average span for this process has been only about twenty years. The original thirteen states were the focus of loyalties accumulated over many dacades, but the newer states (the twenty-seventh state, Florida, was admitted in 1845) soon outnumbered the old. New states were, for the most part, products of quick-grown transient and upstart communities, which acquired political and constitutional existence by legislative fiat.

A constitution, which for centuries European man had continued to think of "not as a creation but as a growth; not as a national code so much as a national inheritance" was now, in one territory after another, conjured up at will. This new sense of control shaped an American functional attitude toward all government. Nothing was more obvious than that men could create new political entities quickly when they wished. And what men could make, could they not also alter for their convenience?

The geographic peculiarities of the new nation made it possible to add one new "state" after another, without encroaching on a strong neighboring power. In the Old World, addition to one nation could not be achieved without extinction of a nation or subtraction from another. The United States could grow by simple addition. Except for the Atlantic Ocean, the United States had not traditional boundary. Thus the new Union was built by an "Add-a-State" plan, as Americans casually created new political units.

A Politics of Involution: Change Is Normal. Gradually and continually, the government of the metropolitan United States was itself reshaped to incorporate the needs, the voices, and the aspirations of the newly added units. As each new state was added, the whole political frame was slightly altered. This is one reason why there has never been a successful violent political revolution in the United States. Involution has made revolution superfluous. The great exception was, of course, the South, which refused to accept the alterations required by expansion, and tried to make rigid the political arrangements which had survived only by their flexibility.

While it is not clear to what extent the framers of the Constitution of 1787 envisaged this development, there are clues that some of them intended the involution that would distinguish the American empire. The census, for example, showed the expectation that, as new territories and states were added to the Union, the center of political power should shift. It expressed belief that the framework of representation in the Congress should remain fluid, to incorporate the new areas in its activities and involve them in the national business. Population-counts had been taken by European governments for one purpose or another. And there was a rough precedent in the periodic seven-year "census of electors and inhabitants" provided in the first constitution of the State of New York. But the Federal Constitutional provision for a decennial census (Art. II, sec. 2) was in many ways distinctive. The need for it grew out of the great compromise between large and small states, which also provided for two legislatures, in one of which representation was to be by population. Obviously, under the Articles of Confederation, since each state had only one vote in the single-chamber legislature, there was no need for a periodic count for representative purposes. But now both direct taxes and representation in the House of Representatives were to be proportionate to figures based on population, "determined by adding to the whole number of free persons, including those bound to service for a term of years, and excluding Indians not taxed, three fifths of all other persons." The facts for this purpose were to be redefined every ten years. In origin, then, this provision was wholly fiscal and political—to provide a fluid basis for taxation and for the composition of the House of Representatives. Not until 1850 did the census become a substantial source of national statistics for other matters.

The United States Census, for the first time, provided that changing numbers of population (and hence the changing rates of regional growth) should become normal elements in the periodic redistribution of the power of the units in the political system. In England and elsewhere in Europe, parties struggled during the 19th century to make individual changes in the basis of representation, but in America a continual process of change had been incorporated into the original scheme. The census figures would in the normal course of events become public: this, too, was a great change, for, at least until the 19th century (and in some countries into the 20th), statistical data were state secrets. Over there the fears of the tax-farmer and of rival nations dominated, but here the claims of different parts of the country to be represented had to be published to the people.

The effect of the decennial reapportionments was especially dramatic in the first century of nationale life. In the First Congress, the constituency of a member of the House averaged about 33,000 persons; in 1840 it averaged about 71,000; by 1890 it would average about 176,000. Instead of redistributing the membership as it existed in 1789, the House allowed itself to grow with the population. This was, of course, only another example of the American penchant for multiplying political units (in this case, congressional districts). Its consequences was not only to alter the apportionment of powers within the House, but substantially to alter the House's character, and its way of doing business. While the House of Representatives in 1789 numbered 65 and in 1790 numbered 106, by 1820 the number had doubled to 213, and by 1860 had increased to 243. The number was finally fixed at 435 in 1910, where it remained until the temporary addition of two more in 1960 after the admission of Alaska and Hawaii.

SELECTIVE
BIBLIOGRAPHY

The current wave of reinterpretation of the origins of American constitutionalism springs from two impulses: the recent research on English political and constitutional thought in the seventeenth and eighteenth centuries and the revision of Charles A. Beard's interpretation of the federal Constitution. Four major areas of English and colonial constitutional thought have received extensive attention: the concept of the mixed constitution (Corrine Comstock Weston, *English Constitutional Thought and the House of Lords, 1556–1832,* 1965; Betty Kemp, *King and Commons, 1660–1832,* 1957; J. W. Gough, *Fundamental Law in English Constitutional History,* 1961); the separation of powers (W. B. Gwyn, *The Meaning of the Separation of Powers,* 1965; M. J. C. Vile, *Constitutionalism and the Separation of Powers,* 1967); the concept of representation (J. R. Pole, *Political Representation in England and the Origins of the American Republic,* 1966; Richard Buel, "Democracy and the American Revolution," *William and Mary Quarterly,* 3rd ser., 21 [1964] 165–190; Michael Zuckerman, "The Social Context of Democracy in Massachusetts," *ibid.,* 25 [1968] 523–544; Michael Kammen, ed., *Deputyes and Libertyes: The Origins of Representative Government in Colonial America,* 1970); and the radical Whig tradition of politics (Clinton Rossiter, *Seedtime of the Republic: The Origin of the American Tradition of Political Liberty,*

1953; Caroline Robbins, *The Eighteenth-Century Commonwealthman: Studies in . . . English Liberal Thought from the Restoration of Charles II until the War with the Thirteen Colonies*, 1959; Archibald S. Foord, *His Majesty's Opposition, 1714–1830*, 1964; H. Trevor Colbourn, *The Lamp of Experience: Whig History and the Intellectual Origins of the American Revolution*, 1965; J. G. A. Pocock, "Machiavelli, Harrington, and the English Political Ideologies," *William and Mary Quarterly*, 3rd ser., 22 [1965] 549–583; J. H. Plumb, *The Origins of Political Stability: England, 1675–1725*, 1967; Bernard Bailyn, *The Origins of American Politics*, 1968; Isaac Kramnick, *Bolingbroke and His Circle: The Politics of Nostalgia in the Age of Walpole*, 1968; Jack P. Greene, 'Political Mimesis: A Consideration of the Historical and Cultural Roots of Legislative Behavior in the British Colonies in the Eighteenth Century," *American Historical Review*, 75 [1969] 337–360.)

Although Charles A. Beard's emphasis on the economic interpretation of the Constitution was the most influential explanation of the adoption of the document from 1913 to 1956, many of the major constitutional scholars never did accept it. Edward S. Corwin, Charles Warren, and Andrew C. McLaughlin ignored or rejected it, some, like McLaughlin, seeing it not as an explanation but as a point of departure. Despite the early criticism, Beard's view became the dominant one, even though he himself altered his emphasis in the 1940s. It was not until the early fifties that widescale revision of the Beardian interpretation began, with Richard Hofstadter, Douglass Adair, and Robert E. Thomas leading the way (Hofstadter, "Beard and the Constitution: The History of an Idea," *American Quarterly*, 2 [1950] 195–212; Adair, "The Tenth *Federalist* Revisited," *William and Mary Quarterly*, 3rd ser., 8 [1951] 48–67; Thomas, "A Re-appraisal of Charles A. Beard's 'An Economic interpretation of the Constitution of the United States,'" *American Historical Review*, 57 [1952] 37–75). Two full-scale critiques shattered the Beardian emphasis: Robert E. Brown, *Charles Beard and the Constitution* (1956); Forrest McDonald, *We the People: The Economic Origins of the Constitution* (1958). As Hofstadter concludes in *The Progressive Historians* (1968), Beard's reputation, "once the grandest house in the province, is now a ravaged survival," an "imposing ruin in the landscape of American historiography." After his negative assault on Beard in 1956, Brown accentuated the positive in his Bacon Lectures, elaborating his views of the federal Constitution as a democratic document (*Reinterpretation of the Formation of the American Constitution*, 1963). Benjamin F. Wright had earlier stressed the linkage between the Declaration of Independence and the Constitution in *Consensus and Continuity, 1776–1787* (1958). For two critical reviews of Beard's interpretation, see Henry Steele Commager, "The Constitution: Was it an Economic Document." *American Heritage*,

10 (1958) 58–61, 100–103, and Cecelia Kenyon, "An Economic Interpretation of the Constitution after Fifty Years," *The Centennial Review*, 7 (1963) 327–352.

Although it seems clear that Beard's particular economic interpretation has been rejected by most serious scholars today, that does not mean that economic factors were not important in the movement for the Constitution. Jackson Turner Main stresses socioeconomic divisions in *The Antifederalists: Critics of the Constitution, 1781–1788* (1961) and in *The Social Structure of Revolutionary America* (1965). He is critical of both Brown and McDonald; see especially his "Charles Beard and the Constitution: A Critical Review of Forrest McDonald's *We the People*," *William and Mary Quarterly*, 3rd ser., 17 (1960) 86–110. But Main, who agrees that he "stands closer to Beard than to his detractors," concedes that "Beard can no longer be accepted without serious reservations." Interestingly enough, Beard's most thorough critic, Forrest McDonald, in *E Pluribus Unum: The Formation of the American Republic, 1776–1790* (1965), makes the politics of the pocketbook the central determinative factor in the creation of the Constitution, though he does not completely rule out ideology, calling the framers—or some of them, at least—"giants in the earth" and the Constitution "the miracle of the age." In his study of *Turner and Beard: American Historical Writing Reconsidered* (1960), Lee Benson suggests that broad social forces were more influential than narrow economic interests in the contest over the Constitution, that ideas about the Good Society rather than ideas about the Good State were the critical factors. Staughton Lynd, *Class Conflict, Slavery, and the United States Constitution* (1968), emphasizes social and economic groups in the formation of the federal charter. In a brilliant article, E. James Ferguson links the problem of constitutional reform to the Revolutionary war debt, but he rejects the Beardian emphasis in his reconstruction of an economic interpretation, refusing to minimize the force of noneconomic motives in the establishment of the national government ("The Nationalists of 1781–83 and the Economic Interpretation of the Constitution," *Journal of American History*, 56 [1969] 241–21).

Of the early writers on constitutionalism, none surpassed Andrew C. McLaughlin, whose *Constitutional History of the United States* (1935) is the only textbook to win a Pulitzer Prize. His article on "The Background of American Federalism," which appeared in the *American Political Science Review*, 12 (1918) 215–240, was incorporated in his Phelps Lectures, *The Foundations of American Constitutionalism* (1932). Other appraisals of the origins of federalism include Charles H. McIlwain, "The Historical Background of Federal Government," in *Federalism as a Democratic Process* (1942) and John C. Ranney, "The Bases of American Federalism," *William and Mary Quarterly*, 3rd ser., 3 (1946).

There was a flurry of interest in the political and constitutional ideas, if not the ideology of the American Revolution, in the 1920s, three major books appearing in 1922–23: Randolph G. Adams, *The Political Ideas of the American Revolution* (1922); Carl L. Becker, *The Declaration of Independence: A Study in the History of Political Ideas* (1922); and Charles H. McIlwain, *The American Revolution: A Constitutional Interpretation* (1923). The recent interest in the constitutional issues of the Revolution stems from the excellent study by Edmund S. and Helen M. Morgan of *The Stamp Act Crisis: Prologue to Revolution* (1953) and the writings on the radical Whig tradition cited previously. The books by Colbourn and Bailyn, already mentioned, and volumes by Robert R. Palmer (*The Age of the Democratic Revolution: A Political History of Europe and America, 1760–1800,* 1959, 1964) and Bernard Bailyn (*Ideological Origins of the American Revolution,* 1967) have emphasized the connections between American Revolutionary thought and experience and English and European traditions. For a provocative interpretation of "The Social Contract in America," see Thad Tate's article in the *William and Mary Quarterly,* 3rd ser., 22 (1965) 375–391.

The most comprehensive accounts of the Revolutionary state constitutions are in Allan Nevins, *The American States During and After the Revolution, 1775–1789* (1924), Elisha P. Douglass, *Rebels and Democrats: The Struggle for Equal Political Rights and Majority Rule During the American Revolution* (1955), and Hannah Arendt, *On Revolution* (1963), which has a fascinating discussion of the "spontaneous outbreak of constitution-making" during the Revolutionary era. The most stimulating study in abbreviated form is "Part Two: The Constitution of the States" in Gordon S. Wood, *The Creation of the American Republic, 1776–1787* (1969). The development of the people as constituent power in Massachusetts is presented in a massive documentary collection edited by Oscar and Mary Handlin (*The Popular Sources of Political Authority: Documents on the Massachusetts Constitution of 1780,* 1966) and in a more selective edition by Robert J. Taylor (*Massachusetts, Colony to Commonwealth,* 1961). Older studies include William C. Morey, "The Genesis of a Written Constitution," American Academy of Political and Social Science, *Annals,* 1 (1891) 529–557, and "The First State Constitutions," *ibid.,* 4 (1893) 201–232; William C. Webster, "Comparative Study of the State Constitutions of the American Revolution," *ibid.,* 9 (1897) 380–420; J. F. Jameson, "Early Political Uses of the Word Convention," American Antiquarian Society, *Proceedings,* n. s., 12 (1897) 183–196; Walter F. Dodd, "The First State Constitutional Conventions, 1776–1783," *American Political Science Review,* 2 (1908) 545–561; and

Benjamin F. Wright, "The Early History of Written Constitutions," in *Essays . . . to Charles H. McIlwain* (1936), pp. 344–371.

The leading scholar of the Confederation period is Merrill Jensen. His books, *The Articles of Confederation: An Interpretation of the Social-Constitutional History of the American Revolution, 1774–1781* (1940) and *The New Nation: A History of the United States During the Confederation, 1781–1789* (1950), are influential and controversial interpretations that view the Articles as the constitutional expression of the philosophy of the Declaration of Independence and the Constitution as the culmination of an antidemocratic crusade. Edward S. Corwin had earlier modified the view that the philosophy of the Declaration had been frozen in 1776, tracing "The Progress of Constitutional Theory Between the Declaration of Independence and the Meeting of the Philadelphia Convention" in the *American Historical Review,* 30 (1925) 511–536. Most of the recent studies of the Confederation period are discussions of constitutional development in the context of public finance, focusing on the nationalist movement of the early 1780s to strengthen the Confederation by adding powers to the central government. See E. James Ferguson, *The Power of the Purse: A History of American Public Finance, 1776–1790* (1961); and Main, *The Antifederalists,* and McDonald, *E Pluribus Unum,* both previously cited.

Herbert Johnson outlines the evolution of institutional arrangements under the Confederation Congress in his brief but provocative article, "Toward a Reappraisal of the 'Federal' Government: 1783–1789," *American Journal of Legal History,* 8 (1964) 314–325. The classic statement which connects the shortcomings of the Confederation government to the theme of legislative sovereignty at the state level is James Madison's "Vices of the Political System of the United States, 1787," Gaillard Hunt, ed., *The Writings of James Madison* (1901) vol. 2, pp. 361–369. The most imaginative elaboration of this theme is in Wood, *Creation of the American Republic,* 393–467. For a valuable summary of historical views on the Confederation period, see Richard B. Morris, "The Confederation Period and the American Historian," *William and Mary Quarterly,* 3rd ser., 13 (1956) 139–156. A revised and updated version entitled "Confederation and Constitution: Fulfillment or Counter-Revolution," appears in Morris, *The American Revolution Reconsidered* (1967), pp. 127–167. For another review of the historiographic hassle over the Confederation, see Stanley M. Elkins and Eric McKitrick, "The Founding Fathers: Young Men of the Revolution," *Political Science Quarterly,* 76 (1961) 181–216.

There have been four useful studies recently of the Philadelphia Convention and the ratification controversy: Catherine Drinker Bowen, *Miracle at Philadelphia: The Story of the Constitutional Convention, May to September 1787* (1966); Paul Eidelberg, *The Philosophy of the American Constitution: A Reinterpretation of the Intentions of the Founding Fathers* (1968); Clinton Rossiter, *1787: The Grand Convention* (1966); and Robert A. Rutland, *The Ordeal of the Constitution: The Antifederalists and the Ratification Struggle of 1787–1788* (1966). For a brief summary of the Convention's actions, see Irving Brant, *James Madison: Father of the Constitution, 1787–1800* (1950), 11–185. For a fuller account Charles Warren's *The Making of the Constitution* (1928) is still useful. John P. Roche's article, "The Founding Fathers: A Reform Caucus in Action," *American Political Science Review,* 55 (1961) 799–816, concentrates on the fundamental agreement at Philadelphia rather than the differences, viewing the Constitution as the product of democratic political procedures. For two intriguing articles on the psychology of the founders and their views on human nature, see Arthur O. Lovejoy, "The Theory of Human Nature in the American Constitution and the Method of Counterpoise," *Reflections on Human Nature* (1961), pp. 37–65, and Benjamin F. Wright, *"The Federalist* on the Nature of Political Man," *Ethics,* 54 (1949). Robert A. Feer, "Shays's Rebellion and the Constitution: A Study in Causation," *New England Quarterly,* (1969) 388–410, concludes that "Shays's Rebellion was not a cause of the Constitution of the United States." There has been a recent reprinting of Conyers Read, ed., *The Constitution Reconsidered* (1938), with a new preface by Richard B. Morris (1968).

The revived interest in the ratification contest was inaugurated by Cecila Kenyon's provocative article, "Men of Little Faith: The Anti-Federalists on the Nature of Representative Government," *William and Mary Quarterly,* 3rd ser., 12 (1955) 3–43; she has refined and elaborated her views in the extensive introduction to the documentary collection, *The Antifederalists* (1966), pp. xxi–cxvi. Other documentary selections include Alpheus T. Mason, ed., *The States Rights Debate: Antifederalism and the Constitution* (1964) and Morton Borden, ed., *The Antifederalist Papers* (1965).

Douglass Adair and Martin Diamond have several illuminating articles on the *Federalist Papers* and the political and constitutional thought of the Framers. For Adair, see "The Tenth *Federalist* Revisited," *William and Mary Quarterly,* 8 (1951) 48–67; "That Politics May Be Reduced to a Science: David Hume, James Madison, and the Tenth *Federalist," Huntington Library Quarterly,* 20 (1957) 343–360; "'Experience Must Be Our Only Guide': History, Democratic Theory, and the United States Constitution," in Ray A. Billington, ed., *The Reinterpretation of Early*

American History (1966), pp. 129–148; and "Fame and the Founding Fathers," in Edmund P. Willis, ed., *Fame and the Founding Fathers* (1967), pp. 27–52. For Diamond, see "Democracy and *The Federalist:* A Reconsideration of the Framers' Intent," *American Political Science Review,* 53 (1959) 52–68; "*The Federalist's* View of Federalism," in George C. S. Benson, *et al.,* eds., *Essays in Federalism* (1961), pp. 21–64; "What the Framers Meant by Federalism," Robert A. Goldwin, ed., *A Nation of States: Essays on the American Federal System* (1963), pp. 24–41; and "*The Federalist,*" Leo Strauss and Joseph Cropsey, eds., *History of Political Philosophy* (1963), pp. 573–593. All these essays stress the common assumptions among James Madison, Alexander Hamilton, and John Jay, the authors of *The Federalist,* but see Alpheus T. Mason, "*The Federalist,* A Split Personality," *American Historical Review,* 57 (1952) 125–143, who argues that there were basic differences between Hamilton's and Madison's contributions. For an intensive analysis of the *Federalist Papers,* see Gottfried Dietze, *The Federalist* (1960). There have been quantitative analyses of the federal convention and the contest for ratification by S. Sidney Ulmer, "Sub-group Formation in the Constitutional Convention," *Midwest Journal of Political Science,* 10 (1966) 288–303, and Charles W. Roll, Jr., "We, Some of the People: Apportionment in the Thirteenth State Conventions Ratifying the Constitution," *Journal of American History,* 5 (1969) 21–40.

On the relationship between constitutional thought and the adding of new states on the basis of equality, see the brilliant article by William T. Hutchinson, "Unite to Divide; Divide to Unite: The Shaping of American Federalism," *Mississippi Valley Historical Review,* 46 (1959) 3–18; Beverley W. Bond, Jr., "Some Political Ideals of the Colonial Period as They Were Realized in the Old Northwest," in *Essays in Colonial History Presented to Charles McLean Andrews . . .* (1931), pp. 299–325; and Daniel J. Boorstin, "A Spacious Republic," *The Americans: The National Experience* (1965), pp. 391–430.